Rudra Gita

Raj Behera

Rudra Gita

Library of Congress Control Number: 2020916527
ISBN-13: Paperback: 978-1-64749-347-9

Printed in the United States of America

GoTo Publish

GoToPublish LLC
1-888-337-1724
www.gotopublish.com
info@gotopublish.com

Contents

Dedication xi
Saranagati xii
Preface xiv
Prayers for Rudra (Rudra Mantra) 1
Meaning of Rudra 3
Difference between Rudra / Shiva / Shambhu / Shankara / Sada-Shiva 5
Rudra's real position 6
Rudra's meditative position 7
Names of Rudra 8
Philosophical birth of Rudra 10
Rudrani 13
Color of Rudra 14
Who was born after Rudra? 15
Another meaning of Rudra's birth 16
Rudra's expansion 17
Rudra's share in Yajna 18
Lord Shiva and Parvati marriage ceremony 20
Rudra–Half man & Half woman (Ardhanarishvara) 25
Real Rudra - Hari-Hara 27
  Ayappa 33
What is Rudra Gita? 35
Rudra's vehicle - Nandi 41
12 Jyotirlingam 43
Lingaraj Temple 44
Kedarnath of Lord Shiva 47
Amarnath of Lord Shiva 48
Shiva in different Yugas 50

Satya Yuga 50
Treta Yuga 51
Dwapara Yuga 53
Kali Yuga 55
Shiva in Multifarious Lila of Vishnu 57
Ram Lila 57
Krishna Lila 59
Vrindavan Lila as Gopi 59
Goloka Lila in Nandagram 61
Goloka Lila as a mountain – Nandgaon 62
Govardhan Chakaleswar – Mosquito 63
Parashuram Lila 64
Mohini Lila 65
Dattatreya Lila 67
Jagannath Lila 68
Rudrayamala 72
Chaitanya Lila 74
Rudra mentioned in various scriptures 76
Rudra in Bhagavad Gita 76
Rudra in Bhagavatam 76
Rudra pleased with Banasura 77
Rudra and Citraketu 79
Rudra and Bhagirathi 80
Rudra and King Salva 81
Rudra and Daksha 81
Rudra instructs Markandeya Rsi 82
Rudra meeting with demigods 83
Rudra and Kamadeva 85
Rudra and Maya 86
Rukmini's prayers to Ambika 87
Rudra in Sri Chaitanya-caritamrta and Chaitanya Bhagavat 90
Vriddha Shiva (Shiva Doba) 93
Rudra in Padma Purana (Gita-Mahatmya) 94
Rudra in Sri Satvata-Tantra 96
Rudra in Valmiki Ramayana 100
Yuddha Kanda 101
Uttara Kanda 101

Rudra in Vyasa's Mahabharata 102
Adi Parva – History of Draupadi 102
Vana Parva – Ganga comes to earth – Lord Shiva appeared 102
Rudra in Skanda Purana – episodes of Simanta Dvipa 103
Simanta Dvipa is represented as Sravanam, Hearing 104
Rudra in Sri Nabadwip Dham Mahatmya 105
Shivashtakam By Sri Chaithanya Mahaprabhu 106
Lord Rudra in Brahma-Samhita 109
Rudra as mentioned in the Varaha Purana 112
Rudra Suktam 117
Garuda Purana – Rudra prayer to Narasimha 118
Lord Shiva – Satyam Shivam Sundaram 124
Master 124
Husband 124
Father 126
Devotee friendly 128
Rudra Gita 128
Rudra and Hanuman 146
Rudra and Moon 148
Rudra and Narada 149
Rudra and Brahma 151
Rudra and the Snakes 153
Rudra and the Crematorium 155
Sankaracharya and Lord Shiva 158
Pregnancy impact by Lord Rudra 163
Mayavada Bhasya and Lord Shiva 164
Lord Shiva is Ashutosh 166
Lord Shiva and the Rudraksha mala 167
Lord Shiva's residence – Kailash mountain 168
Lord Shiva and the Bael (Wood Apple) 172
Lord Shiva and the Damaru 174
Unified Vision for the Trimurti - Lord Shiva, Brahma, and Vishnu 177
Lord Shiva as a Tamasi or Tamo guna Adhikari 179
Does Lord Shiva drink Marijuana (Ganja)? 181
The real meaning of Shiva Ratri 182
Criticism against Lord Shiva 184

Lord Shiva and Goddess Kali 187
Lord Shiva and Kamadeva 190
Lord Shiva glorifies Markandeya Rsi 193
Lord Shiva and Brhaspati 195
Lord Shiva as a Mahajana 197
Lord Shiva with Mohini 198
Lord Krishna saved Lord Shiva 201
Lord Shiva and descent of Mother Ganges 203
Lord Shiva and Vrkasura 204
Sivoham 209
Shiva-Jvara and Vishnu-Jvara 210
Shiva or Vishnu (Yogurt or Milk) 213
Rudra Sampradaya 215
Rudra's humility in Daksha Yajna 219
Arjun acquired the Pashupati-Astra 222
Banasura, Lord Shiva and Krishna 223
Essential teachings of Lord Shiva 224
Acknowledgement 228
References 229

Dedication

To our dear most grand spiritual master, HDG A. C. Bhaktivedanta Swami Prabhupada, founder-acharya of the Hare Krishna movement, author of the precious gem, Srimad Bhagavatam, and many more Vedic literatures. I am deeply grateful to my spiritual master, H. H. Gopal Krishna Goswami, my spiritual teacher, H. G. Vaisesika Das, and Team ISV. My special homage to H.H. Bhakti Caru Swami for his outstanding service in translating Srimad Bhagavatam to the Bengali language. I am also known as Balimardana Das in the ISKCON community.

I want to thank my parents (Sriman Gagan Bihari Behera and Srimati Surama Behera) and my parents-in-law (Sriman Achyutananda Mishra and Srimati Bharati Mishra) for giving me the valuable connections with the divinity. To all my SAP colleagues, Odia friends, and Parasar Behera and Mishra family members. Without the support of my family, this book would not be possible.

To my dear wife, Anita (Ananda), my two sons, Abhay and Balaram, and all my readers.

Saranagati

Finally, it is tough to know the Guru Tattva, Vishnu Tattva, and the Shiva Tattva. I don't have the right qualifications to attempt to write in the subject of Rudra Tattva. Somehow, by the divine mercy of Guru and Gauranga, I made this humble attempt. It was Nandisvara of Lingaraj temple, Bhubaneswar, who inspired and blessed me to write this book. According to Vedic literature, Nandisvara is also the spiritual teacher of the four kumaras popularly known as *catur-kumaras*. It is a custom that whoever whispers any wish on the ear of Nandisvara in the Lingaraj temple, such wishes are fulfilled by the grant of Lord Shiva through the via medium of Nandisvara, the spiritual messenger of the prayer of the devotees. Lord Shiva never returns empty handed to His devotees. By the causeless mercy of Nandisvara and Harihara, I am presenting this gem *"Rudra Gita"* to all my readers. In my childhood days, I used to frequently visit a Shiva temple near Bhimkhoj, Dharamgarh, and the ancient Shiva-linga temple in Chakuli. Everything is a source of His inspiration only; I am very much grateful to such a rarest personality of this universe.

I beg forgiveness from all the readers to excuse me for any mistakes I have made in this book publishing effort. I am very nervous in publishing this book as *Rudra Gita*, mainly a compilation from the Srimad Bhagavatam fourth canto chapter twenty-four. Based on my deficit in spiritual talents and understanding, I might have presented with incomplete realization or interpretations even though I have read several times the scriptures of the acharyas of our *parampara*. This book is compiled for the pleasure of all the Vaishnavas and Shaivas in the world after undergoing due diligence in various spiritual scriptures with substances. My humble prayer at the Lotus feet of Srila Prabhupada and his disciples to accept me as a neophyte spiritual practitioner and to forgive me any mistakes done unknowingly. I am sure that I lack the qualities to express the Srimad Bhagavatam's views and conclusions because of my inadequacy and less qualification.

One offers the Ganges water back to the Ganges for the pleasure of the Lord. Similarly, I am using the same principle in writing this book. Please shower your blessings and forgive me for all my offenses. I hope you will like this book – "*Rudra Gita*" and receive the mercy of Lord Rudra.

Preface

Rudra Gita is a song sung by Lord Shiva in the glorification of the Supreme Personality of Godhead, Krishna. By his causeless mercy, Lord Rudra instructed this message to the ten Pracetas, who were elevated saintly kings, the sons of Prancibarhi, in the dynasty of king Prithu. Lord Brahma recommended king Barhisat, popularly known as Prācīnabarhi, to marry Satadruti, the daughter of the god of the ocean. This song is as good as Bhagavad Gita, spoken by Lord Krishna. This great song is found in the fourth canto of the spotless literature, Srimad Bhagavatam. As Vidura asked the details about the glorious conversation between Rudra and Pracetas, Maitreya explained this song very nicely for the entire humanity. By reciting this divine song, one will undoubtedly attain the love of Godhead and will be clear of all misgivings of one's life. It is fascinating to note why Pracetas were chosen for this instruction and why Lord Shiva appeared in front of them. This transcendental symptom is naturally the import of the causeless mercy of the great personality, Lord Shiva. As Srila Sukadeva Goswami has given the individual treaties to Parikshit Maharaj, he is equally anxious to give the ultimate instructions of Srimad Bhagavatam. In this medium of instruction from one teacher to the students, all of humanity gets benefit in the parampara system of descending knowledge process.

The unique characteristics and qualities of Lord Shiva are presented in this book. Lord Shiva is regarded as the qualitative incarnation of God, one of the Mahajanas (12 great personalities), His exhibition of uncommon pastimes such as drinking the poison during the churning of Milk Ocean, being tolerant as a tree when cursed by Daksha, and giving the benedictions to all His devotees including the demons. There is the mysterious birth of Lord Shiva even though he is beyond the conception of birth and death like an ordinary living entity, His marriage to Sati and later to Parvati are so pleasing to the heart of the pure and liberated souls. There are so many mysterious pastimes of Lord Shiva in connection with the service to the Supreme Lord Krishna in His Lila in Vrindavan, Vraj Mandal Dham, and Jagannath Puri.

Lord Shiva is as good as God concerning the understanding of transformation from milk to yogurt. Vishnu and Shiva are considered as milk and yogurt respectively. Lord Shiva is eternally situated in the Kailas Loka, which is beyond the Brahma Jyoti or Brahman effulgence. Lord Shiva showers benedictions to one and all without discriminating between demons and demigods, similarly Lord Chaitanya has distributed the Krishna-Prema to everyone without any discrimination.

Any person desiring to free himself from the karmic reactions should rise in the brahma-muhurta period and chant the hymns composed by Lord Rudra. Also, one who encourages others to sing the song, is equally qualified to receive the mercy of the supreme Lord.

|| Hare Krsna Hare Krsna Krsna Krsna Hare Hare

Hare Rama Hare Rama Rama Rama Hare Hare ||

|| OM Namo Narayanaya!! ||

|| OM Namo Bhagavate Vasudevaya!! ||

|| OM Namo Shivaya!! ||

|| OM Namo Rudraya!! ||

|| Hare Krsna Hare Krsna Krsna Krsna hare hare

Hare Rama Hare Rama Rama Rama Hare Hare ||

Prayers for Rudra (Rudra Mantra)

Rudra mantra is also popularly known as the Maha-Mrityunjaya Mantra, and it is found in the Veda, such as Rigveda (RV 7.59.12). This unique mantra is also found in the Yajurveda (TS 1.8.6.i; VS 3.60). I offer my prostrated humble obeisances unto the lotus feet of Lord Rudra, and by His causeless mercy, one can glorify the Supreme Lord in relationship to Lord Rudra. This mantra is widely used by various sects of people in the world for purification, perfection, and happiness.

Om Haum Joom Sah!! Om Bhur Bhuvah Svah!!

ॐ त्र्यम्बकं यजामहे सुगन्धिं पुष्टिवर्धनम् ।
उर्वारुकमिव बन्धनान् मृत्योर्मुक्षीय माऽमृतात् ।

oṃ tryambakaṃ yajāmahe sugandhiṃ puṣṭi-vardhanam
urvārukam iva bandhanān mṛtyor mukṣīya mā 'mṛta.

It is an auspicious invocation to Lord Shiva; we worship the three-eyed Shambhu, who is fragrant as the spiritual substance, increasing the nourishment of our inner heart, from these many bondages of the material cycles similar to the cucumbers tied to their creeper, may I attain the supreme and infallible destination by the mercy of Lord Shiva.

This below verse is collected from Srimad Bhagavatam twelfth canto as a prayer to the Supreme Personality of Godhead, and even this mantra is also pleasing to Lord Rudra. One who utters this mantra, undoubtedly, one will attain the taste of devotional service to Lord Krishna. Let us repeat the same for the pleasure of the ultimate cause of all causes. At the beginning of the spiritual journey, such prayer is worth reciting and chanting.

ŚB 12.13.1

sūta uvāca
yaṁ brahmā varuṇendra-rudra-marutaḥ stunvanti divyaiḥ stavair
vedaiḥ sāṅga-pada-kramopaniṣadair gāyanti yaṁ sāma-gāḥ
dhyānāvasthita-tad-gatena manasā paśyanti yaṁ yogino
yasyāntaṁ na viduḥ surāsura-gaṇā devāya tasmai namaḥ

Sūta Gosvāmī said: Unto that personality whom Brahmā, Varuṇa, Indra, Rudra, and the Maruts praise by chanting transcendental hymns and reciting the Vedas with all their corollaries, pada-kramas and Upaniṣads, to whom the chanters of the Sāma Veda always sing, whom the perfected yogīs see within their minds after fixing themselves in a trance and absorbing themselves within Him, and whose limit can never be found by any demigod or demon — unto that Supreme Personality of Godhead I offer my humble obeisances.

Meaning of Rudra

Before starting this book, we need to understand the meaning of Rudra from authoritative sources such as the Brahma sutra or its explanation known as Srimad Bhagavatam. After the four kumaras were born from Lord Brahma, they were advised to get married to expand the population of the world; however, they declined to accept the offer of their father, the creator of the universe. They did not want to be engaged in family life, rather wished to remain celibate and pursue the path of brahman realization. Having heard the words from his sons, Lord Brahma got mentally angry as the kumaras refused to oblige to his order. From the anger of Brahma, a personality appeared from his eyebrows, and His name was Rudra because, from the wrath of Brahma, he was born. This personality was crying from the very beginning, *rodana,* so his name became Rudra. No matter the cause, Rudra is the most famous name in the Puranas and in the entire world. Based on these beautiful names, I dare to compose this book known as Rudra Gita. Lord Krishna has given the divine gift and song of God as Bhagavad Gita, and it is found in the Mahabharata, the greatest epic. Similarly, Rudra Gita is also found in the Srimad Bhagavatam, and this song is very dear to Lord Krishna. Whoever sings it, reads it, or distributes it (Bhadra Purnima); naturally, he will attract the loving devotional service towards Lord Krishna by the mercy of Rudra.

As per Srimad Bhagavatam 4.4.14, *yad dvy-akṣaraṁ nāma gireritaṁ nṛṇāṁ..,* Shiva means auspicious and Sati was mentioning to her father Daksha that the two syllables "Si" and "Va" purify all sins of the world and brings all promising to the world as a whole. Lord Shiva was the most beloved of each creature of the creation of this world. Shiva glorifies even if a person has negligible quality and bestows all kinds of benedictions to him. Since Lord Rudra is the most magnificent soul among the living entities within this material world, his name, Rudra or *Shiva* is very auspicious for persons who are not even qualified in their positions. Lord Shiva is always pure and transcendental beyond the jurisdiction of the Vedic rules and regulations. Lord Brahma honors him by accepting the flowers offered to his lotus feet and placing them with great respect on his heads.

If anyone takes shelter of Lord Shiva, gradually he will understand that he is not the material body but are spirit soul. *Shiva* means Mangala, or auspicious. Within the body, the soul is propitious. Ahaṁ brahmāsmi: "I am spirit soul,» whatever material activities one does are inauspicious. *Shiva* means "auspicious," and devotees of Lord *Shiva* gradually come to the platform of complete understanding in true brahman spirit.

In Rg Veda, it is mentioned in Rudra's glorification, "O Rudra, through the cures administered by you, may we pass through a hundred winters. Drive away from us haters. Wreck our sins and destroy the spreading of sicknesses." (Rig Veda II.33.2)

In Yajur Veda, Adhyaya 39, it is mentioned that "*bhavasya kannyechha rudrasyonta parsyam mahadevasya yakrrchhesye vanisnu puritatah*," meaning - Bhava is what is on the throat, Rudra is what is between the ribs: Mahadeva is the liver, Sarva is the rectum, Pashupati is the pericardium. Yajurveda is meant for the fire sacrifice and ultimately pleased to the Supreme Lord via the agency of demigods. *The yoga* practice is more recommended to attain the goal, the master of all such yogis is Lord Shiva, as he is the best yoga practitioner known as

Yogīśvara. Lord Krishna is the master of all yogic siddhis and bestower to all yogis and known as Yogeśvara.

DIFFERENCE BETWEEN RUDRA / SHIVA / SHAMBHU / SHANKARA / SADA-SHIVA

Sometimes we ponder in our mind, if there is a difference in the names of Rudra, Shiva, Shankara, Sada-Shiva, Bholenath, Bhutanath, Ashutosh, Mahadev, Umapati, etc. Technically, it's the same person as he exhibits different qualities in relationship with his devotees or unique pastimes thus the name is more prominent. In this age of Manu, he is known as Shankara as Lord Krishna describes himself as Shankara in Bhagavad Gita. As per Bhagavad Gita 10.23 *rudrāṇāṁ śaṅkaraś cāsmi, amongst Rudras, I am Shiva.* Ashutosh means one who is easily pleased by anyone's prayer. It applies to my humble self as I am not so qualified to write a book like this; however, Ashutosh empowered me to write about His glories from the authoritative point of view and his relationship with Lord Krishna. He is also called Mahadev because he is the chief of all the demigods like Indra, Agni, Surya, Chandra, etc. He is worshiped by the demigods even. Numerous living beings pronounce the name of the Lord as it is suitable per their relationship and worship methods. Lord Shiva / Rudra is very simple and straightforward, so that he is known as Bholenath by many devotees. Lord Shiva, by nature is sincere, humble and honest, he is called Bhutanath. Lord Shiva is also known as Umapati, the husband of Uma and celebrated as the father of Ganesha and Kartikeya.

Lord Shiva has unlimited names, and Shambhu is one of the prominent as we chant Jaya Jaya Shiva Shambhu, Hey Jaya Jaya Shiva Shambhu, the meaning of Shambhu is found in the scripture as follows,

Sham Bhavayasi ca Bhavase Sham ca Bhavasi ceti va deva

Tvam Devedaruvipine linge prathitosvata Shambhu!!

Meaning: O the Lord of all, you are the generator of all bliss. You enjoy all pleasure (embodiment of joy) and eternity. Your aniconic form of Lingam that is found (installed or self-manifested) in pinewood forest is called Shambhu Lingam. Therefore, you are known as Shambhu.

In SB 12.10.8, *ity uktvā tam upeyāya bhagavān sa satāṁ gatiḥ īśānaḥ sarva-vidyānām īśvaraḥ sarva-dehinām;* Having spoken thus, Lord Śaṅkara — the shelter of pure souls, master of all spiritual sciences and controller of all embodied living beings — approached the sage. Sukadeva Goswami often uses the word Bhagavan for Lord Shiva also.

RUDRA'S REAL POSITION

There are three principal deities of Vedic systems like Brahma, Vishnu, and Shiva, and often they are attributed as the mode of passion, mode of goodness, and mode of ignorance in the same order. Brahma is the living being, whereas Vishnu is the Supersoul, has Shiva been considered an ordinary living being or Supersoul, or the transient form of spirituality? Shiva is not a living being like us as well as he is not the supreme Lord like Lord Vishnu. Shiva's position is eternally the spiritual being extended in all planets and universes. No one will become Shiva, as Shiva is Shiva himself. After the dissolution, Shiva remains in the spiritual sky, as mentioned in Brahma Samhita and the eternal residence as the Kailash mountain. Shiva is as good as God, and one should remember the verse from Padma Purana that Shiva or Brahma is still not equal to Vishnu, and one must consider Shiva as the position servitor God in terms of Vishnu and Krishna. Any living being if performed the *varnasrama dharma* for hundred life then his is eligible to become Brahma, As Brahma is a position and one living being has the chance to grow in any of the universes as per his qualifications and

Lord's mercy to take that position. However, no one can take the position of Rudra / Shiva as Shiva is eternally remaining in his original position. It's challenging to understand Shiva's absolute truth in connection with Vishnu; however, with the mercy of Shiva, one can know about Him as well as Lord Vishnu in full reality.

As per Srimad Bhagavatam SB 2.3.7 *vidyā-kāmas tu giriśaṁ dāmpatyārtha umāṁ satīm..,*the meaning of this verse: If one desires to be a much learned man he should worship Lord Shiva, and if one desires an excellent marital relation he should worship the chaste goddess Umā, the wife of Lord Shiva.

RUDRA'S MEDITATIVE POSITION

On many occasions, we find the pictures of Shiva in a complete trance, and that's his true identity, Rudra is always meditating on the supreme personality of Godhead, Sankarsana. The verse in Srimad Bhagavatam suggests us to know the real position of Lord Shiva, it is mentioned by penance and austerity, there is a scope for one to approach the supreme Lord and then to Lord Shiva, it is applicable to similar procedures.

When a child is annoying his mother, she requested him to sit down quietly in one place so that she can produce better results by cooking efficiently. On the other hand, she can engage her children in the cooking process, also if they are interested in cooperating and listening to the instructions. We tend to follow a principle or follow a leader of high integrity. This is natural for all humanity. Lord Brahma advised Rudra to help in the expansion of the growth of the population in the universe. By means of severe penances, only once can invoke the mercy of the Absolute Truth. The results are different as Lord Rudra produced the population ready to devour the existing one without discrimination; this is contrary to what Lord Brahma wanted to have. So, Lord Brahma again asked Rudra to perform meditation on the supreme so that every being can get benefit out of such actions. It is essential to know whenever the creation is in progress, annihilation needs to be delayed; this is the will of the Lord, so Rudra is always meditating under a banyan tree for eternity, and we find the picture which is very fascinating to our mind. With the results of such actions, the followers and sons of Rudra refrained from the annihilation principles and remained calm to satisfy their master, Lord Rudra. With the advice from Brahma, Rudra started meditating on the Sankarsana – the source of His energy and qualities. Most of the time, we see the picture of Lord Shiva in meditative form due to this reason.

NAMES OF RUDRA

When the creation of the world started, several daughters of Daksha were given to different personalities in marriage for propagating the population of the world by the direction of Lord Brahma. Brahma was pleased that Daksha was performing better than any other Prajapati in discharging his duties. One of the daughters of Daksha, known as Sarupa, got married to the Bhuta. And Bhuta produced millions of Rudra. Are the Rudras the same as Lord Shiva? No, they are the classification of the Rudra category and remain associates of Rudra eternally.

As per Srimad Bhagavatam ŚB 6.6.17-18

sarūpāsūta bhūtasya
bhāryā rudrāṁś ca koṭiśaḥ
raivato 'jo bhavo bhīmo
vāma ugro vṛṣākapiḥ

ajaikapād ahirbradhno
bahurūpo mahān iti
rudrasya pārṣadāś cānye
ghorāḥ preta-vināyakāḥ

“Sarūpā, the wife of Bhūta, gave birth to the ten million Rudras, of whom the eleven principles Rudras were Raivata, Aja, Bhava, Bhīma, Vāma, Ugra, Vṛṣākapi, Ajaikapāt, Ahirbradhna, Bahurūpa, and Mahān. Their associates, the ghosts and goblins, who are very fearful, were born of the other wife of Bhūta.

Sarupa, one of the wives of Bhuta, became the mother of the eleven Rudras of this universe. Bhuta had one more wife besides Sarupa, and she became the mother of the ghosts and hobgoblins and many more associates of Rudra. This is interesting to note the growth of the Rudra-gana in the material world at the time of universal creation.”

When we try to differentiate an intuitive personality, it is challenging to analyze it unless we refer to the conclusion of the sages and especially Srila Vyasadava. Shiva is all auspicious, and Vedic mantras chanted for Lord Shiva, such as “*Om Namah Shivaya*” or “*Om Rudraya Namah,*” are invoking mercy from Lord Rudra. Shiva is also called Mahadeva, the greatest of all the demigods, and sometimes Shiva is referred to as the Supersoul of the universe. There is nothing in such statements, and one has to understand the context, situations, and means of the prayers. The self-effulgent identity of the universe is known as the Paramātmā because Lord Shiva is directly an incarnation of Lord Vishṇu. Sukadeva Gosvami mentions *“patiṁ viśvasyātmeśvaraṁ śāśvatam.”* Lord Shiva is eternal, and he is the Supersoul also. In other instances, we can understand the meaning of Supersoul as it is referred to by various names *such as Achyuta, Shiva*, and Mahesvara. Here we can appreciate the import of the Veda that Shiva is also known as the Supersoul.

Rudra is also a class of society where they follow Lord Shiva; generally, we should understand as Rudra-Gana or the populace of Rudra or Rudra’s direct expansion to assist the original Rudra in the destruction of the universe. In the sky, when we see there are many stars and one moon, similarly Rudra is one, and his

Rudra associates and Shiva Gana are enormous. One should know the absolute position of Rudra in totality.

PHILOSOPHICAL BIRTH OF RUDRA

Whenever the concept of birth is there, there is an end of this element as death or transformation from one element to another. The principle of reincarnation is still found in the Dalai Lama, sect of the Buddhist ideology in Tibet. Krishna mentioned in Gita that his birth and activities are always non-material and completely spiritual. That means he takes birth to expand his limitless pastimes in the earthly planets. Rudra has close to the same principle; however, the presence of the Rudra principle is understood in a different meaning. As soon as the light is there, we understand the presence of the sun, and the coolness of the night is brought forth by the presence of the beautiful moon, so as the intense anger in any human is considered the presence of the Rudra. As the body is composed of senses, mind, intelligence, and ego, so the principle of Rudra is known by the level of the mood of ahankara. Let's talk about the philosophy of the ego or sometimes called false ego. Anger is generated from lust and becomes the killer of the world. Lust means, the uncontrollable desires to enjoy with full extent and unlimitedly. However, such enjoyment is not possible in the material world, so the obstructions in enjoyment develop a sense of anger. It could be any form of anger by words, body gestures, movement of the hands and legs, heavy breathing, red eyes, and biting the teeth also.

One has to overcome the enjoying spirit and situate in the mode of goodness to control over the biggest enemy, anger, or *krodha.* The principle of anger is controlled by the ego, as one living being thinks himself as the doer of everything and controller of everything. He gets frustrated because of the conception of oneself to be the center of the world. Once the conceptions of the subjective principle destroyed by external means, natural disturbances, other forms of attacks, the person gets infuriated and comes under the control of anger. Rudra acts as the ahankara, and it could be influenced via the mode of goodness, passion, and ignorance also. Mode of ignorance mixed with the Ahankara would certainly produce havoc in the society. The symbolic representation of the human being's different bodily limbs such as hands as Indra, nostrils as the Asvini-Kumara, eyes as the sun, mind as the moon, and the ahankara as the Rudra and many more. Rudra's philosophical birth is due to the cause of the anger; similarly, the birth of Rudra in this world occurred due to the anger of Lord Brahma.

Before the birth of Lord Rudra, Lord Brahma had not been angry with anyone, and he was blessed by Lord Vishnu to expand the universe. Lord Rudra existed in the *Kailasa loka, Sada-Shiva Loka,* before his appearance in the material world. The only reason he appeared was the starting point of Brahma's being angry for the first time in his lifetime; otherwise, there is no need for Rudra to come to this world. With the element of anger, the modality and mixture of transformation started, and that is called the cycle of samsara. Rudra is an essential ingredient to run the samsara and destroy the samsara. Once he was influenced by the anger, Rudra appeared in the world. In one sense, it is good; on the other hand, we need to be careful in pleasing Rudra so that we can become free from anger.

Sometimes, we argue that Shiva is more powerful than Brahma and has more qualities than Brahma and more ancient than Brahma, then how could he later take birth after the appearance of Brahma? Varaha also appeared very late in cosmology. Does it mean that Varaha is younger to Brahma? No. We must understand the philosophy of Rudra's birth in a similar context. Rudra, in the form of original Sada-Shiva, is always present in the spiritual world, and he comes to the material universe when Brahma becomes angry, the anger is mixed with the mode of passion and ignorance brought forth by the system of expansion for the philosophy of Rudra. when the Rudra principle is attributed to Brahma, he did not exhibit the form of words or actions of any kind of body movement; rather, he shows within his mind. Rudra lies in the heart's core in the form of false ego and displays its power as the spirit soul is influenced by lust and anger. This ahankara or false ego is the result of the interaction of egocentric ideas of the spirit soul. Lord Brahma also thought as the center of the universe and thought that whatever he wants, it should happen. Kumaras were reluctant to follow the order of Brahma, and it caused anger. Brahma was mixed with the mode of passion and false ego, resulting in anger. This is the first appearance of Rudra in the material world.

Rudra always resides in the heart of all living beings as long as one considers himself the body, mind, intelligence, and real doer. The real doer of all the actions is the Supreme Lord, and none of us could claim the title, in case we do, that's the resultant combination of passion and false ego. Rudra principle is so subtle, and one must cultivate by following the real Rudra, who is always chanting the name of the absolute truth, by doing so, one could come out of the influence of anger and the Rudra principle.

Rudra's philosophical birth could be found in various instances and topmost personalities like sage Durvasa, son of sage Samika, Shringi, king Indra, Brihaspati, Brahma, and what to name of the current days' mortals. One will be considered pure if the Rudra principle of the material world is entirely absent in him, and he surrenders to real Rudra, Sada-Shiva. Lord Krishna mentions that shark, lion, banyan tree, and many objects of articles of worship are the opulent manifestations of Him. Similarly, the snake, tiger, ghosts, dhutura, marijuana, etc. are the expansions of Rudra-principle in the mode of ignorance. There is a big cyclone or tornado that happens in the ocean, and it is considered the furious god, Rudra. In Hawaii, they call the lava, Pele, the god of volcanoes, and Paka, the anger of the wind, the anger of the mountain of Hawaii, a different set of the incarnation of God. Those are the forms of Rudra. In some religions, anger is expressed in the form of worship and warfare; they are known as the Rudra principle.

The philosophical birth of Rudra to be understood seriously, and one should discern from the real Rudra philosophy and advance in the spiritual life. If someone is excessively influenced by such principles of anger and ahankara, then certainly, the result would be falling down from one's original spiritual position.

RUDRANI

In Bhagavad Gita, we usually know that there are eleven Rudras, and Krishna is known as the chief Rudra as Shiva. Eleven Rudras have corresponding energy expansion as their wives known as Rudrani, and their names are mentioned in Srimad Bhagavatam ŚB 3.12.13 as follows:

dhīr dhṛti-rasalomā ca
niyut sarpir ilāmbikā
irāvatī svadhā dīkṣā
rudrāṇyo rudra te striyaḥ

O Rudra, you also have eleven wives, called the Rudrāṇīs, and they are as follows: Dhī, Dhṛti, Rasalā, Umā, Niyut, Sarpi, Ilā, Ambikā, Irāvatī, Svadhā, and Dīkṣā.

When God descends to the material world, they are always associated with the respective energy expansion. Lord Vishnu descends with mother Laxmi and Lord Shiva with Parvati. The eleven Rudra have the corresponding energy expansion as Rudrani, and they are also famous in the world.

In Srimad Bhagvatam, 12.5.1, *yasya prasāda-jo brahma rudraḥ krodha-samudbhavaḥ;* from whose satisfaction Brahmā is born and from whose anger Rudra takes birth. We can refer the conceptual ideas from the discourse of Srimad Bhagavatam. In addition to this, Srimad Bhagavatam (12.12.11) mentions about the birth of Lord Rudra as *rudra-sargas tathaiva ca*. All the references are very much helpful in understanding the appearance of rudra and rudrani.

COLOR OF RUDRA

Sometimes we get confused with the original color of Rudra or Shiva. Do the color of the body of Shiva matter to our understanding? The color of Krishna is blackish blue, and the color of Lord Chaitanya is molten gold. Many more incarnations of God have a different color in different time and age. Lord Shiva has many expansions in this material world with varying degrees of His body color, and He can manifest those attributes based on His mood and qualities. And the verse is found in Srimad Bhagavatam ŚB 3.12.15, *bhagavān nīla-lohitaḥ,* the color of the body of Lord Rudra is *nila* and l*ohita*, *nila* means blue and *lohita* means red, when the two color mixes, blue and red, the uncommon color of bluish red is the natural color of Lord Rudra. This is the statement from Sukadeva Goswami as he is explaining the color of Rudra. Lord Rudra has all manifestations of color of his body like that of Lord Krishna.

Most of the time, we see a picture of Lord Shiva as a blue or white with meditation posture, why his color in the cover page is golden hue? This incident took place when Shiva appeared to bless the ten Pracetas, as if he assumed the form of Lord Gauranga to manifest His pastimes. Nevertheless, God's form, attributes, qualities are unlimited, and I am sharing few details only. My limited mind has reached to a certain extent of the Lord's body. It will be my impudence only if I limit the size of Lord Shiva or His transcendental body color to something one to the mundane world. God is the source of all colors, and we can see the beautiful color, such as the blackish cloud color of Krishna, as the most common form of worship.

Similarly, the golden hue color is also a stunning form for both the devotees of Krishna and Lord Shiva. This brief information will help the readers understand the meaning of God's body color so that it can establish the importance of the form of God, and Lord Shiva is not formless or colorless. He possesses the beautiful feature, and it attracts even the great demigods of this universe, what to speak of mere mortals of this planet earth.

WHO WAS BORN AFTER RUDRA?

Sometimes we tend to explore the chronological and sequential order in the universal creation. As per the Veda, Rudra was born just after the great sages known as four Kumaras namely Sanat, Sanaka, Sanatana, Sanandana. These four kumaras were born from Lord Brahma, and subsequently, Rudra came into being. Does it mean that Rudra did not exist before His birth from Lord Brahma? No, it's like sunshine is not seen in our mundane eyes at midnight; we can't conclude here that there is no sun in the sky; however, the sun is somewhere else on the planet. Similarly, Lord Rudra appeared to assist in the service of the Supreme Personality of Godhead. Rudra's birth is very mystical; Lord Boar appeared via the nostrils of Lord Brahma as he sneezed. But whenever we sneeze, there could be many viruses. Nowadays people in general fear the coronavirus, and we are afraid of spreading the COVID-19. Based on the scriptural references, we can understand that the three principal qualitative incarnations or *Gunavatara* are beyond our perceptions and understanding. We must depend on the *Sruti / smrti and Puranas* to know the glorious birth of the Lord. Shiva is as good as God, and He is also the supreme servant of Lord Vishnu.

After Rudra was born, various sages were born from Lord Brahma, and they are listed below in the shloka. These great personalities were born to assist in the expansion of the population and the welfare of the universe under the directions of Lord Brahma. After Rudra was born from between the eyebrows of Lord Brahma, Lord Brahma also expanded various sages from His internal potency without the help of any female energy. This creative energy is so powerful, and these qualities can only be found in Brahma, Vishnu, and Shiva but not with any other demigods.

Seven sages and other important sages were born after the appearance of Rudra in this universe such as Vasistha, Angira, Kratu, Pulaha, Atri, Bhrgu, Marici, Pulastya, Marici, Daksha and Narada. Daksha was born after Rudra's appearance and one should not be confused with the cosmological age factor.

ANOTHER MEANING OF RUDRA'S BIRTH

There are unlimited potencies of Lord Shiva as well as his birth has many sources of references and one interesting reference from Srimad Bhagavatam ŚB 5.25.3.

yasya ha vā idaṁ kālenopasañjihīrṣato 'marṣa-viracita-rucira-bhramad-bhruvor antareṇa sāṅkarṣaṇo nāma rudra ekādaśa-vyūhas try-akṣas tri-śikhaṁ śūlam uttambhayann udatiṣṭhat.

"At the time of devastation, when Lord Anantadeva desires to destroy the entire creation, He becomes slightly angry. Then from between His two eyebrows appears three-eyed Rudra, carrying a trident. This Rudra, who is known as Sāṅkarṣaṇa, is the embodiment of the eleven Rudras, or incarnations of Lord Shiva. He appears to devastate the entire creation. "

Srila Prabhupada explains the devastation procedures of the cosmic manifestation, as anger is the starting point, and anger remains the endpoint for the devastation. One should note that the reason behind Rudra's anger. Rudra is helping every living entity to try to go back to Godhead and aspire for liberation from the material bondage, the shackles of Durga Maya. Rudra gives benedictions, assistance, punishments, and establishes a perfect example so that the living entities could get a chance and think of going back to Vaikuntha. When he sees that there are still many people loitering in this world with the material boons, he really gets angry at this point, that's the starting point of his anger, and he manifests the devastating identity from Sankarsana and receives the power to destroy the three worlds. All of the eleven Rudras become prominent at the time of cosmic annihilation. They laugh, dance, and make the world fearful and destroy it by the will of Lord Sankarsana.

In this annihilation process, we can only know that Shiva is beyond the jurisdiction of Lord Brahma's creation as he has expanded from Lord Shiva, and He has eternally remained beyond the Brahma-Jyoti radiance of the Lord. Lord Shiva expanded himself into eleven Rudras, as discussed in the earlier section.

RUDRA'S EXPANSION

Does Rudra expand Himself? Rudra is considered as the qualitative God, and he is also the knower of past, present, and future. Lord Rudra is known as *Trikalanja*. He knows every living beings' desire and intention. In many instances, Lord Shiva descends from His abode from the mount Kailas and manifests Himself according to His devotees' mood and prayers. Lord Shiva also descends to places where Krishna's devotees need spiritual realization, as we found in the case of Pracetas. Lord Shiva appeared in front of the Pracetas and gave them religious instructions. Rudra Gita is popularly known as one of the best songs in the entire Vedic scriptures, and the glories are unlimited who glorify the essential meanings to others. Lord Shiva and

Brahma do not perform the Lila like Lord Krishna. They act as the servitor of Lord Vishnu in his earthly pastimes, and they take more jubilation in such services.

It's fascinating to note the Rudra principle and know its impacts, what a human being should do to please Rudra to attain the ultimate goal of life. There are many earthly creatures who always represent the Rudra element. The snake, tiger, and lion are still representations of Rudra. Rudra descends to various planets to give mercy to the living beings, and he is easily pleased with anyone with a pure offering to him. Narada muni has distributed loving devotional service to the fallen souls, and Lord Shiva bestows the material opulence of persons in need, if He sees someone is frank, there is no hypocrisy or malice in his heart, even though he approaches for a material boon, he offers the highest award such as knowledge of the supreme being and how to attain Him. Lord Shiva expanded in all the Dham of Vishnu, such as Vraja Mandal, Navadvipa Mandal, Jagannath Puri Dham, and many more. He personally expanded himself into many beings as Lingas and received the worship of devotees on the bank of the Ganges in Varanasi etc. When the Rudra principle is exhibited by persons who are not engaged in the devotional service of the Supreme Personality of Godhead, the angry person falls from the peak of his improved position.

RUDRA'S SHARE IN YAJNA

Yajna means sacrifice and generally performed with the fire element. In the fire sacrifice, all the demigods' hymns are mentioned, or they partake the offering of the Yajna in different meanings. These processes are based on the ritualistic fruitive activities, and the satisfaction of the Supreme Lord, the combination of both determines the outcome of the Yajna. Technically all the demigods play a significant role in the Yajna like Indra, Candra, Varuna, Surya, Kuvera, etc. and Lord Shiva should not be part of this share of the sacrifice. During the

Vajapeya Yajna conducted by Daksha, with the dispute of not respecting to Daksha properly, Daksha uttered the curse that Lord Shiva should not be part of the share of the Yajna sacrifice as it's generally offered to many demigods, Shiva being utterly aloof from the ceremonial offering, felt happy within for bereft of the ritualistic reactions.

All our activities are meant to please the Supreme Personality of Godhead, and the same action is attributed as a sacrifice. By the arrangement of the divinity, Daksha has cursed him out of anger and envy that Lord Shiva will be bereft of all share of sacrifices from any Yajna performed at any time. In another way, he was relieved from the gross karma Kanda theory and roamed in His divinity and was completely independent. As per Srimad Bhagavatam SB 4.6.53, *yajñas te rudra bhāgena,* Rudra's share should be given in the execution of the fire sacrifices, Lord Brahma is fully conversant with the real religion and the position of Rudra and he is mentioning that any sacrifice and especially the Dakha Yanja will not be fully complete and yield results unless Shiva accepts the offering of the oblations. This is the mystery of the Vedic science and one has to be fully conversant on the topic of the outcome of the yajna. In Kali Yuga, the yajna is very simple as Sankirtana Yanja, only chanting of the Maha mantra.

On the contrary, we find that Daksha was envious of Lord Shiva. A great personality dared to offend and curse him, the curse uttered by Daksha, as mentioned in Srimad Bhagavatam. ŚB 4.2.18, *saha bhāgaṁ na labhatāṁ,* there is no scope for Lord Shiva to obtain any resultant output of any sacrifices however all the demigods like Indra and Varuna will get the benefit. Shiva could not get the share of the yajna performed by human beings; we can understand the envious attitude of Daksha towards Lord Shiva. Anyway, it was a blessing in disguise for Lord Shiva.

Sometimes a curse becomes a boon by the will of providence. For example, when Narada cursed the sons of the Kuvera; they got the darshan of Lord Krishna in the Vraj Dham. Similarly, the curse of Daksha was a blessing for Lord Shiva. Shiva is aloof from the ritualistic Karma Kanda activities, and there is no need for him to take part in them like the demigods. It is clear that Shiva is not a demigod and beyond the conception of the demigods like Indra, Surya, Chandra, Varuna, etc. It does not make sense for Shiva to participate in the Yajna share and be afflicted with the result of Karma Kanda or Upasana Kanda activities. The essence one can get from this situation is that Shiva is happy within, and his position as superior to a demigod is established by the sweet will of Lord Vishnu. By not offering the sacrificial result to Shiva, he is not bereft the godly opulence outcome as he is independent on the human sacrifice items. He is entirely dependent on the Sankarana's power.

LORD SHIVA AND PARVATI MARRIAGE CEREMONY

Srimad Bhagavatam describes the detailed description of the marriage of Shiva and Sati and how Sati left her body in the presence of all the assembled priests and guests at her father, Daksha's place. In summary, in *dakṣa-yajña*, the Lord Shiva's devotees, massacred all the *yajña* arena due to the demise of their goddess Sati. It is natural to have such a level of anger when they saw Sati burnt into ashes in front of her father; he did not prevent it from happening. Mahārāja Dakṣa was also cut off by his head, and he was put in a goat's head, in this way. So, after the death of his wife, Lord Shiva was very much aggrieved. He went to the forest and engaged himself in meditation. Social order was disrupted by the ferocious fight between demigods and demons. Because there was always fighting between the demigods and the demons, so to kill the demons, there was a need for a very great soldier who must be borne by Lord Shiva, by the semina of Lord Shiva. So, at that time Sati, Dākṣāyaṇī, after death she has taken another body as the daughter of King of Himalaya, Pārvatī. Therefore, her name was at that time Pārvatī. Pārvatī means "the daughter of Parvata." Parvata means mountain.

So, the plan was that within the womb of Pārvatī and by the semina of Lord Shiva, one son must take birth, and later he did, his name was Kārttikeya. Kārttikeya was born. So, Lord Shiva was in meditation, and Pārvatī was not married at that time with Lord Shiva, although she was destined to marry Lord Shiva. Because in the transcendental world, the husband and wife, they are also eternal. Even if the wife or husband changes the body, again, they become husband and wife. This is a higher sense of understanding. They do not separate. Lord Shiva was in deep meditation. And it is tough to break his meditation. Pārvatī was engaged in worshiping Shiva-liṅga, the genital of Lord Shiva while he was meditating without any cloth in His body. As per the Vedic culture, there is worshiping of Shiva-liṅga. So Pārvatī was engaged to worship the genital of Lord Shiva. Indeed, there was touching by a young girl, but he was not agitated. We become excited by seeing one beautiful girl. But the most beautiful girl, young, was touching the genital of Lord Shiva; still, there was no disturbance. This is the actual position of Shiva.

Once upon a time, the God of the mountain Himalaya is known as Himavat, and his wife, Mena, received a great boon from the divinity in the form of a beautiful child - a daughter and named as Parvati. She is also considered as the reincarnation of Sati, who left her body at her will at the fire sacrifice of the Daksha - the Prajapati. Narada came to the house of Himavat and announced that this girl is certainly going to marry Lord Shiva. Parvati has been trying to impress Shiva by the advice of the Demigods so that they lock into a Vedic wedding and a divine son to be born to protect the devas as nothing is attainable without austerity. Parvati is also known as Gauri because of her fair complexion. She performed severe penances at the Triyuginarayan place.

Currently, there is a Gauri Kund in this place for the memory of her austerity. This is also the baseline spiritual connection point to the Kedarnath pilgrimage tour. By the divine arrangement, both happened to marry. Still, some people say that Lord Shiva proposed to Parvati in the Guptakashi area. They got married in the Triyuginarayan village, the confluence of Sone-Ganga and Mandakini river, part of the Uttarakhand province.

As demigods were harassed by the demon known as Taraka and he is destined to be killed by the son of Lord Shiva and Pravati. They are anxious that Shiva is in complete meditation and has no sign of engaging in Parvati's conjugal service. Demigods sincerely prayed to Mother Parvati to serve Shiva and allure Him for quick marriage. They employed the Kamadeva to go to Mount Kailash and use his power on Shiva to fulfill their mission. When Lord Shiva opened his eyes and saw Parvati, he developed a sense of affection towards her and later realized that this was a trick from Kamadeva, and he burnt Kamadeva into ashes.

After that, Lord Shiva wanted to test Parvati's genuine love for Him, so he appeared as an old brahmin and requested her that there is no need to marry a person who is wearing a tiger skin or smeared with ashes on his body. He said, "I don't see any good quality in Lord Shiva, and please refrain from getting married to Him." Parvati was sad and furious against the old brahmin, and she mentioned the unlimited glories of Lord Shiva. She also revealed that she is none other Sati and Shiva is her eternal husband. There is nothing in the world that could change her marriage with Shiva. She felt unconscious by uttering such statements to the old brahmin. Shiva was pleased with the feelings and devotions of Parvati for him. Lord Shiva showed His true form and identity and promised to marry Parvati.

Sthula Purana depicts the marriage and points to the place where the actual wedding took place between Shiva and

Parvati in the presence of all the demigods, including the Supreme Personality of Godhead Vishnu and first creator of the universe Lord Brahma. Vishnu acted as the brother of Parvati in this marriage ceremony as Krishna acted as the brother of Yogamaya in the Krishna Lila, and they are eternally the brother and sister and Maya acts on behalf of Vishnu's potency. Brahma was appointed as the priest of the ceremony, and there is *shila* called *Brahma-shila* signifies the certificate of the marriage and a legendary note for the generations to come and to seek blessings from the divine couple. Whoever visits this place, Triyuginarayan and the temple where the marriage ceremony took place undoubtedly have a sophisticated marriage life and develop a love of Godhead by the mercy of the trinity deity.

Many demigods were invited for the marriage ceremony, and there were arrangements for the holy bath in four ponds known as Brahma Kund, Vishnu Kund, Rudra Kund, and Saraswati Kund. It is understood that the water is flown into the remaining three kunds from the Saraswati Kund. That is getting the transcendental water from the navel of Garbodaksayi Vishnu as the kund's water has unlimited potency such as curing many diseases and also it gives immense strength for spiritual cultivation.

After the marriage ceremony was over, all the demigods departed to their abode, so as Lord Shiva and Parvati to Mount Kailas.

RUDRA–HALF MAN & HALF WOMAN (ARDHANARISHVARA)

Vedic scripture suggests changing the sex by the will only, Parvati converted any person visiting the forest to woman where both Lord Shiva and Parvati reside. Just by entering the area where Parvati made the clause, any male can turn into female by the will of Parvati. There are many such examples, such as taking a bath in a pond, a king turned into a female. As per Srimad Bhagavatam ŚB 12.12.11, Sukadeva Goswami mentions about the birth of Rudra as "*rudra-sargas tathaiva ca*" as well as the possibilities of the half man and half woman gods such as "*ardha-nārīśvarasyātha*". Nowadays, scientists always pursue the path of gender change process but there is no evidence of the half man and half woman feature in one personality. One must admit that some inconceivable attributes are uncommon qualities in Lord Shiva and Goddess Parvati. It proves that there are possibilities of a half man and half woman scenario in Vedic ages.

Srimad Bhagavatam Canto 4.4.3 mentions, "*premṇātmano yo 'rdham adāt satāṁ priyaḥ*"- meaning is that Lord Shiva, who had given her half his body due to affection. Lord Shiva and Sati are together, and they make one unit and complete it. Ardhanarishvara is a Sanskrit word, and the meaning is "Lord Who Is Half Woman" composite male-female deity of the heavenly God. This form of the deity is so beautiful and enchanting that half of the figure is represented with the male (Shiva) with the beautiful hair, the partial third eye on the forehead, and serpents coiled in the neck, tiger skin for the half of the body. The second half of the central figure's left side is ornamented with the combed hair and silk garment on the body with girdles, an anklet, a red dot on the forehead with a developed breast. Both Lord Shiva and Parvati share half of their body in the unique androgynous form, and wife is always on the left side so-called *Vama Bhagama*. The Ardhanarishvara feature is the mysterious form of Lord Shiva. This shows the entire cosmos of the material world with the combination seed of Shakti and Shiva, the essential ingredient of the material creation. In SB 8.7.30, *"netra-trayaṁ sattva-rajas-tamāṁsi"*, Lord Rudra's three eyes represent the three modes of material nature such as ignorance, passion, goodness and ignorance is manifested in the third eye which is rarely used except the methods of destructions.

When we refer to the *Brihadaranyka Upanishad*, the first being created with one absolute whole and subsequently the being to expand further. Then, it divides the infinite whole into two such beings as energetic and energy with the equal power of the universal system. Such type of unity of male and female is inseparable and brings the formula of the existence of the material world. The spiritual world has the same concept, with Radha as the energy and Krishna as the energetic. The only difference between the two views is the former becomes distorted views in the mundane world. This symbolic presence of the male and female gives us the guiding principles to follow the tradition of the Varnasrama system with the system of family life and ultimate attainment at the end of the universal cataclysms. Ardhanarishvara is considered an anthropomorphized manifestation of the non-dual Brahman and emanates the essence of the material world. Generally, it is also known as the Shiva and Shakti, and both have equal importance in our life system.

Sada-Shiva or Parashiva, the abstract in brahman conceptual ideas, Shiva is comparable in His metaphysical properties to Brahman, sometimes the non-dual substance as such, the essence of the universe. The energy emanating from the spiritual *brahmajyoti* is the cause of this material universe's sustenance, where Lord Shiva acts as the transcendental agent of the supreme being.

When we refer to Rg Veda 3.38.4, Visvarupa, the divine God of heaven, manifests as an androgynous form with the half-bull half-cow form in one sacred unit, it can self-generate though. A similar conceptual process was mentioned in the Brihadaranyaka Upanishad. One singular absolute form of Brahman, as Jiva Goswami said in his *Nama Vyakarana*, is the *Brahman* as neutral linga. Even Lord Krishna expanded from His left body to the most beautiful and the expansion of the energy form of the Lord as Sri Radha. Lord Chaitanya is known as *"Sri Krishna Chaitanya Radha Krishna nahi anya*." which means Lord Chaitanya is a combination of Radha and Krishna. This form, Ardhanarishvara of Lord Shiva and Mother Parvati is the androgynous feature of the Brahman as symbolized as the most compassionate mother as well as the elongation of the companionship of the spiritual essence.

In Srimad Bhagavatam SB 9.1.32, *tad idaṁ bhagavān āha priyāyāḥ priya-kāmyayā sthānaṁ yaḥ praviśed etat sa vai yoṣid bhaved iti;* Thereupon, just to please his wife, Lord Shiva said, "Any male entering this place shall immediately become a female!" This is the power of Lord Shiva, and at his will He can assume any form He desires, and He can transform anyone into any form of the body available in the material world.

REAL RUDRA - HARI-HARA

Rāma and Kṛṣṇa are the Supreme Lord, and Hare means Harā. So Harā means the potency, pleasure potency of the Supreme Lord. It is addressed as Hare. So, Hare Kṛṣṇa means Rādhā-Kṛṣṇa and Hare is the principal energy of the supreme Lord. Hara implies Hari's manifestation in the material world, which is another name of Lord Shiva. As per Brahma-Samhita, Maya, the shadow potency of the energy is sitting and requesting mercy from the supreme Lord. There is a festival in India called "Hari & Hara Milan"- the meeting of Lord Shiva and Lord Hari during the Shiva Ratri period. Lord Hari visits the temple of Lord Shiva, and the meeting is celebrated in great jubilation. In my native place in Odisha, India, they do celebrate this festival and procession takes place from Jagannath temple towards Shiva temple. This is unique and symbolizes Hari and Hara unity and, of course, the followers of both the Lords.

The potency of the Supreme Lord, Harā is often addressed as Hare like a vocative form of invocation. Hari, Hara, Hare, and Harā have four different identities and meanings; one should be very careful to know its impact and benefit. So Harā means potency, pleasure potency of the Lord. There is no ambiguity in deciphering the meaning of Hari. Hari means Lord Vishnu; His spiritual energy is called Hare or Harā. However, Hara is the shadow energetic from the Lord (milk to yogurt) in the material world. Whether we understand the technicality of the holy name or not, we chant in ecstasy the *"Hare Krishna Maha Mantra"* so that our condition may be fallen; we can still take this instruction of the Shastras and chant incessantly. Lord Hara is going to help us when we chant the name of Lord Hari with the help of mother Harā (hladini potency).

Hare is pronounced from the śabda or word as hara, ah, From Harā, just like *latā-śabda, latāḥ.* So, addressing, Harā means the energy. Hari or the Supreme Personality of Godhead and He is always present everywhere, in every atom and molecule. God has unlimited potencies and energies with various transformations to sustain the material and spiritual universe. The Maya or Gauri or Durga energy is one of the manifested energies of the Supreme Lord, it is also called as the illusory energy. Durga means the fort or the superintendent of the jail, this material world is considered as the jail. Māyā śakti is also His śakti.

sṛṣṭi-sthiti-pralaya-sādhana-śaktir ekā

chāyeva yasya bhuvanāni vibharti durgā

[Brahma-saṁhitā 5.44]

Durgā is also His śakti. In the mantra, we could infer the variety of Krishna's expanded energy and the reciprocal ways to address the energy. One should not end with the energy rather approach the energetic. That's the basic principle of the emanations of the methods of connecting with the divine. Hare Krishna is a way of addressing the energy and energetic form of the Supreme being and Hare Rama has the similar potent and bonafide approach., then we are addressing Krishna and Rama, Varaha, Parashuram, Balarama and many more incarnations of the God. Many of us have the same question as to why are we addressing the Supreme Lord? Of course, for His mercy and love. The address is vocative and called as Hare instead of Harā. O my mother or Oh my God, or Oh my Lord, etc. I hope this definition is clear now.

The Advaita principle is a non-dual substance in the oneness of brahman as discussed here in the name of "Harihara". We find a similar concept in Chaitanya Lila as Advaita Prabhu, an incarnation of a combination of Lord Mahavishnu and Lord Sada-Shiva. Sometimes Lord Shiva and Lord Vishnu give their oneness in one form as Harihara, a similar deity, is found in the most famous temple of Lingaraj lingam at Bhubaneswar. The concept of unity is to be understood simultaneously one and different with varying degrees of quality and attributes.

Shiva is the deity of the mind. He is the son of *Chaturmukha* Brahma & thus the grandson of Lord Vishnu. Shiva receives the name "Shiva" - "the auspicious" and He was pleased to receive the sanctified water poured by four-headed Brahma to the feet of Lord Vishnu. Hara is the abbreviation from "Harati." which means that one who snatches or clears away. For the sattvic souls, the Lord of the mind snatches away all the obstacles. He makes their perception of devotion towards the Supreme Brahman (Lord Vishnu) and His family of deities/demigods. For the tamasic souls, the Lord of the mind distracts from the good and righteousness and makes their account attached against the Supreme Brahman. This could also be through distracting their thoughts by creating fascination towards worldly pleasures. There are many quotes in the Shiva Purana, Skanda Purana, wherein Lord Shiva himself proclaims that Lord Vishnu is the Supreme Brahman. Vedas and other branches such as Upanishads already proclaim Lord Narayana to be the Supreme Brahman.

Unlike in humans where the name is nothing, in particular, the Supreme Brahman is nameless to the senses; He does not have a single name that identifies Him. All the names through which He is referred to, have more profound meaning on the attribute of the Brahman. For example, Narayana (pronounced as *Naa raa yanaa*) means that one who has no defects, one who is the essence of all the souls, one who sleeps on the ocean of pralaya Samudra, one who is filled with promising attributes in complete form. As per Srimad Bhagavatam ŚB 4.2.25, "May those who are envious of Lord Shiva, being attracted by the flowery language of the enchanting Vedic promises, and who have thus become dull, always remain attached to fruitive activities."

We should not get confused with Harā with the name hāra as both are different meanings. And in another place of Srimad Bhagavatam ŚB 10.46.45, *calan-nitamba-stana-hāra-kuṇḍala,* their hips, breasts, and necklaces moved about. In this connection, the Vraja gopis movement and the wearing of the ornaments are described, and the import of the hara is significant as the garland of flowers or necklaces worn by the *Vraja-badhu*. If we reflect more from Sastra, then we will be bewildered that how the word 'hara' is used significantly, and the meaning and pronunciation are different to each usage in the hymn. We should not get confused with Harā with the name *hāra* as both are different meanings. And in another place of Srimad Bhagavatam ŚB 3.25.24, *saṅga-doṣa-harā hi te,* here we can find out the meaning of hara as the remover of pain or someone who counterfeit the miseries in the heart as the word suggests complete counteraction of the pernicious effects of material attachment.

Again, we take the meaning someone steals your mind, heart, or distress, can also be called as hara. We should not get confused with *Harā* with the name hara as both are different meanings. And in another place of Srimad Bhagavatam ŚB 3.8.27 *mukhena lokārti-hara-smitena*; he also acknowledged the service of the devotees and vanquished their distress by His beautiful smile. In this connection, we can see the meaning of the hara means someone who vanquishes the pain by providing a beautiful smile.

For us to better understand the deeper meaning of Hari, Śrīla Bhaktisiddhānta Sarasvatī Ṭhākura referred to the beautiful verse from Nārada Pañcarātra:

ārādhito yadi haris tapasā tataḥ kiṁ

nārādhito yadi haris tapasā tataḥ kim

antar bahir yadi haris tapasā tataḥ kiṁ

nāntar bahir yadi haris tapasā tataḥ kim

"If one is worshiping Lord Hari, what is the use of performing extraneous penances? And if one is not worshiping Lord Hari, no such penances will save one. If one can understand that Lord Hari is all-pervading, within and without, what is the need of performing penances? And if one cannot understand that Hari is all-pervading, all his penances are useless." A Vaishnava is always absorbed in executing his devotional service to Kṛṣṇa. If a devotee becomes falsely proud of performing severe penances and austerities and meditates on accepting and rejecting material objects instead of thinking of his service to Kṛṣṇa, his so-called austerities become an impediment to devotional service."

We always seek blessings from the Mahajan, spiritual master and saintly persons, demigods, and any source channel to receive the mercy of Lord Hari. There are many people who are bereft of spiritual mercy such as *vaisya, sudra* and woman class of living beings. It is always necessary that the great Mahajan appear and offer all kinds of benedictions so that they also come to the level of equality. Every great sage thinks of the welfare of others and meditates on how to bring the level of everyone to God consciousness and they work in that direction. Vedas suggest that any learned person must see everyone as equal.

Was that Hari, Hara, or Hare or Harā.?

HARI means the person who is expert in stealing the best of someone, stealing in expert but in return awards, the best, who else is known as the butter thief, also called as the Hari. Sometimes it is understood that Lord Hari takes away all of our misgivings, illusion, bad habits, and all kinds of *anarthas*. Hara means joy or who is the first person to be joyful by chanting the name of Hari. Lord Shiva is mostly joyful because He is always chanting the name of Hari as Rama and Sankarsana (Balarama). This is the mystery of Hari-Hara.

HARI refers to Lord Vishnu or Lord Krishna, the supreme personality of Godhead. HARE is the vocative form of Hara, the supreme energy of God, Krishna and Rama are connected with the power of the Lord. Hare Krishna mantra is complete in the absolute sense, and it gives pleasure to the ultimate absolute. All the demigods are pleased when one utters the energy and energetic form of the Lord. The chanting of the holy name is especially recommended in this age of Kali. HARA also refers to Lord Shiva in terms of the name Harihara or "*Hara Hara Mahadev*" etc. Harā is also the feminine aspect of the Supreme Personality of Godhead, known as hladini Shakti. Harā is eternally the principal energy of Lord Hari, known as Radha, Lalita, Visakha, Candravali, Laxmi, Rukmini, Satyabhama, etc.

Hara is the name of Shiva as popularly chanted across India as "*Har Har Mahadev*" .. Shakti, the wife of Lord Shiva, is also sometimes considered the shadow energy of Hari and sometimes known as Mahamaya and Yogamaya when she appeared as the sister of Lord Krishna. Even in the Nandighosa cart, Ratha of Lord Jagannath in Puri, one of the nine Parva deva is Harihar. We could know the mood of Lord Jagannath and He wanted to keep the form of Harihar in his Ratha also.

Please don't get carried over with all the literal meanings instead focus on the sound vibration with implicit faith in the holy name and always chant the Maha-mantra, Hare *Krishna Hare Krishna Krishna Krishna Hare Hare - Hare Rama Hare Rama Rama Rama Hare Hare!* Then, you will please both Lord Hari and Lord Hara also and you can feel their effect regardless of whether we understand the meaning. Be a better person to understand the glories of the holy name and even the philosophical meaning. Nevertheless, the sacred name is going to bless the sincere seeker.

Ayappa

The appearance of Ayyappa in the dynasty of Pandya was mysterious as the Pandya empire ruled over Madurai province and beyond. King Rajasekhara is considered the foster father of Lord Ayyappan. Ayyappa is a very famous Lord in south India, and He is worshiped by one and all. As per the Hindu scriptural reference, Lord Ayyappa was born from the combination of Shiva and Mohini (Vishnu's incarnation). When Mohini bewildered Lord Shiva, and He was captivated after Mohini murti and discharged semen, with the preservation of the semen, Lord Ayyappa was born, and he was considered as a son of Hari and Hara. In this connection, Lord Ayyappa is also called as Hariharan.

As per the legend and historical facts, Lord Shiva and Vishnu, with their divine will, left the child in the care of the childless dynasty Pandya or Pandalam, the king is Rajasekhara. Both Lord Shiva and Lord Vishnu have a gift of a golden bell for their child, and hence Lord Ayyappa was known as Manikandan. As he was childless, King Rajasekhara accepted the award from God, the divine child, and took care of him very nicely.

Lord Ayyappa left the mortal world with the instructions of installing a deity of Him in the sacred Sabarimala mountain range. Lord Parashurama built the deity of the Lord Ayyappa on the bank of the river Padma (Ganga) and the town as Sabarimala (Kasi) in Kerala. Sabarimala is the most famous pilgrimage place in India, and millions of people offer their homage by visiting the holy site and receiving the blessings of Lord Ayyappa.

Guruvayurappan is an original form of Lord Vishnu in Kerala, this is a beautiful child form of Krishna and associated with the God of wind, heavenly priest and Lord Shiva. The meaning of Guruvayurappan means Guru means the spiritual master of the world, i.e., Brihaspati, he is celebrated as the spiritual master of the heavenly planets. As per Bhagavad Gita 10.24, *O Arjun, amongst priests, I am Brihaspati.* And Vayu means the God of wind, Appan means Lord or father. Once upon a time, after the dissolution of Dvaraka in water as it was submerged within the Arabian sea, Brihaspati was selected to collect the deity of Lord Krishna's childhood form as exhibited to His parents Vasudev and Devaki. However, Brihaspati was not able to get hold of the deity of Lord Krishna even though it was visibly floating on the sea. With the help of God of wind, he was able to collect the sweet deity of Lord Krishna, and they were discussing on where to install the deity and happened to reach Kerala province by the sweet arrangement of Lord Parashuram. When they were able to determine the exact spots to install the deity, they found Lord Shiva and Parvati were already dancing in joy in the spirit of waiting for the Lord to arrive at that place. Vishwakarma built the temple and arranged the beautiful surroundings for the deity to be installed, Lord Shiva was the first Lord to offer His worship to Lord Krishna and he declared the name of the deity to be called as Guruvayurappan. Brihaspati and the wind god proclaimed that anyone visiting the place will find solace from the disturbances of the iron age, Kali Yuga. Lord Shiva and Parvati, along with Ganesh and Kartikeya, were shifted to the opposite bank of the lake known as Mammiyur. One comes for the pilgrimage to the Guruvayur place, and his journey is not successful unless he visits the area / Lingam of Lord Shiva. It is also mentioned that Janmejaya also visited this place for getting a cure from a disease, and he also visited the Shiva Linga temple in Mammiyur.

According to the prayer by Murari Gupta in the book called as Sri Krishna Chaitanya Carita Maha Kavya,

upavisan nava-kambala-samvte I hari-haro 'tra vicitro rarama sura-ghe nija-loka-samavte I varada avavdhe nija-tejasa

Covered by new outfits at all festivals, their astonishing Lordships Hari-Hara (Gaura- Advaita) were seated in the temple, surrounded by intimate devotees. They revealed to the pure devotees and awarded boons whoever comes with pure intentions and respects.

WHAT IS RUDRA GITA?

Is Rudra Gita the same book as Bhagavad Gita? Lord Krishna spoke Bhagavad Gita to Arjuna on the battlefield, and Lord

Rudra spoke Rudra Gita to Pracetas in the forest. This episode is found in Srimad Bhagavatam, the greatest of all Puranas. This particular section is so dear to the devotees and to Lord Krishna that anyone who recites, reads, preaches about this song can undoubtedly attain the love of Godhead.

Once upon a time, there was a great king in the dynasty of Prthu Maharaj named Barhisat. He is the son of the great king Anthardhana. Now the generation follows: king Barhisat and then Prācīnabarhi and then Pracetas are born from him. Rudra happened to meet the Pracetas while they were seeking for perfection. This episode is a discussion between Maitreya and Vidura, and sage Narada is also explaining the glories at the same time.

Sage Maitreya is explaining to Vidura about the descriptions of the Prthu dynasty and its importance in world history. Vijitasva is the son of Prthu, out of affection and manner of equality; he distributed the kingdom to his brothers. This is the etiquette of the ancient civilizations; currently, we need to go to the court for justice for sharing the wealth, property amongst brothers. He divided four sections like eastern, western, southern, and northern provinces and offered his brothers to rule it with full sovereignty. When Vasishta cursed the fire god for descending in the mortal world, the three gods named Pavaka, Suci, and Pavamana appeared as the sons of Anthardhana, who is the son of Vijitasva. The three sons looked so bright and luminous like the fire, and their reputations have no limit. It was customary for the kings to marry many women, and polygamy was allowed earlier, Anthardhana married to another wife, Nabhasvati and fathered a child named Havridhana. Anthardhana also gave the liberty of releasing Indra during the time of horse sacrifice of Prthu Maharaj. Havirdhāna by the grace of Lord Krishna, fathered six sons, named Barhiṣat, Śukla, Gaya, Kṛṣṇa, Satya, and Jitavrata.

Vidura is very much eager to hear this pastime of Rudra and Pracetas from the lotus mouth of his spiritual master, Maitreya Muni. When disciples ask the right set of questions, the spiritual master reveals confidentiality in a deeper mood. Vidura asked five questions to Maitreya, and Maitreya answered them in a satisfactory manner. These elements are as follows:

1. Why Did Lord Shiva appear in front of Pracetas without worshiping to Shiva?
2. Why were Pracetas qualified and heading towards the forest, leaving aside the opulent kingdom?
3. The intriguing questions related to the revelations, why did Shiva deliver the message of Krishna to Pracetas however he rewards material benediction to whomever he meets?
4. What was Shiva's assurance to Pracetas, and what lessons should we take from this conversation?

Maitreya was curious to tell the details as to how the pious Pracetas happened to see Lord Shiva and all it happens by the causeless mercy of Lord Shiva. The omniscient Lord Shiva knew very well the purpose of their journey towards the jungle, the reason for their quitting the opulent life, and pursuing the path of seclusion into the forest. In ancient ages, even the kings leave the palace to pursue the path of self-realization in full sincerity. Lord Shiva knew the heart of Pracetas that there was no impurity in their heart, they were sincere seekers of the absolute truth, and there was no tinge of material motivation in their pursuit. Lord Shiva is also *dharma-vatsala*, and He is very much eager to serve the aspiring devotee of God or Krishna. Pracetas have only one determination; that is nothing other than to satisfy Lord Vishnu by their austerity. Even if they are fully qualified in the spiritual values and knowledge, they still need a mentor, a guru, to give the torchlight of knowledge for further deepening their meditation. Shiva appeared in front of the Pracetas for these reasons and preached the gospel of God in the form of Rudra Gita.

People generally think that Shiva offers various material rewards, benedictions, and heavenly pleasures to the worshipers. Vidura knew very well that Shiva even offered the Pasupathi Astra to Arjuna. Why did he not give the love of Godhead to Arjuna? Shiva is fully aware of Arjuna's position as the loyal and best friend of Arjuna, and he aspires to get his association, what to speak of giving love of Godhead. As a great war was about to happen on the battlefield of Kurukshetra, Arjuna needed special weapons by Krishna's advice. Lord Shiva knew the will of Krishna very well and provided the Astra to Arjuna. In this situation of Pracetas, Lord Shiva awarded the love of Godhead as they are true recipients of such knowledge, and they received it without asking from Shiva.

Since Lord Shiva does not incarnate himself unless there is some special reason, it is tough for an ordinary person to get darshan of Him. However, Lord Shiva does descend on a special occasion when he is ordered by the Supreme Personality of Godhead. There is an example of the appearance of Shankaracharya to bewilder the pseudo seculars. It is stated in the Padma Purana that Lord Shiva appeared as a brahmana in the Age of Kali to preach the Māyāvāda philosophy, which is nothing but a type of Buddhist philosophy.

On the bank of the serene lake near the great forest, the ambiance is so cool and enchanting, there is no question of disturbance in mind. In this age of Kali, we have anxiety and disturbances all around, and we are frustrated in every action also. Pracetas' mind was transparent and fresh, and when they approached the lake, there was a deep awakening in the heart for self-realization. Various birds, flowers, lotus, bees, trees, and mixed sounds from all the living beings in the natural environment are undoubtedly favorable for spiritual cultivation. The trees are smiling and joyful whenever the bumblebees roam from tree to tree for the collection of honey. Swans are making Olympiad champions in the midst of the lake and smelling the fragrance of the blue, red lotuses, lilies, and many other water flowers in the lake. It feels as if there is a competition of enjoyment amongst the swans in the water, bees in the plants, birds like the parrot, cuckoo in the sky and monkeys, rabbits, squirrels in the land. Who is enjoying the beauty of other beings' activities? The surrounding trees around the lake shades are so cooling that there is no need for an air conditioning system as desired by the modern civilizations. Enchanting music, the sound of the water birds, bees are making a scene of Kailasa Hill, and Sukadeva Goswami describes that the Pracetas reached the actual planet of Lord Shiva.

Suddenly in the sky, the Pracetas saw the magnanimous personality with the golden hue, snake in the neck, three-eyed Lord, and the bluish throat. He was not accompanied by Gauri; rather, many of the Gandharvas and Kinnaras were with him. They all were glorifying Lord Shiva with various kettledrums, musical instruments, and singing. Upon such a level of music, singing, Shiva's presence in the scene captivated the mind of Pracetas. Pracetas fell on the ground and offered various prayers to Lord Shiva and cried in joy with the emotions of love. Lord Shiva is no doubt, Ashutosh, the easily satisfied God, was very much pleased to see the Pracetas near the lake. Sometimes it is mentioned that Shiva is the real *dharma-vatsala*, and Krishna is the *bhakta-vatsala*. There is no difference, but who maintains the religious duties as per the Veda, he is favored by Shiva and ultimately becomes a devotee of Krishna. Then Krishna favors the devotee, and He is famous as *bhakta-vatsala.* Demons, whenever they find the opportunity to see Shiva or worship the Shiva Linga, they immediately ask for many benedictions, but Pracetas were not asking for any blessings from Shiva. This type of behavior is the symptom of a pure devotee of Lord Vishnu, and Shiva is the best of the Vaishnavas, and he is the happiest when he meets another Vaishnava. Ordinary persons would immediately ask for many boons and power from Lord Shiva upon seeing him. Shiva is also called *dharma-vatsala*, and many times, demons worship him in the mode of ignorance. Being favored for the dharma of the *tamasic guna*, Shiva appears before them and offers many boons so that they would come to sense some days. On the contrary, the outcome becomes very disturbing as the living being is puffed up by getting such boons. But when he sees a person in the mode of goodness like Pracetas, he opens his heart and mind and ultimately offers the best of the jewel of gifts, Krishna Prema to such devotees.

Lord Shiva wished all good fortune to the Pracetas, he told them the reason for his coming to them, and he told Pracetas that he knew very well their intention and purpose, such as how to worship and remember Lord Vishnu. He was willing to provide the nitty-gritty of the Vedic regulations, mantra, and other techniques so that Pracetas could advance in spiritual life. One does not need to please a demigod out of the context of Vishnu worship, because demigods are always willing to aid the devotees. This is a brilliant example of the meeting of Pracetas to Lord Shiva, even without worshiping Lord Shiva. He came in front of them and provided all blessings. We should always worship Krishna directly with any combination of the demigod worship. By considering Shiva as a Guru or the greatest Vaishnava, one can worship him with the mantra of the Hare Krishna sound vibrations.

Lord Shiva continued giving His gospel to Pracetas as "*Any person who renders service, remembers, chants the name of Vasudeva, the absolute Lord of both the material and spiritual world, is naturally very dear to me also*". Lord Shiva is truly the protector of dharma in this age of Kali also. One has to take refugee unto the lotus feet of Vasudeva, he corroborated the same principle of the mantra chanted at the beginning of the Srimad Bhagavatam as '*Om Namo Bhagavate Vasudevaya*", he explained in detail about the positions of the material nature, demigods and Vasudeva's transcendental position. *Yaṁ brahmā-varuṇendra-rudra-marutaḥ stunvanti divyaiḥ stavaiḥ* (Bhāg. 12.13.1): Kṛṣṇa is worshiped by Lord Brahmā, Lord Shiva, Varuṇa, Indra, Candra, and all other demigods. This is expressed herein openly. The conclusion is that a devotee of Lord Shiva is not dear to Lord Shiva, but a devotee of Lord Kṛṣṇa is very dear to Lord Shiva.

RUDRA'S VEHICLE - NANDI

Nandi is the bull carrier of Lord Shiva, and it's installed as a gatekeeper of every Shiva temple, similarly Garuda and Jaya and Vijaya are found as the doorkeeper at the Vishnu temple. Even though Nandi is the carrier of Lord Shiva in the bull form, he is the most knowledgeable and self-realized person. He also instructed to eight sages such as Sanatkumara, Sanaka, Sananda, Sanatana, Vygrapada, Patanjali, Tirumular (Thirumoolar), and Shivayoga in the matter of devotional service to the Supreme Personality of Godhead.

There is a beautiful deity of Nandishwara in the Lingaraj temple, and the mystic process is to speak some wish in his left ear, and Nandi relays it to Lord Shiva, and your request will be fulfilled. I was fortunate to visit the same place with my family members. In Ramayana also, Ravana mocked Nandi for his monkey-like appearances, and Nandi cursed Ravana that he will be killed by the monkey army only. While going to attend the Daksha Yajna, mother Sati sat unto the back of Nandisvara and left for her father's abode with all the Shiva's associates. Nandi is always eager to serve Lord Shiva in the same spirit as Garuda used to serve Lord Vishnu. Nandi is also serving Lord Shiva in the bull form and bull is generally considered as the father of the religion. Nandi remains as the gatekeeper of all the Shiva temples in the world. We pray that Nandisvara gives his blessings to all of us to remain in the Supreme Personality of Godhead service.

12 JYOTIRLINGAM

There is a conversation between Sanat Kumar and Nandishwara about various topics of spirituality and the origin of Shiva Linga. Nandisvar is answering the origin of Lord Shiva and the benefit of worshiping it. A long time ago, there was an innate fight between Lord Brahma and Lord Vishnu, so Lord Shiva intervened as a pillar in between and pacified the two Lords with His pleasing characteristics. Both Lord Vishnu and Lord Brahma applauded the intelligent intervention, and henceforth the Linga worship was started by the humans as it was done for the protection of the earth.

There are twelve jyotirlingas in India, and they are prominent, and Lord Chaitanya used to visit a few of them while touring India.

1. Somnath in Gir Somnath, Gujarat (first pilgrimage site to begin with)
2. Mallikarjuna in Srisailam, Andhra Pradesh (Lord Chaitanya and Nityananda visited this Linga, and it is also worshiped with Shakti-Peeth)
3. Mahakaleshwar in Ujjain, Madhya Pradesh (self-manifested Linga; south-facing and Sree Rudra Yantra perched upside down)
4. Omkareshwar in Khandwa, Madhya Pradesh (An island of Narmada river)
5. Kedarnath in Rudraprayag, Uttarakhand (Lord Shiva's eternal abode Mount Kailas; snow-clad Himalayas; pure ghee is applied here)
6. Bhimashankar in Maharashtra (having quadrangular Shakti around the Linga and decorated by a Upavita as per the Puran)
7. Vishwanath in Varanasi, Uttar Pradesh (oldest city and the most sacred pilgrimage place of Lord Shiva)

8. Trimbakeshwar in Nashik, Maharashtra (linked with the origin of Godavari river)
9. Baidyanath in Deoghar, Jharkhand (Ravana worshiped and offered his head here; Shiva gave the boon and became the doctor for Ravana and cured him)
10. Nageshwara in Dwarka, Gujarat (mentioned in Shiva Purana)
11. Ramanathaswamy in Rameshwaram, Tamil Nadu (Lord Rama performed Abhishek of this Linga)
12. Grishneshwar in Aurangabad, Maharashtra (sometimes referred to as the Dhushmeshwar temple)

Lord Chaitanya visited the Lingaraj temple before going to Jagannath Puri. Lord Chaitanya mentioned that if you would like to receive the real mercy of Lord Jagannath, then you should visit the Lingaraj temple in Bhubaneswar and then go and see Jagannath in Puri. Bhubaneswar is the capital of Odisha (formerly known as Utkal) and is around 70 km from Puri.

LINGARAJ TEMPLE

Lingaraj temple is situated in the city of Bhubaneswar, also known as *Ekamra Kshetra,* the name *Ekamra Kanana* was found in Skanda Purana (Vedic times) as well as in the Ekamra Purana (13th-century Purana), and the meaning is one mango tree, the Linga was self-manifested here.

It is interesting to note that Shiva is worshiped as the dual combination of Hari and Hara, both the Tulasi leaves and Bael leaves are offered to the Lingas, and it's also a combination of the *Salagram Shila* and Shiva Linga. Lord has manifested in the form of Shiva and Vishnu to give mercy to all the fallen souls of this age of Kali. There is a connection of cultural influence from the Jagannath temple from the Ganga dynasty.

The *Ekamra Kanan* Story was described by Jaimini and it is found in the Skanda Purana 12th chapter of Ekamra Kanan section which glorifies Lord Shiva. The great sage Jaimini narrated a story of the establishment of the city of Bhubaneswar and how Lord Shiva and Parvati made this place as their residence. It is said that Lord Shiva married Parvati and stayed with his in-law's house for a few years. Shiva does not have a residence, and Parvati wanted to stay at her father's place in the Himalayan mountain range. Once while walking in the forest, Parvati and her mother, Hima, her mother jokingly told 3 points of Lord Shiva, I know your husband is so poverty-stricken, no home, no wealth and no beauty. You are staying with us without any further hope. She said to her daughter that please consider this as a joke only, and I don't mean to hurt you. Generally, a woman does not take anything lightly, and she petitioned Lord Shiva one day that, "You are the master of the universe, and you don't have a place to stay." Considering the plea of his wife, Lord Shiva manifested His glorious pastimes.

He found the place Kasi and his *Koti Lingeswara* is still worshiped on the bank of Ganges, and this place is known as Varanasi also Kasi Viswanath is a trendy name, and Lord Chaitanya visited this place and gave the instructions to Sanatana Goswami on the devotional service. Later on, Kasi was destroyed by Lord Krishna as a dispute between the king of the Kasi and Lord Krishna. Lord Shiva tried to save this city; however, with the power of Krishna, it is not possible to counteract the sweet aggression of the Lord. He knew that His master is all-powerful and merciful. In that event, Lord Krishna advised Lord Shiva to go to the Ekamra Kanan, Bhubaneswar, and settle there, and Lord Krishna said that He would also appear as Lord Jagannath in the city of Puri and assist Him in his Leela. Lord Shiva was thrilled to receive the news from His master and decided to go to the great city of Ekamra Kanan. This was so beautiful, and Lord Shiva bestowed this place with the *Koti Lingeswara* deity, and he was worshiped as Lingaraj with the mixture of Hari.

This temple has immense beauty of worship of Tulsi and Bael together as the top portion is Salagram Shila, and the bottom part is Shiva Linga. We find a high potency in this temple. My humble self was bestowed with mercy from Nandishwara to write this beautiful book as I visited this temple in 2019 with my family members and got the inspiration to write this book from the deity, Lord Shiva and Lord Hari. I am very much thankful to Lingaraj Mahadev for granting the boon to me for writing this book as an insignificant attempt to please the greatest devotee of Supreme Personality of Godhead, Vaisnavanan Yatha Shambu. As Srimad Bhagavatam suggest ŚB 12.13.16

nimna-gānāṁ yathā gaṅgā

devānām acyuto yathā

vaiṣṇavānāṁ yathā śambhuḥ

purāṇānām idam tathā

"Just as the Gaṅgā is the greatest of all rivers, Lord Acyuta the supreme among deities and Lord Śambhu [Shiva] the greatest of Vaishnavas, so Śrīmad-Bhāgavatam is the greatest of all Purāṇas."

Lingaraj temple is considered to be the holiest of tirthas and a very sacred place for the *Koti-Lingeswara* deity of Lord Shiva. It is believed that the name Bhubaneswar comes from Shiva's Sanskrit name Tribhuvaneshwar – meaning Lord of the three worlds – as it was one of the favorite places of Lord Shiva.

Lingaraj temple is no doubt the ancient and old structure of the world heritage, possibly a 100 years old temple in the heartland of Utkal. Lord Shiva even glorifies the importance of the city Bhubaneswar as dearer than Kasi. Parvati was stuck with awe and wonder while listening to Lord Shiva, and she favored the town as well by her divine presence.

The sacred Shiva Lingam was supposed to have been self-manifested here by the divine will of Lord Shiva. He chooses the place to be more scared and holier. Of course, wherever Lord Shiva resides, that place becomes the place of pilgrimage. As this is a combination of both Lord Hari and Lord Hara, the worship methods and practices are very similar to Lord Jagannath. It's quite befitting to see the doorkeeper of the temple is Jaya and Vijaya. The trident is found at the entrance and snakes, and all symbolic representations of Lord Shiva are depicted alongside the temple structure. The original deity of the Lord is a Lingam, and it's made of granite and Salagram Shila. The top portion is Salagram Shila, and the bottom part is Shiva Lingam. Both of the Lord gives an audience of majestic views, and I was fortunate to see the Chandrachuda Besa Srinagar in one of the days I visited the temple. Pujaris worship every day with milk, water, Tulsi and Bael and flowers, and many more *Naivedya* for Hari-Hara's pleasure. As Parvati stays alongside her husband, we can find the deity of Kartikeya and Ganesha also. So beautiful draperies and ornaments for the Srinagar of the goddess in the Lingaraj temple. Lord Chaitanya's regular visit to the Lingaraj temple is mentioned in various scriptures, and he recommended every devotee to follow his footsteps and take the permission of Lord Shiva before going to the Jagannath temple in Puri.

KEDARNATH OF LORD SHIVA

Who else can deny the beauty of the Himalayan range, Kedarnath is the best place in this mountain range, and this description of Kedarnath is also found in the Skanda Purana? The meaning of Kedar as per Sanskrit is the field and Nath is Lord, so the Lord of the field or the crop of liberation grows in this sacred holy place. Legend says that Pandavas built the Kedarnath temple. However, there is not enough historical evidence in this matter.

Kedarnath is a place where Lord Shiva released the divine Ganga from His matted hair, and Ganga was born from Lord's hair. Bhagirathi and his forefathers are saved from the mercy of Lord Shiva and Ganga. Ganga liberates the places it flows through all over India. As this temple is situated almost 12,000 feet above sea level, during the winter season, the temple is closed for darshan, and the Utsav murti is generally transferred to the *Guptakashi*. In this place, Shiva and Parvati got married. Kedarnath's importance is found in *"Kashi Kedar Mahatmya"* and Madhva's *"Sankshepa-Shankara Vijaya"* episodes. Some say that Adi Shankaracharya attained samadhi in this place; however, others, like Anandagiri's Prachina-Shankara-Vijaya, refuted and mentioned that Adi Shankaracharya attained samadhi in Kashi. There are descriptions of the meeting of Lord Shiva and Nara-Narayana rsi at this place, Nara-Narayana rsi also performed severe austerity at the Himalayas range like Badarikashrama, this is quite possible for them to meet and think about the welfare of the entire humanity. Kedarnath is one of the twelve jyotirlingas of Lord Shiva and most celebrated amongst the practitioners of the spiritual values and ultimate goal of life.

AMARNATH OF LORD SHIVA

Amarnath means Lord of immortality, Lord Shiva resides in this place eternally, and it is one of the adventure mountainous terrain pilgrimages to the Amarnath cave. Amarnath is located in Jammu & Kashmir, India. According to a scriptural reference, Amarnath is the holy land where Shiva explained the mysterious symptoms and origin of life and eternity to His divine consort, Parvati. Sometimes it is understood that Lord Shiva instructed the Srimad Bhagavatam Katha to Mother Parvati in this place inside the cave. This cave is always covered with heavy snowfall, and only a few months in summer, it is opened for darshan. Shiva lingam is molded when the liquid trickles from the mountain rock roof and gets amassed; subsequently, it starts freezing on the floor. Sometimes it is understood that the based on the waning and waxing of the moon, the size of the Lingam varies, I could not find any scientific evidence in this connection, As Krishna is Bhavagrahi Janardana, Shiva is always transcendental and could exhibit the same principles as He holds the crescent moon in His head. Wherever Shiva resides, especially His eternal associate and wife Parvati manifest there and two more ice foundations occur in the cave that is supposed to be of Mother Parvati and their son Ganesh.

Once upon a time, mother of the universe, Parvati asked Shiva about wearing the beads of the skull head. On this question, Lord Shiva pondered for a while and explained to Parvati whenever you were born, it is counted as a bead. Mother Parvati was very curious to know about the science of immortality, generally known as Amar Katha. Amar Katha talks about the Srimad Bhagavatam as Parikshit Maharaj also attained immortality and beyond, i.e., love of Godhead. In the same way, Lord Shiva spoke the "Rudra Gita" to Pracetas for the highest benefits of the saintly king. He is very merciful, so how could He not give the same knowledge to Mother Parvati. They explored for a secluded place where no living being is there to hear the talk of immortality. Now Shiva, by His sweet will, decided to describe the great transcendental topic to Mother Parvati and headed towards the cave. On His tour, he left His bull Nandi at the village Pahalgam; He always wears the crescent moon on His head, He left the moon at Chandanwari, Lord Shiva's extraordinary garland, the snake, He bade farewell to His snake at Sheshnag, His child Ganesh at Mahagunas mountain, at Panjtarni, He left the *Pancha-Mahabhuta*. Now Lord Shiva and Parvati headed towards the vast cave.

Lord Shiva with His meditative position and seated on a deerskin, He took complete samadhi, in a trance of merging in the love of Godhead. He made the last stage of coverings with His Rudra fire known as "Kalagni" and commanded him to set fire around the cave. He started describing the holy talk on the highest goal of human life, Pancha Purusartham, love of Godhead, Amar Katha. By hearing, no one will again take birth in this material world. Lord Shiva wanted to ensure that such great topics should be heard by the qualified persons and need to be favored by great Mahajan like Lord Shiva. Despite the effort, a pigeon egg was found inside the deerskin, this is mysterious, and many pilgrimages still found the pigeon couple in this cave now also. Pigeons are still found in the cave as they were there in the cave while Lord was telling Parvati. Many speak about the parrot also, and the parrot became Sukadeva Goswami as Lord Shiva was angry at the parrot, and he ran after the parrot. The parrot went to the ashram of Vyasadeva and entered the womb of Vyasadeva's wife and later became the speaker of Srimad Bhagavatam. This is coming from the story of Mahabharat. Kedarnath and Amarnath pilgrimage are two important milestones for the devotees to trek on at least once in their lifetime for the glorification of Lord Shiva.

SHIVA IN DIFFERENT YUGAS

Satya Yuga

Satya Yuga is the first Yuga of the millennium or the start of the Brahma's day, and Shiva remains visible to all living beings and bestows His mercy in all ages. Even though Shiva is beyond the calculation of any yugas, He remains calm and poised and always in a trance in the absolute Brahman. Most likely, Lord Shiva fought with the Tripurasura and awarded the Mrityu Sanjeevani mantra to Sukracarya in the Satya Yuga phase. Lord Shiva spoke the Rudra Gita to Pracetas in Satya Yuga. Lord Shiva drank the poison after churning the ocean in Satya Yuga. Lord Shiva is present in all Yugas, and He is enlightening the entire living beings by His causeless mercy.

Treta Yuga

Lord Shiva met Lord Ramachandra, and Ramachandra performed the Linga Abhishekam of Lord Shiva in Rameshwaram before crossing the Lanka canal, Palk strait, Ram Setu or Adam bridge.

Ravana tried to lift the Kailasa mountain and how Lord Shiva tricked him and awarded him various boons. This unusual incident about Ravana being corrected by Lord Shiva is very much astonishing, and the detailed illustration is found in the Ramayana episode.

In Treta Yuga, Lord Ram showers His mercy to all the world's residents, including the demigods, humans, monkeys, and bears. Ravana was the ferocious demon and made all havoc in the society even though born in a family of a learned brahmana named Vishrava and demon princess Kaikesi. Ravana's mother was a great devotee of Lord Shiva, and she used to make the sand Shiva Linga every day to worship it, when she comes to the shore of the ocean the next day, the lingam will vanish like the sandcastle. It is again her turn to prepare the sandcastle again, and it becomes a ritual every day. One day she pleaded to her son Ravana to bring a Shiva-linga for her.

Ravan thought of getting the Linga directly from Lord Shiva only, and he went to the Himalayas for severe penances to please Lord Shiva. Even after performing several decades of austerity in the heavy snow and rain, there is no sign of Shiva to appear before Ravan. Ravan was still full vigor in his asceticism, and later, he decided to offer his head as an oblation to the sacrifice. He started offering one after another his head to Lord Shiva, when he was about to offer his last head, tenth head, then Lord Shiva appeared in front of Ravan and asked him what benedictions he needed. Ravan offered prayers and salutation in the glories of Lord Shiva and requested a Shiva-linga for worship at Lanka. Lord Shiva, pleased with Ravan's austerity and devotion, said, "I offer you this linga, special in its quality as it descends from my own abode Kailas. This linga is unique and carries high significance in spiritual essence; please place it in the area where you intend to start worshiping it. Please remember that it cannot be removed after it is placed once in the ground. Take it back to Lanka with care and attention and continue the worship."

Upon hearing the incredible boon received from Lord Shiva, demigods were very afraid that Ravan would again be invincible with the attainment of the causeless mercy of Lord Shiva. Of course, the powerful self-manifested Shiva-linga and presented by his lotus hand to Ravana will positively impact Ravana's strength. So, the demigods devised a plan to refrain the linga to go to Lanka along with Ravana. They requested Ganesha to help in this regard. Ganesha agreed to the proposal of the demigods and transformed himself as a little brahmin boy in a place where Ravan is flying in the sky. As the evening is approaching, Ravan has not even reached Lanka yet, and he is a faithful follower of ceremonial activities. He needs to perform the Sandhya ablutions in the evening time. At the same time, Ravana remembered the word of Lord Shiva not to place the linga in the ground. Finally, he found the little brahmin boy and asked him to hold the linga for some time to finish his evening Sandhya rituals. The boy used to say that it's too heavy, and I can't hold that long; however, Ravan could see the sun is about to set in the west, and without delay, he shifted the lingam at the hand of the little brahmin boy and went inside the river. With the divine arrangement, the boy is groaning and screaming that this linga is very heavy and please come and take otherwise I have to keep it in-ground, after repeated saying for three times, Ravan had to rush back by finishing his Sandhya rituals, at the same time the little brahmin boy also placed the Linga in the ground.

Upon seeing the Linga in the ground, Ravan was furious, and he tried to uproot the Linga, but by the words of Lord Shiva, it could not be moved out. Ravan then hit the boy, and he transformed into Ganesh. Upon seeing Ganesha, he understood the plan of the demigods and of Lord Shiva. He prayed to the Linga there and left for Lanka.

Where the Linga was placed is known as the Mahabaleshwara temple on the shore of the Arabian sea. The Shiva linga is also called Mahabaleshwara – the strong one, for it could not be pulled out of the ground. The top slice of this linga is perverse, as Ravan tried to pull out from the field but in vain. Besides, there is also a deity of Ganesha in this place near to the linga to showcase the reason for the linga to settle here. The head of Ganesha has trivial indenting where Ravana is supposed to have knocked him. Also, his feet are diminutive under the pulverized soil, as if strapped in by the strength of the blow from Ravan. Similarly, Ganesha also prevented Vibhisana to take the deity of Raghunatha at Srirangam temple. This incident is the mystical exhibition of Lord Shiva and Ganesha to protect the real religion for the benefit of the demigods.

Dwapara Yuga

Lord Shiva existed in Satya Yuga and Treta Yuga, and now we can see his activities are mentioned in Dvapara Yuga. In ancient times Lord Shiva established the beautiful Kashi city in the bank of Ganges. Later, many kings ruled this city and became ardent devotee of Lord Shiva. Lord Shiva gave all protections to the residents and the king and awarded many boons to the pious souls. It is fascinating to note that in a fight between the king of Kashi and the Yadus, Lord Krishna destroyed the city of Kashi, and there was a fight between Lord Shiva and Lord Krishna on account of the king, who was an ardent devotee of the Lord.

Banasura pleased Lord Shiva with his thousand hands to play the drum for the pleasure of Lord Shiva. In Dvapara Yuga, we know the daughter of Banasura, Usha, who fell in love with

Aniruddha, the grandson of Lord Krishna. Many of the incidents can be found in the chapter of Banasura and Lord Shiva in this book.

In Dvapara Yuga, we have heard a lot of the glories of Arjuna. He received many boons from demigods and obtained celestial weapons as well, Arjuna fought with Lord Shiva and obtained the Pasupathi Astra.

There are various episodes of Lord Shiva in the Dvapara Yuga. I have mentioned a few to let readers know about the presence and existence of Lord Shiva.

Being so insulted by Bhima after losing the battle as a result of kidnapping Draupadi, Jayadratha was in full anger and decided to take avenge against the insults by the Pandavas. In such a situation, no one other than Lord Shiva came into mind of such an angry and envious person like Jayadratha. He decided to go to the Himalayan range near to the Gangotri area for practicing severe penances for pleasing Lord Shiva. Upon the appearance, the Lord, Ashutosh, gave benedictions to king Jayadratha that he could defeat Pandavas at least once in the battlefield. Jayadratha was a mysterious personality, as whoever is the cause of his head to fall down will die immediately without fail. Lord Krishna advised Arjuna to use the brilliance of killing Jayadratha and ensured to send the head fall unto his father, who is practicing austerity at the Samanta panchaka ashram. In one arrow, Arjuna served two purposes; killed Jayadratha and his father during the Kurukshetra war. Lord Shiva's boon helped Arjuna's skills in the battle and his glorious victory over all the demons who opposed Lord Krishna, internally Lord Shiva desires the same objectives even though He awarded the rewards to the demons out of formality.

In Srimad Bhagavatam chapter one and fifteen, the episode of Jayadratha in connection to Lord Shiva in Dvapara Yuga is mentioned.

It was by His causeless mercy only that in an ensuing fight, I was able to astonish the most auspicious god Lord Shiva and his wife, Uma, the daughter of Mount Himalaya. Arjuna informed his elder brother Yudhishthira that how he obtained various weapons from demigods as well as the special *pashupati-astra* from Lord Shiva. This is a special boon Arjuna received from Lord Shiva and he seemed very confident to win the upcoming war against the Kurus. Of course, the mercy of Shiva is always favorable towards Draupadi as well as to Arjuna. Shiva knew the position of Arjuna in relation to Krishna and He was ready to offer all kinds of benedictions to the Pandavas. Arjuna is explaining the uncommon feats to Yudhishthira Maharaj on how he obtained the Pasupathi Astra.

Kali Yuga

Generally, demigods and Gods are not revealed to the common man in this age of Kali because people are so fallen in the iron age; however, they still remain in the temple, in scriptures, in the holy names, and in the discourse of the saintly personalities. Lord Shiva manifested himself to Sanatana Goswami in Vraj Mandal, Goverdhan. Lord Shiva manifested himself to Narasimha Brahmachari by his prayer. Lord Shiva bestowed him the mantra of the holy name of Krishna and taught the process of obtaining mercy from the Supreme Personality of Godhead.

When Gopesvar Mahadev wanted to bless someone, then nothing can stop in the mortal world and nothing more to gain also upon receiving the mercy of the Lord. One of the exciting incidents happened to a great saint known as Narsingh Mehta, born in Telaja, Bhavnagar district of Gujarat, in the year 1414. He lost his parents at the age of five and was then cared for by his grandmother, Jaya Gauri. Narsingh Mehta was known as Narsi Mehta or Narsi Bhagat. It is hard to believe that he could not speak a single word until the age of eight. Lately, he got married to Manekbhai, and they lived as a joint family with his brother's family. By the ill-behaved attitude of his brother's wife, taunts, and insults had no bounds in his life to perform pure devotional service to the Lord. One day he could not tolerate the abuse and left the house without anyone's knowledge. He went to Lord Shiva temple and completely surrendered to Him by performing severe penances with no food or sleep. Lord Shiva is known as Ashutosh. He was pleased with Narsi Mehta and appeared in front of him and asked for a boon. Being a very simple devotee, he requested Lord Shiva that whatever is very dear to him, please give him the most beloved object. By pleased with the sincere, humble approach of Narsi Mehta, Lord Shiva bestowed him the path to love of Godhead in the Vraj Bhakti procedures.

The most favorite pastime of Lord Shiva is Rasa Leela or Maha Rasa, as we know He wanted to become a gopi and dance with Krishna, and this story is famous in the entire Vraj Mandal Dham. Henceforth, there is a temple known as Gopesvar Mahadev, who even guards the Vraj Mandal Dham for any danger or calamity.

Delighted with his commitment, Lord Shiva presented him the best of the gem from His heart. Narsi was so content with the audience of Lord Shiva and receiving the most beloved Nectarian message '...Mahadeva offered him the nectar of Govinda's *'Rasa Lila'* in Vraj Mandal. What a majestic gift from God, obtaining the Vraj Bhakti from Lord Shiva. It is also mentioned that Lord Krishna instructed Narsi to reveal his blissful understanding of the conditioned souls in the form of extraordinary poems and songs. He composed around 22,000 verses of songs, and the most popular one was the *'Vaishnav Jana to'* – the famous song which enthused Indian independence warrior Mahatma Gandhi.

It was by the benedictions of Lord Shiva, designated as the greatest Vaishnava in Srimad Bhagavatam, that a follower of Rudra, Narsi Mehta, became an illustrious Vaishnava saint.

Followers of the system of Aghora and Tantra consider that Krishna and Shiva are the two aspects of the supreme absolute like milk and yogurt substance. The practice of Bhakti is the utmost level of spiritual realization, and one can gain access to the love of Godhead by the mercy of Shiva, there is no doubt about this fallacy. It is self-evident in all the revealed scriptures. We will find the system of aghora practice in this age of Kali.

SHIVA IN MULTIFARIOUS LILA OF VISHNU

Ram Lila

King Janaka obtained the most beautiful daughter from his land while plowing the field. Thus, the name of his daughter was popularly known as Sita or Janaki. Janaka kept the divine Shiva Dhanu or Shiva bow, and once playing with the bow, Sita got hold of this bow and placed it in a different place. Seeing the bravery of Sita, king Janaka was mesmerized and thought that she is no ordinary child and pledged that anyone who will lift the Shiva Bow is eligible to gain his daughter's hand. Who else can match the strength of Shiva bow except for the power of His master, Lord Ramachandra? Ramachandra not only picked the bow, but he broke it as an event and thus irritated the mood of Lord Parashuram, and subsequently, he was calmed by Lord Rama. This is the glorious deed of Shiva, Rama, and Sita from Ramayana.

Lord Rama also installed the beautiful Shiva Linga at the Rameshwar temple before His departure to Lanka for the battle. Ahiravan kidnapped Rama and Laxman to the sub-terrain range of Patala. No one knew where the two Lords are now. Hanuman took the task of finding his masters and ultimately reached the sub-terrain range of Patala. Ahiravan was planning to sacrifice Ram and Laxman before Goddess Kali, as the same incident happened in Srimad Bhagavatam for Jada Bharat. Hanuman emerged, thrust Kali to the subterranean range, and killed the demon Ahiravan to rescue Rama and Laxman. When mother Kali had trodden in on the upper body of Lord Shiva in an incident long time ago, in order to counter the incident of this, this appeared in Treta Yuga with the pastime of Hanuman, who is considered as the partial incarnation of Lord Shiva, shoved mother Kali in this episode.

Again, according to a South Indian Version of Shiva Purana, Hanuman was the son of Lord Shiva and Mohini (the female avatar of Lord Vishnu). Thus, the birth story of Hanuman has been merged with that of Ayyappa of Sabarimala.

Millions of years ago, during the churning of the ocean of the milk, disputes occurred during the distribution of nectar between demons and demigods, Mohini intervened the situation and helped the demigods to obtain it. Lord Shiva was not part of the nectar distribution category as Lord Shiva is always an eternal associate of the Lord, both in the mundane and spiritual world. However when it came to His notice that Mohini was so charming and beautiful and tricked the demons, Lord Shiva wanted to see the same elegant form of Lord Vishnu and thus requested Lord Vishnu for the same, Pleased with His plea, Lord Vishnu exhibited the Mohini form again in front of Lord Shiva, Completely bewildered, agitated with the beauty of the divine angel, Mohini, Lord Shiva ran after Her and tried to touch and have union with Her. This is the potency of Vishnu Maya; one has to submit to the Lord for one's spiritual discipline. As the semen discharged Lord Shiva from the embrace, the seven sages kept the semen and placed it in the womb of Anjani, the saintly woman praying for Lord Shiva for a progeny. Thus, pleased with the prayers and the help from the wind god, Anjani received the semen of Lord Shiva by the directions of the seven sages. A great child was born from her, named as the pavan-suta Hanuman. Lord Shiva took the form of Hanuman to serve Lord Rama directly and get His association of His master eternally. Lord Rama killed Ravana and restored the real dharma with the help of Hanuman, Sugriv, and many monkey warriors.

KRISHNA LILA

Vrindavan Lila as Gopi

Many mystical incidents are described in the Srsti-khanda of Padma Purana. All the energy expansion of the Lord wanted to serve in Vraja bhaktas; even Laxmi was jealous of participating in the rasa dance. Gayatri, the best of the hymn, wanted to be a gopi and serve Radha and Krishna. She manifested from the sound of the flute and Krishna blessed her too. As Krishna was performing His Maha-rasa in Vrindavan and He was playing the flute, the sound of the fifth note of the flute penetrated the whole universe, and it reached the domain of Kailasa. Lord Shiva, upon hearing the transcendental flute sound, he was entirely in a trance, samadhi. He followed the sound until the real abode of Lord Govinda was reached, where He found so many Gopis surrounding Krishna. Lord Shiva desired to enter the arena with an intense mood of joining the rasa dance. However, He was stopped by the internal energy of the Lord, Yogamaya. Yogamaya told Him, you are not allowed inside the rasa dance as only females are allowed, if you desire so, then meet Vrinda Devi. Lord Shiva then searched for Vrinda Devi and begged her to help Him to make a female. Vrinda Devi took Lord Shiva to the nearby Manasarovar pond in the Vraj Dham and asked Him to receive a full deep into the lake. Upon finishing His bath, Lord Shiva was turned into a beautiful Gopi. Then the Lord in the form of a Gopi was allowed inside the rasa dance.

Then the rasa dance commenced, and the most attractive Lord Shyamasundara danced along with the Vraja-Gopis; fortunately,

Shiva in the form of a Gopi also danced with Syamasundara elegantly. Little later, the dance in an ecstatic mood, all the Gopis felt satisfaction. They wanted to take a rest for a while. Lord Krishna mentioned to His chief Gopis, especially to Lalita, "Something is not in order as I am feeling uncomfortable with the dance, and I do not have the same mood as usual; is there someone outsiders in our group? Please check." Lalita went on checking with everyone and found no one suspicious, then Lord Krishna asked to check again, and now with due diligence of the search, they found someone having three eyes and brought her to Lord Krishna. Lord Krishna was laughing and rolling upon seeing the new Gopi, and no one could understand what's going on, and then Lord Shiva revealed His true identity as Lord Mahadev in the assembly of the rasa dance. Krishna spoke, "This rasa dance is meant for Vrajavasi only; however, with the mercy of Vrinda Devi, you already fulfilled the cherished desire by now. I will bestow you to give the position of dwara-pala or the gatekeeper of the rasa dance and, of course, of Vraj Dham. I award the boon to you that all the Gopis will offer homage to you and seek your blessings to get the real gopi bhava. I also bequeath you the benediction that, henceforth, all the Gopis will approach you and seek your blessing to become like a Gopi or attain the Gopi-bhava."

Gopeshwara signifies that Lord Shiva is the controller or the Isvara of the Gopis. Krishna voiced him to enter the rasa ballet entrance and that no one would be permitted to come in the rasa-mandala without Shiva's approval. The Vraja Badhus, Gopis of Vrindavan, always worship Lord Shiva, popularly known as Gopeshwara. There is a beautiful temple of Gopeshwar Mahadev near the bank of the Yamuna. Gopis do not worship Lord Shiva for material benefit as they are pure devotees of Lord Krishna, and they want Krishna as their husband. Gopis are elevated souls, and there is no question of worshiping demigods. By the divine will of Lord Krishna, gopis are inspired to worship both Goddess Katyayani and Lord Shiva for getting Krishna's favor.

Generally, one receives the mercy of Krishna by not the direct medium of Krishna but the authorized agents of Krishna. That's the beauty of Vraja Bhakti, and Lord Shiva plays a vital role in these pastimes.

One should follow the footsteps of Gopis while approaching Lord Shiva, any Vaishnava who sees Lord Shiva and Lord Vishnu as simultaneously one and different as referred to the analogy of the transformations of milk and yogurt, he is to be considered as a true seer. Lord Chaitanya taught us the principle of "*achintya bheda-abheda tattva*" by this principle, God is everything; however, everything belongs to God, and everything cannot be God on its own quality. Lord Shiva is considered as the topmost Vaisnava, that's the conclusion of the Vedic Sastras.

vrindavanvani pate jaya soma soma

maule sanandana sanatana naradeya

gopishvara vraja vilasi yuganghri padme

prema prayaccha nirupadhi namo namas te

"O Shiva, O gatekeeper of Vrindavan! O you who are accompanied by Uma! O you who carry the moon in your hair! O Lord worshiped by Sananda-Kumar, Sanat-Kumar, and Narada Muni! O Gopeshwara, the worshipable deity of the Gopis! Desiring that you bestow upon me, love for the divine couple, Sri Sri Radha Madhava, who perform joyous pastimes in Vraja, I offer my obeisances unto you again and again." *(Srila Visvanatha Chakravarti Thakura, Sri Sankalpa-Kalpadruma)*

Goloka Lila in Nandagram

Once Lord Shiva visited Krishna's house in Nandagram and when mother Yasoda saw someone standing with a dambaru and snake in the neck, she was very much afraid, and she thought of Krishna as a small baby, and he will be very much apprehensive of this scene. Lord Shiva requested to have darshan of the sweet baby Krishna; however, Yasoda-mayi said you couldn't have darshan of my Lala as you are wearing a snake in your neck and ashes on your body. Lord Shiva pleaded a lot; however, mother Yasoda was reluctant to permit Shiva to have darshan, and Shiva was determined and fixed that he would not move out without having a darshan of the Lord in this place. Lord Shiva waited for several years as when Krishna came out of the house and played with his friends and calves. It was only possible when Lord Krishna had gone out for a play, at that time Lord Shiva had darshan of Lord Krishna. Such is the rare interaction of Shiva and Krishna in his childhood pastimes. There is a beautiful temple of Shiva in Nanda-gaon.

Goloka Lila as a mountain – Nandgaon

Brahma, Vishnu, and Maheswhara are also extending their forms as mountains in the Vraj Dham, such as Brahma expanded as the mountain in Barsana Dham, Lord Shiva expanded as mountain in Nandagram, and Lord Vishnu expanded as mountain Goverdhan. Lord Shiva is taking much pleasure by transforming him as a mountain and giving comfort to Bala Gopala.

Lord Shiva has unlimited names like Lord Krishna, and He wanted to associate with all phases of Krishna Lila, including the Kaisora Lila, Balya Lila, and so on. Lord Shiva, known as the master of Nandi, performed severe austerities to participate in the Balya Leela of Lord Krishna. Upon pleased with the sincere desire of Lord Shiva, Lord Krishna granted him to reside in the Vraj Mandal Dham. Nandisvara accepted the boon of Krishna as to serve the Vrajdham as a hill and give transcendental pleasure to Lord Govinda. He took the form of gigantic Nandishwar Hill in the village of Nandgaon. Nandgaon is named after the father of Krishna, Nanda Maharaj. Three principal deities are represented as Govardhan Hill (Vishnu), Nandishwara Hill (Shiva), Barsana Hill (Brahma) in the Vraj Mandal Dham. In this way, the super most relationship between Lord Shiva and Lord Krishna is manifested in the sweet Balya Lila of Govinda.

As an afterthought, a holy place of the Nandagram Temple, there is a Shiva-linga called (Nandishwara), which is said to have been introduced by Vajranabha. This linga of Lord Shiva lives everlastingly in Nandagram performing bhajan to Lord Sri Krishna. This unique Linga is one of the five presiding Shiva-Lingas of Braja. This Shiva-linga shields the Vraj Dham, the most divine and sacred dhama of the universe, from any irritating components to enter inside of it.

Govardhan Chakaleswar – Mosquito

Lord Shiva blessed Sanatana Goswami during the time of Lord Chaitanya's pastime in this world. A great saintly person named Sanatana Goswami used to live in Vraj Mandal Dham. His chief service to Lord Chaitanya was to write devotional books, chanting the holy name of Lord Krishna, instructing Brajabasis and circumambulating the twenty-four miles perimeter of the Govardhan Hill. He used to perform his daily Bhajan near the Manasi Ganga area. He was severely disturbed by the mosquitos and decided to quit this place and go to another location. We must be steady and undisturbed while serving the Supreme Personality of Godhead. While Sanatana Goswami was considering the situation like this, the presiding deity of this temple Chakalesvar Mahadev, was very sorry to lose the greatest Vaishnava in this planet, he came as a disguised form of a brahmin boy. He inquired from him about the wellbeing of Sanatana Goswami. Sanatana Goswami revealed the current mosquito problem to the Brahmin; the Brahmin told him to stay one night and continue his chanting; see if the situation does not change, then he could decide tomorrow. Lord Shiva then ordered the demigod in charge of the mosquito and insects not to disturb this area. With the order from the master, there was no trace of a single mosquito in the Manasi Ganga area near the ashram of Sanatana Goswami. One should note that pure chanting of a pure Vaishnava can transform the place virus-free as people are suffering from coronavirus or COVID-19. By the mercy of Lord Shiva, one can overcome the difficulty, and the solution is one that needs to chant the holy name of Hare Krishna maha-mantra always. Sanatana Goswami did not leave this place until the end of his life and served Radha Krishna without any disturbance of the insects etc. and by the assistant of Lord Shiva. All the demigods are pleased upon a Vaishnava, and they are ready to serve them also.

Parashuram Lila

Shiva happened to meet Parashuram during the time of the annihilation of the kshatriyas by Lord Parashuram. Lord Shiva was the guru of Parashurama; his ax was given to him by Lord Shiva. Lord Parashuram is the divine incarnation of Lord Krishna and known as the sixth incarnation as per the Dasavatara stotra of Jayadeva Goswami. He is one of the seven Chiranjeevi of the world who remains forever. He performed severe austerities to please Lord Shiva. He received the special weapon "ax" known as Parashu, an unconquerable and immeasurable weapon, and thus, his name was famous in the three worlds as Parashuram. He was instructed by Lord Shiva to protect the pious devotees and annihilate the demons, ill-behaved kings, puffed up beings for power, and the extremists too.

Once, Lord Shiva confronted Sri Parashuram in an encounter to examine his talents and skills in combat. The spiritual master Lord Shiva and the disciple Parashuram were sealed in a ferocious battle. This horrible duet persisted for twenty-one days. No one is winning, and no one is losing the fight as if the sun and moon appeared in the sky together and encountered a nuclear battle. The trident (Trishul) of Lord Shiva was untouched and so was the ax of Parashuram. Gaining a momentary upper hand, Lord Parashuram attacked Shiva's forehead thrusting a wound in His forehead. Shiva was extremely pleased with Parashuram, so as He was pleased with Arjuna's fighting spirit. He showered uncommon blessings to Parashuram and prayed for the welfare of the entire world.

The Kalki Purana forecasts the emergence of Lord Parashuram during the appearance of Kalki Bhagavan with his horse. Lord Parashurama will act as the martial and spiritual guru of Lord Kalki as Dronacharya served as the martial guru for the Pandavas and Kauravas. Lord Kalki will please Lord Shiva to obtain the celestial weapon to annihilate the Kali Yuga's mlecchas. Lord Rudra is the God of the annihilator, and He serves the supreme Lord in this connection also.

Mohini Lila

Mohini incarnation of Lord Vishnu appeared during the churning of the milk ocean for receiving the nectar. The incident of the churning of the milk ocean informed us about four incarnations in the line such as Lord Vishnu himself appeared along with Garuda for transportation of the Mandara mountain, Kurma holding the Mandara mountain, Vasuki, the servant of Vishnu as a rope for the churning, Ajita, the master and leader of all demigods as Lord Vishnu and appeared on the top of the mountain, Shiva at the time of drinking of the *kalakuta* poison and finally Mohini murti. Lord Shiva was not present at the time of Mohini distributing the nectar to the demigods and how she bewildered the demons. Lord Shiva is the greatest devotee and always desires to learn about Lord Vishnu's exceptional qualities and explore in detail. Shiva made an entourage to the *Svetadvipa* along with Parvati, Nandi, *Bhutagana*, and many more associates like ghosts, Yaksha, and goblins. It is a great fortune for all the ghosts and goblins to associate with Lord Shiva and receive the mercy of the advanced devotees and participate in the discourse and as well as darshan of Lord Vishnu. It is evident that one has to seek a spiritual master to come to the stage of the darshan of

God and Vishnu. Upon seeing Lord Shiva, Lord Vishnu, with open heart, welcomed and satisfied all the associates with pleasing words and his gentle behavior. With such generous hospitality of Lord Vishnu, all of them were fully joyful and happy and eager to hear the upcoming discourses between Lord Shiva and Lord Vishnu. Lord Shiva desired to see the beautiful form of Mohini, and he persisted even though Lord Vishnu said that the Maya is difficult to overcome. With the sincere and genuine interest of his beloved friend and master, he was compassionate towards Lord Shiva. He exhibited the beautiful form of the Mohini, the most celebrated and attractive woman in this world. Even the apsara like Urvasi, Menaka, Rambha are nothing in comparison to the beauty of Mohini. All of the three worlds could be captivated by the glance of the Mohini, the most uncommon beauty of the feminine form of the Lord. Whoever can resist the beautiful form of the Lord, Lord Shiva forgot his identity and ran after the beautiful form of the Lord. He did not even consider the presence of the associates, Parvati, and many sages in the forest where they traveled where Shiva ran after Mohini. After such intimate transactions with Mohini, Shiva discharged his semen which subsequently transformed into gold, silver, minerals in this material world. Lord Vishnu and Lord Shiva's combine interest to give the best ornaments to the modern civilization for decorations and luxurious living standards. One can learn that nothing goes in vain in the matter of interactions with either Lord Shiva or especially Vishnu. This is one of the mysterious events and interactions between Lord Shiva and Lord Vishnu, and more details can be found in the great literature, Srimad Bhagavatam.

Then, Lord Shiva and all the associates, along with Parvati, left for his own abode, Kailasa Hill. Śukadeva Gosvāmī concludes this chapter of Mohini Lila by explaining the innate qualities of Lord Vishnu and Mohini and advising us to continue hearing and chanting about them regularly.

Dattatreya Lila

Dattatreya was born from the great sage Atri and his most chaste wife, Anasuya. The three Lords have tested the chastity of Anasuya and given blessings to her to be their mother. In Srimad Bhagavatam, fourth canto chapter one, the appearance of Dattatreya is mentioned in detail. The two brothers of Dattatreya are named Chandra (moon) and Durvasa (angry sage), and all are considered the partial incarnation of Vishnu, Brahma, and Shiva, respectively. Some Puranas state that Dattatreya is the combination of all the three gods and he holds six hands and three heads. One portion of the head and the pair of his hand is referred to Lord Vishnu with lotus and disc in his hands; the other set of pair of a head and two hands carry kamandalu and a bead for the representation of Brahma; the last set of the pair of a head and two hands depict the drum and a trident of Lord Shiva. In this verse, Sukadeva Gosvami has mentioned the three lords' representation as follows: «ātma-īśa-brahma-sambhavān.» Ātma means the Supersoul or Maha Viṣhṇu, īśa means Rudra or the controller, and Brahma means the creator of the universe. When we understand the partial representation, it's the example of the candle and expansion of the light via many other candles. Lord distributes His energy in a similar process. To further elaborate in the arithmetic language of the Supreme Personality of Godhead's quality and attributes, Kṛṣṇa, who has all one hundred percent of the qualities of God. All other Vishnu-tattva have ninety-four percent of possessions of the original Lord; they are a little bit dimmer than Lord Krishna. Then the Shiva-tattva has eighty-four percent of the original light or Godhead, so Shiva is a little bit dimmer than Vishnu or Krishna. Now comes the comparison of Lord Brahmā, who possesses seventy-eight percent of the quality of the Supreme. All of us have the capability to become like Brahma but not to the point of Shiva or Vishnu. This is the real arithmetic of learning the science of God and His qualities.

Dattatreya has also preached about the Avadhuta-Gita and the importance of the twenty-four Gurus to follow. Many of the states of India like Maharashtra, Gujarat, Karnataka and South India follow Dattatreya as their Adi Guru and the instructions taught by him. Dattatreya taught with simple language with the mood of simple living and high thinking principles. Some notable institutions follow the different aspects of Dattatreya iconography with the animals in a place like a cow and four dogs. It is understood to know that the four Vedas are four dogs, and the cow is the mother earth who is eternally providing nourishment. Lord Shiva is also considered the Adi Guru for many followers of Dattatreya of the nine sects of Shaivites and nine sects of Vaishnava school of the ideology based on the teachings of the Nath sampradaya.

Jagannath Lila

Lord Shiva has so many intimate pastimes with Lord Jagannath in Nilachala Dham, and there is no end to the glories of both the Lord, such as Mahaprasadam, Kasi Vishwanath, Kapala Mochan Lila and so on.

Kashi Vishwanath temple: - This temple is situated in the east corner of Baisi Pahacha. It is a Shiva temple. The size of the temple is too small. The gate of the temple is towards the west. The idol (linga) is made of marble stone, according to the descriptions of one of the greatest Odia poets Upendra Bhanja. " The Lord of Kashi (Kashi Vishwanath) is staying at Puri as the Kshetra has been the head of all tirthas.

Agnishwara Mahadeva: - After crossing 22 steps, one enters into the inner compound known as Kurma bedha. Turning to the left towards the south, one can see a small temple where Agnishwara Mahadeva is installed in a deep seat. The temple is situated on the way to the kitchen. Agnishwara Mahadev is known as the protector of the fire of the temple kitchen. It is also believed that due to the grace of Lord Agnishwara, half-cooked Maha Prasada becomes fully cooked while passing through him. One will be free from all sin when he sees Lord Agnishwara.

Siddheshwara Mahadev temple: - This temple is situated on the western side of the temple on the way to Nialacala upaban (the flower garden of the world). It is said that devotees get siddhi by worshiping this Lord.

Bedha Lokanatha: - On the east of Sitala temple, Lokanath Shiva temple is situated. It is named as Bedha Lokanath temple.

Parashunatha temple: - In the south of Ganesha temple, Parashunatha Shiva temple is situated. This temple is also known as the Kasinatha temple.

Dhabaleshwar temple: - Dhabaleshwar temple is situated near the Parashunatha Mahadeva temple.

Vaikunthanatha Mahadeva temple: - On the gateway of Koili Vaikuntha, Vaikunthanatha Mahadeva is worshiped in a dilapidated temple.

Ishaneshwara temple: - The temple is situated in the corner of the inner wall and outer wall; it is a Shiva temple. Lord Ishaneshwara Shiva is placed near about 20 feet deep on the temple. According to madala panji, this temple was constructed by Dhrubakesari. An image of Hara (Shiva) and Parvati is installed on the way to the temple. It is believed that River Ganga flows through this temple. Unique festivals are arranged in this temple on the day of Shivaratri.

Harisahadeva: - Turning south on the left one can see a small temple where Harisahadeva Shiva is worshiped. It is believed that Harisahadeva, the protector of the cows of the Lord.

Devotees get lovely results by worshiping the Lord to reap the benefit from cattle rearing.

Panca Mahadeva: - In front of Bata Mangala, there are 5 Shiva temples. These Shiva temples are known as Panca Mahadev temples. These panca Mahadeva are Sri Lokanatha, Sri Yamesvara, Sri Nilakantha, Sri Markandeya, and Sri Kapala Mochana. These Shiva temples are also situated outside the temple premises. These five Shiva's are known as the guardian deity of Sri Kshetra.

Markandeya temple: - Near Sarva Mangala temple, the temple of Markandeya rsi is situated. It is Shiva linga, which is placed seven to eight feet deep. This linga is cracked as of now also because Lord Shiva manifested from this Linga to protect Rsi Markandeya from the clutches of Yamaraj.

Kshetrapal Mahadev temple: - This temple is near Ananta Vasudev temple. Lord Kshetrapal is known as the protector of Sri Mandira. Devotees get permission to visit Jagannath after worshiping Ksetrapal Shiva. This temple was constructed during the time of Ananga Bhima Deva.

Muktesvara Mahadev temple: - Muktesvara Mahadev temple is on the side of the Multi Mandapa, where Brahmin's used to sit. It is believed that by reciting Maha Mrytunjaya mantra gets liberation before Muktesvara Mahadeva.

Pataleshwara temple: - This temple is situated near Sri Rama temple towards east of the main temple of Jagannath. Pataleshwar temple has nine Shiva shrines. Half of the temple is submerged in the soil. Since the linga is below the earth, it is called a Pataleshwara temple. Legend says that Vamana put his third step on Bali's head while pressing him to Patala, Bali stayed here by becoming the associate of Pateleshwara Mahadeva.

Mahaprasad Lila – This episode of the availability of the Mahaprasad to the entire world by the mercy of Mother Parvati is so fascinating and astounding. The bhoga offered to Lord Jagannath then it's offered to Vimala is considered as Mahaprasadam. Once upon a time when Narada used to visit Vaikuntha and see both Laxmi and Narayana. Laxmi served delightful offerings to Lord Narayana, and Lord mentioned to her that please don't give my remnants to anyone. One day, Narada asked Maha-Laxmi to allow to eat some maha prasadam, out of affection, and in an intelligent manner, Laxmi somehow tricked one plate of sweet rice just as Kshira-Chora Gopinath stole the pot of sweet rice for Madhavendra puri. When Narada received the special mercy, after eating the sweet rice, he completely transformed into a person filled with the love of Godhead and went to the Kailasa hill to share his feelings. When Lord Shiva saw Narada in full ecstasy and nonstop dancing, he could not understand the import of the activities, Narada explained the details how he received the maha prasadam from Lord Narayana by the mercy of Laxmi. Upon looking at Narada, Shiva inquired about receiving some maha prasadam; however, Narada forgot that he had none except a bit piece in his small finger. Quickly Lord Shiva grabbed the finger of Narada and sucked it with full vigor; after getting the small portion of maha prasadam, Lord Shiva went into deep ecstasy, and both danced as if the earth and the universe were shaking totally. When mother Parvati arrived at the scene, she was asking what's going on and the reason for being so happy and jubilant. They explained all the details about Maha Prasadam, and Parvati asked about her share, they could not give any answer. Parvati, out of anger, went for severe austerity to please Lord Narayana, and Narayan awarded the boon that in the age of Kali, at Jagannath Puri Dham, Parvati in the form of Bimala will receive the first Maha Prasadam from Jagannath. So, after that, it will be distributed to all the devotees, we should thank Mother Parvati as because of her prayers and goodwill, we are able to receive the mahaprasadam. All glories to Jagannath Mahaprasad.

Vimala Bhabita Namnam Hari Kaivalya Modita

Vaisnavi Parama Maya Kalau Khyata Bhavisyati

Eight types of Rudras are installed in the Puri temple – 1) Kapalamocana 2) Yamesvar 3) Ishanesvar 4) Markendasvar 5) Billesvar 6) Nilakantha 7) Batesha 8) Lokanath (Mahesha)

There four types of chandis are placed as guard to the Sri Kshetra dham in each side of the dham such as south, north, east and west along with four types of Hanuman are placed in each direction of the dham. The most opulent and gorgeous Ram chandi, Hara Chandi, Smashani Chandi etc and Bedi Hanuman, Mahavira hanuman and makardhvaja Hanuman are also present in all gates of the Puri dham.

Rudrayamala

Rudrayamala is a sacred conversation between Lord Shiva and Shakti and this scripture is found in the ancient times. Sometimes it is calculated as prior to the Tantra scriptures. One verse is found for the pleasure of Lord Jagannath and the nearby sacred places adjacent to the Purusottam dham.

Mahakanda Basi Mahananda Basi

Puragram Basi Mahapithadesa

Jagannatha Bakshya Sthalastyo Barenya

Brutananda karta Shivananda karti

Sometimes, Rudrayamala teaches the seed mantra for each deity and its invoking prayer as well as the methods it is worshiped. The Bija mantra of Sudarshana is Om, Jagannatha is Klim, Subhadra is Hrim, and Balabhadra is Srim

Kapala-mocana temple – Lord Shiva killed one head of Brahma, and then the temple is known as kapala mocana. This incident is found in Skanda Purana.

Markendesvara – Markendeya saw the Lord after the annihilation, and he decided to reside here.

Yamesvara: - Yama was awarded by Mahalakshmi to stay in Puri. The temple is 100 feet below the ground level. Both Garuda and Vrishabha are side by side. A synthesis of the Hari and Hara cult. Eight Shiva images inside the temple, similarities of Lingaraj temple, and here at Jagannath Puri. Devotees worshiping Lord Yamesvara could achieve the fruit of worshipping crores of Shiva Linga in many places.

Lokanatha temple – Lauki was given by locals to Lord Rama, and He worshiped Shiva here and fulfilled his search for Sita.

Maa Mangala: - Mangala is also the expansion of Shakti and the female energy of Lord Rudra. Maa Mangala Temple is a sacred temple in Kakatpur, in the state of Utkal. Utkal is glorious with the presence of Lord Jagannath and the associated gods around Lord Jagannath. Nava-kalevar is the famous festival of Lord Jagannath, and it occurs in the almost twelve years cycle of change of the body of Lord Jagannath (depending on the calculation of the Tithi). The journey of the search of the transcendental wood starts from the great temple of "Maa Mangala" at Kakatpur. This temple is situated at the Bay of Bengal as well as the river Prachi. Mangala is worshiped as Vana Durga as she is one of Lord Shiva's consorts or Durga's manifestations. The worship of goddess "Maa Mangala is so systematically done and the detail rituals can be found during the Nava Kalevara ceremony. This Shakti peeth is part of the Odia culture, and it relates to Lord Jagannath. The deity's curving smile and the gracious presence gives an insight into the worship style of the Odia devotees. The temple was constructed around the 11th century with the architectural view of Utkaliya Peedha Vimana style and always brings auspiciousness to everyone. I am fortunate to be there once, as Maa Mangala is our Ishta Devi. My grandparents Bidulata Devi and Prasanna dada used to worship the deity every day with firm faith and conviction. Mangala is revered first before preparatory for the Nava Kalevar of Jagannath, and both Lord Shiva and Maa Parvati are in complete service of the Lord Jagannath in full ecstasy.

Chaitanya Lila

Lord Shiva and Mother Parvati had intimate pastimes with Lord Chaitanya in the Rudradwipa of the Nadia. Whenever people does not take to the path of devotional service to Lord, Lord Rudra gets angry; however, Lord Rudra was not angry with the fallen souls in the age of Kali, and in the manifestation of Advaita Acharaya prayed to Lord Chaitanya with sincere crying. Lord Shiva was named as Lord Rudra because of His raudana or crying after taking birth from Lord Brahma. Lord Sada-Shiva, in the incarnation of Advaita Acharya, sincerely prayed to Lord Chaitanya for giving them the ultimate mercy, love of Godhead. Advaita Acharya is an incarnation of the combined form of Sada-Shiva and Mahavishnu. Lord Rudra is always meditating on the welfare of conditioned living beings, and he has inaugurated a sampradaya to take back home to the fallen conditioned souls.

In Caitanya Caritamrta Madhya Lila chapter nine, the descriptions of Lord Chaitanya's visit to South India is so auspicious to all of us. Lord Chaitanya visited Mallikarjuna temple on the bank of Krishna river. One of the twelve Jyotirlinga in the world and the most famous Mallikarjuna and the linga is so powerful that any desires can be fulfilled by the will of Lord Shiva. Gauranga Mahaprabhu was so happy to visit the temple. On the other hand, Lord Chaitanya converted all the devotees of Lord Shiva into Vaishnava dharma by inducing them to chant in the holy name of the Hare Krishna Maha mantra. Lord Shiva was extremely happy to see Lord Chaitanya, both Gauri and Shiva appeared in the form of a brahmana boy and brahmani and served Lord Chaitanya with prayers, food, sitting arrangement and many varieties of paraphernalia for worship. Lord Chaitanya also worshiped the linga in each Shiva temple such as Sri Shailam Kshetra and many more. Lord Chaitanya also visited many other important Shiva and Vishnu pilgrimage areas such as Shiva Kanchi, Vishnu Kanchi, Skanda-kshetra, Siyalia Bhairava, Vrdhakasi and many more.

CC Madhya 9.38

tāṅre kṛpā kari' prabhu calilā āra dine vṛddhakāśī āsi' kaila Shiva-daraśane

"After showing mercy to the brāhmaṇa, Lord Śrī Caitanya Mahāprabhu left the next day and arrived at Vṛddhakāśī, where He visited the temple of Lord Shiva."

The ancient Shiva resided in the place so known as Vrdhakasi and this is similar in the Navadvip Mandala dham's Vrdhakasi linga also. There is always a connection between Shiva and Vishnu by the brother of Ramanujacarya, who served the Shiva temple for many years as Ramanujacarya served Lord Vishnu for many years. Shiva Kanchi is the most favorite place of Lord Shiva and popularly known as Kanchipuram and the sarees are very famous also and this is the Banaras of southern India also. Lord Chaitanya visited the important place of Lord Shiva where two birds used to come and pay respects to the linga and eat prasadam and leaves. Lord Chaitanya was amazed to see the linga and the temple and the place is known as Pakshi-Tirtha.

RUDRA MENTIONED IN VARIOUS SCRIPTURES

Rudra in Bhagavad Gita

Lord Krishna is sharing His opulence to Arjuna on the battlefield, and in Chapter 10: The Opulence of the Absolute, Lord Krishna talked about Rudra as follows. Lord Krishna declares himself as Rudra "rudranam sankaras casmi", of all the Rudras, especially the chief eleven Rudras, krishna is known as Sankara. This is one of the opulence of the Supreme Lord in relationship to Lord Rudra.

Rudra is a managerial post that keeps changing in every Kalpa. Hence manifestations of Rudra also change along with the Rudra. (Brahmas and Rudras in all universes are the Jiva-atmas like Indra). Shankara was one (best) of Rudra's 11 manifestations in that Kalpa, during which Bhagavad Gita was revealed. Sada-Shiva remains eternal in the spiritual sky, and He is the source of all the Rudras in the material world.

Rudra in Bhagavatam

Rudra drinking the poison after the churning of the milk ocean is so sweet to hear.

In Srimad Bhagavatam, Sukadeva Gosvami described the pastimes to Parikshit Maharaj about Lord Shiva drinking the poison after churning the ocean of milk. Once upon a time, demons and demigods made a truce to obtain the nectar, With the great force of determination, they reached at the shore of the milk ocean for churning the ocean to obtain the *amrta*, the drink of immortality. They needed a rod and a rope, which is the Mandara mountain and the snake Vasuki. Upon roping the snake unto the Mandara mountain, they failed to move an inch because of the hefty mountain sinks to the bottom. Harassed by the failure of such attempts, they looked for divine help,

Lord Vishnu assumed the form of a tortoise and supported the Mandara mountain so that the churning could continue and the Kurma god could get some sorts of gentle message on His gigantic body. Instead of the nectar, the fumes and the kalakuta or halahala poison accumulated in the shore. Demigods and demons were completely in distress upon seeing the poisonous effects and the poison around them, when there is no hope, people tend to pray just like the situation of COVID-19, Lord bestows His causeless mercy. Now Lord Shiva took the responsibility to consume the poison and save the demons and demigods. His wife Parvati nodded the attempt of Lord Shiva to drink the poison as she knew very well the importance of Lord Shiva and His unlimited power. Once she allowed this endeavor, Lord Shiva got hold of the kalakuta poison in his palm and drank it without any effort. And he kept the poison in his throat, and his throat became bluish, and so he was known as Neelakantha, and He demonstrated such an excellent task for saving all humanity. Few drops fell from his lotus palm, and cactus and poisonous plants consumed it as well as the snakes, rats, dogs, and jackals ate few of the drops fallen from the palm of the Lord. This is described in the eighth canto, the seventh chapter of Srimad Bhagavatam, and one can relish the mellows more.

Rudra pleased with Banasura

Most of the demons are favored by Lord Shiva, and they created great havoc with their power. At an ancient age, the grandson of Prahlad Maharaj named Bali Maharaj was there for whom Lord Vamana appeared on this planet. Bali Maharaj had one hundred sons like Dhritarashtra, and the eldest son named Banasura was exactly like Duryodhana. One should know the art of pleasing Lord Shiva and obtain the best of the rewards. By his musical instruments' knowledge, Banasura played with his thousand hands for the Shiva *Tandava Nrtya*, one of Shiva's famous art, the Nataraj. Banasura received the benedictions from Lord Rudra that he will become the gatekeeper of the capital city of Banasura named, Śoṇitapura. Lord Vamana became the gatekeeper for Bali Maharaj, and here Lord Shiva became the gatekeeper of Bali's eldest son. Even Lord Gauranga is pleased with anyone who plays *karatal* and *mrdanga*, and the music invokes Lord Gauranga to dance in ecstasy. Upon receipt of the rewards from Lord Shiva, Banasura was puffed up with his possessions, and powers dared to ask even his own master no one other than Shiva could have fought with me. Lord Shiva was annoyed with Banasura's false claim and declared that Banasura would be defeated by his worshipable Lord, and his pride will be crushed like Ravana.

Banasura had a beautiful daughter named Usha, and one night she dreamed of a young man, and suddenly the dream came shattered when she awoke from the dream and found herself surrounded by maidservants. Usha's best friend, Citralekha, was a great painter, and she depicted the various person's images based on the descriptions by Usha. She even made the picture of Krishna, Pradyumna, and Aniruddha, and finally, Usha selected the picture of Aniruddha to be her hero. We know the love story of Pradyumna and Mayavati in another section, and now we hear the love story of Usha and Aniruddha. Citralekha, by the guidance of Narada as Narada gave the secret code, mantra to enter Dwaraka. The city of Dwaraka is so subtle that you need to go inside by a code, and then it is unlocked. Citralekha kidnapped Aniruddha and brought him to Śoṇitapura for the pleasure of her friend Usha. They had conjugal love in the palace, and it came to the notice of Banasura, and he attacked the castle with hundreds of military men and captured Aniruddha with the Shiva's weapon Snake rope or called "Naga-phasa". Then a battle happened between Lord Krishna and Banasura with the assistants from Lord Shiva. Ultimately Lord Krishna was victorious in the battle, and Usha married Aniruddha. Lord Shiva was pleased with the entire outcome and worshiped Lord Krishna. We find such beautiful narrations in

Srimad Bhagavatam and Sukadeva Gosvami glorifies both Lord Shiva and Lord Krishna.

Rudra and Citraketu

Citraketu, by the grace of God, got the gift of roaming around the world with his girlfriends but always singing the glories of the Lord. Once, he was passing around the beautiful Kailash hills; and he happened to see Lord Shiva and the assembled sages while Lord Shiva was giving a discourse on Srimad Bhagavatam. Citraketu appreciated the exalted position of Lord Shiva, and therefore he remarked at how wonderful it was that Lord Shiva was acting like an ordinary human being. He appreciated Lord Shiva's position, but when he saw Lord Shiva sitting amid saintly persons and working like a shameless, he criticized Lord Shiva, he did not offend Lord Shiva like Dakṣa. Dakṣa considered Lord Shiva to be insignificant. Sukadeva Gosvami describes the detailed incident about Citraketu and Lord Shiva in Srimad Bhagavatam's sixth canto seventeenth chapter.

In a mundane sense, the marital affairs between wife and husband should be conducted privately for the civilized people; however, here, Citraketu saw Lord Rudra is embracing Parvati in the assembly of the saintly person and not only that he is also sharing his realization about the absolute truth with the sages there. Lord Shiva is considered the best of the yogis, and he can control his senses, and there is no one superior to him in being a dhira. The best of the brahmacharis worship Lord Shiva for their spiritual advancement in celibacy. Citraketu wanted to appreciate the great wonder exhibited by Lord Shiva in a joking manner. One should not joke while someone in the Vyas Asana or with the learned sages or in other circumstances. As per the social custom, it was a direct criticism to Lord Shiva by seeing the contrast glories in such a manner. Lord Rudra is hardly angry with anyone, and if He gets angry, then he can annihilate the whole world. Lord Shiva did not say anything to Citraketu and remained silent. When Daksha criticized Rudra in the assembly, Lord Rudra did not retaliate. This is the proper etiquette of a Vaisnava. All the assembled sages were silent in this context as they saw Lord Shiva is not speaking anything towards Citraketu. However, Parvati, the wife of Shiva, felt offended by the words used by Citraketu towards her husband, and she could not tolerate them exactly as Sati, she could not tolerate the insulting attitude exhibited by Daksha.

Therefore, the powerful consort of Lord Shiva, Parvati, spoke as follows to Citraketu, who thought himself better in all respects than Lord Shiva in controlling the senses and mind. Of course, such a person is the lowest by assuming Shiva to be like this, who is the spiritual master of the three worlds, and the creator of the universe even glorifies, and all the demigods seek the lotus feet of Lord Shiva. This lowborn Citraketus must be punished because he is not behaving like a kshatriya by insulting Lord Shiva. Parvati cursed Citraketu to take birth as a Rakshasa, a kind of demon as he deserves to be so.

Rudra and Bhagirathi

A king of the Sagara dynasty, Bhagīratha satisfied Lord Shiva by performing austerities in order to liberate the cursed forefathers. When King Bhagīratha approached Lord Shiva and requested him to sustain the Ganges' forceful waves, Lord Shiva accepted the proposal of Bhagiratha as he loved his sincere prayer and devotion. Also, ultimately Lord Shiva wanted the welfare of all living beings by bringing the mother Ganges to the earth. He said, "Let it be so. Your wish is fulfilled." Lord Shiva had to sustain the immense flow of the Ganges on the top of his head, and the Ganges is ever flowing from the lotus toe of Lord Trivikrama, Vishnu. Bhagiratha was the first cause of bringing the Ganges to the earth to release his forefathers from their sins who were in the form of ashes. This is the causeless mercy of Lord Shiva upon the great king.

Rudra and King Salva

King Salva was envious of Lord Krishna, and he wanted to destroy the city of Dvaraka, so he wanted to please Lord Shiva to get a boon. As many people know that Lord Shiva is Ashutosh, Jayadratha wanted a boon, king Jarasandha wanted a boon, and many more demoniac kings wanted material boons from Lord Shiva. This description is very nicely mentioned in Srimad Bhagavatam tenth canto chapter seventy-six. King Salva went to the forest for severe penances to please Lord Shiva, and however, after a year passed, there was no sign of Lord Shiva to appear in front of him. Lord Shiva, out of his own will, appeared in front of Markandeya and Pracetas. In this connection, He was not interested to come because he knew that the intention of king Selva was not pure; not only that, he wanted to take avenge against Lord Krishna. Lord Shiva knew very well that this is not going to work even though he himself blesses king Selva. Lord Shiva, Ashutosh, and Sukadeva Gosvami mention that saranam agatam, anyone taking shelter of Lord Shiva, never returned him with empty hands. That's the position of Lord Shiva; one should not conclude that position of Lord Shiva as against Lord Krishna. Lord Shiva is always and fully aware of the position of Lord Krishna. Lord Shiva awarded the boon to king Salva, the special weapon of mass destruction; however, this will be fruitless in the city of Dwaraka.

Rudra and Daksha

Daksha is the son of Brahma, and he is made into the chief of Prajapati, progenitors of the whole world. Daksha is very fond of family life, knowledge, beauty, prestige, and position of social status. Such boons sometimes fall from the path of spiritual realization, and one should be cautious in spiritual life as how to develop humility rather than be envious and proud like Daksha. Daksha happens to be the father-in-law of Lord Shiva also as Sati married to Lord Shiva. In this way, they have a relationship in terms of the body. Lord Shiva is the master of the whole world and the spiritual teachers of four Kumaras, Narada, and many more. Daksha wanted respect and adoration from Lord Shiva, and he considered himself superior being the position of the father-in-law of Lord Shiva. This is over demand for respect from an elevated personality, and that becomes detrimental in the path of spiritual realization. In Srimad Bhagavatam's fourth canto, chapter two, the relationship and turmoil in the relation with Daksha and Shiva are described, and Sukadeva Gosvami explains the situation and conclusion for our understanding in this matter. Lord Shiva is the greatest Vaisnava, and he should be respected even from Daksha, the great Prajapati, if one knowingly offends Lord Shiva, then his fate will be repeated like Daksha. We should humbly beg at the lotus feet of Lord Shiva, and by his mercy, we will attain Krishna Prema.

Rudra instructs Markandeya Rsi

Markandeya Rsi is the son of a great sage Markanda, and he was a great ascetic. Whenever a sage or a devotee attains the stage of perfection, Lord appears in front of them and awards various boons. Lord Shiva and Parvati are flying in the sky as Citraketu and Kardama muni perform the traveling journey. Lord Shiva, being the controller of the material world, nothing is impossible for him. Upon the request of Parvati, they decided to have a stopover at the place of the Markandeya rsi's ashram. In chapter ten of Srimad Bhagavatam's twelfth canto, the detailed description of Markandeya Rsi and Lord Shiva is described. Upon seeing the beautiful form of Lord Shiva, Markandeya offered obeisances and glorified him with prayers. In full ecstasy, he offered a sitting place for Lord Shiva like Gajendra offered the lotus flower to Lord Vishnu.

Markandeya offered sweet words to Lord Shiva. Of course, Lord Shiva, being the name Ashutosh, was very pleased with the behaviors of Markandeya rsi, and he asked for any benedictions as he desired. Mārkaṇḍeya offered his prayers again and again to Lord Shiva, being a pure devotee of the Lord, he requested for Lord Shiva to grant him steadfast love of Godhead to Lord Krishna, and also develop the desire to serve the devotees of Lord Krishna and Lord Rudra. Lord Shiva was very much pleased with Markandeya with his level of austerity and devotion. He granted them all with additional boons such as being famous in the three worlds, ever youth and no disease whatsoever, Trikalnja like himself, being a spiritual preceptor of the Vedic literature.

Sukadeva Gosvami highly recommends his readers to chant and read this section carefully, and upon doing so, they will be free from karma and ultimately attain love of Godhead by the mercy of Markandeya rsi, Lord Shiva and Lord Krishna.

Rudra meeting with demigods

Whenever there is a need for service by humans, beasts, ghosts, demons, they think of Lord Rudra for an easier solution. Demigods also approached Lord Shiva for many instances as we see when they needed help in churning the milk ocean as well as pacifying Lord Shiva after the death of his wife, Sati. There is evidence in Srimad Bhagavatam; it is mentioned how Lord Shiva is meeting with all the demigods for universal welfare. As we find in SB 4.6.39, all the demigods are offering their homage to Lord Shiva as mentioned *"vyupāśritaṁ giriśaṁ yoga-kakṣām"*, Sometimes the accuracy is mentioned in Vedic literature that what kind of dress Lord Shiva is wearing and how He is sitting so that we can understand the mood of Lord Rudra and the interaction pattern with the demigods. When Lord Shiva is wearing a saffron dress and seems very grave, it is to be noted that he is considered a foremost sage in the whole world, truly he is the protector and the spiritual master of the demigods also.

We can understand that all the demigods are respectful towards Lord Shiva, and they know very well the real position of Lord Shiva. It is interesting to note that Lord Shiva is wearing a saffron color dress similar to the dress code of Lord Gauranga. He exhibited the devotional mellows or the feelings in the Sri Harihara Kshetra of Godruma dvipa in Navadvipa Mandala Dham. Whoever dies in this place, Lord Shiva chants the name of Gaura in this place and prays to Lord Gauranga for the ultimate attainment of that jivas. Lord Shiva is always thinking about the welfare of living beings, and he is not uselessly speculating on the arbitrary understanding rather situated on the absolute platform. In this verse, *brahma-nirvanam* is very important as Lord Rudra is entirely in a union of the thoughts and darshan of his master, Sankarshana. Even though his wife left the body, He was still situated in the bliss of the Brahman and teaching us how we can remain in the state of joy in all situations of life. Lord Shiva exhibited various spiritual ecstasies and manifestations, and therefore it is understood that he was eternally absorbed in the state of the bliss, brahmānanda. Yoga-kaksa means the sitting posture and Lord Shiva's sitting posture is always a spiritual posture for all to meditate, either during the time of teachings to the sages and while engaging the teachings to the Shiva-Gana, Narada or four Kumaras. His sitting posture is of utmost the best for spiritual elevation. For proper chanting, we need to use a better sitting posture to maximize our results. Lord Shiva is always using his intelligence and his position to think about the welfare of the general population as to how they can attain the Brahma nirvana state. Even the demigods are approaching Lord Shiva for guidance and solution in their life, so what to speak of the mere mortal? We should take advantage of the situation and take shelter of Advaita Acharya who is non-different from Sada-Shiva and attain Krishna Prema by the mercy of Lord Advaita Acharya.

Rudra and Kamadeva

In Srimad Bhagavatam second Canto, chapter seven, we find the analogy of the competition between lust and anger who has much formidable power over other, Lord Rudra used his anger (rosa) to burn the Kama(lust) by using *"kāmaṁ dahanti kṛtino nanu roṣa-dṛṣṭyā"*, There is no possibility of lust entering the heart of Rudra because He is transcendental however the anger "rosa" has the chance to come closer to Rudra and take shelter at His lotus feet and Rudra needed to use against the lust. Rudra is known as the anger personified and he incarnated as Durvasa as the form of anger to show that anger can devastate the person's accumulated pious activities. Rudra is beyond such duality of modes and he is the master and controller of the anger and he knows well how to use it. Although Lord Shiva was able to control the kama or lust however he was angry at Kamadeva, all such transcendental activities happened by the divine will of Lord Vishnu.

One should not get confused with the name Mayavati and Maya, whenever I speak about Maya, the consort of Lord Shiva, however Mayavati (Rati) is the consort of Kamadeva., the cupid in this material world. Real cupid "*kandarpa koti kamaniya shobha*" is Madan-mohan, Krishna. Kamadeva was burnt to ashes by the wrath of Lord Shiva when he tried to throw his arrows unto him for sexual agitations for Parvati. Rati and Kamadeva are eternally united to serve the Lord. In Dvapara Yuga, they took birth as Pradyumna and Mayavati. Pradyumna is also an expansion of Lord Vishnu, and Jiva Goswami explained in Krsna-sandarbha in detail about the appearance of Pradyumna and how the Kamadeva merged in the body of Pradyumna. When Kamadeva's body was completely turned into ashes by the supreme anger of Lord Rudra, Rati, the wife of Kamadeva, worshiped Lord Shiva to award a suitable body for her husband. At the same time, the fisherman Sambara also reached Lord Shiva for a benediction. Upon seeing Rati, he was captivated by her and he forgot the reason for coming to Lord Shiva and asked for a boon, however, Lord Shiva knew that Rati approached her first, being omniscient of the true identity of the Kamadeva and Rati he awarded the boon to Sambara first and Sambara desired for Rati. By the illusory potency, Rati maintained her integrity at the home of Sambara, and due course of time by the arrangement of providence, Pradyumna was kidnapped and left in the shelter in residence at the palace of Mayavati. Even though Mayavati acted as a mother of child Pradyumna, she showed conjugal love towards him, and both came to know about their real identity as Kamadeva and Rati. By the mercy of Lord Shiva, Rati and Kamadeva reunited again and remained as a direct association of Lord Krishna at Dwaraka.

Rudra and Maya

Maya is considered as an illusion, but in spiritual reality, Maya is also a person, and she is also the wife of Lord Shiva. It is not the interest of any of the Lord to associate with Maya; however, in order to impregnate and continue the material universe, they play a role. Lord Vishnu also gives assurance and hope to Lord Shiva that Maya cannot captivate him. Similarly, Lord Krishna reassures Sukadeva Gosvami that Maya wouldn't touch him, he should come out from the womb of his mother. Maya is also a servant of the Lord, Mahamaya helps in the material world, and Yogamaya helps in the spiritual world. An individual Jiva must be situated either in the criminal law or in the civil law of the government directed by the Supreme Personality of Godhead. The entire material world is created and annihilated by the three lords of the three modes of material nature. As per (Aitareya Upaniṣad 1.1.1-2), *Sa īkṣata lokān nu sṛjā. Sa imāḻ lokān asṛjata*, Mother Parvati is in charge of the Maya and cooperating the Supreme Lord Vishnu. Lord Krishna says in Bhagavad Gita 9.10, *mayādhyakṣeṇa prakṛtiḥ sūyate sacarācaram*: "The material energy, another manifestation of Maya works under My direction, O son of Kuntī. In Brahma-samhita, it is mentioned that *sṛṣṭi-sthiti-pralaya-sādhana-śaktir ekā chāyeva yasya bhuvanāni bibharti durgā*, Durga is the superintendent of the jail and she is cooperating with Lord Vishnu in the material world. Whenever Durga is present, that means Lord Shiva is present, and vice versa, and both of them are working under the directions of Lord Vishnu as per Bhagavad Gita, Aitreay Upanishad, and Brahma-Samhita.

Rukmini's prayers to Ambika

The interaction with Rukmini and Ambika is mentioned as the Gopis in Vrindavan pray to Katyani, and Lord Shiva resides in Vraj Mandal to shower blessings to attain the Vraja Bhakti and develop the mood of Gopis. In Srimad Bhagavatam, ŚB 10.53.46, *sva-santāna-yutāṁ Shivam,* Rukmini is praying not only to Ambika only but also her own families including the two sons of Parvati. Ganesh is known as the obstacle remover and Ambika blesses her to receive a good husband. Rukmini prays with humility and prays to her that she should receive Krishna as her husband. We should take lessons from Rukmini by being humble to pray everyone to become a devotee of Krishna.

Rukmini is the eternal consort of Lord Krishna and what is necessary for her to pray to Parvati to get the hand of Krishna in marriage. Krishna created a situation in the material world that we don't have any options than to pray to the Lord. In this situation one can argue that Rukmini could have prayed to Lord Krishna directly instead of praying to Ambika. Actually, Ambika is the ista devi of the dynasty of Bhismaka. In order to follow the traditional path of the family she adopted and secondly when Krishna was present on the planet, her elder brother did not believe in Krishna's supremacy, nor he allowed Rukmini to marry Krishna even though she desired so. Rukini was in a helpless condition and she followed the same path of the Gopis in Vrindavan, all of them knew that Krishna had given a blanket contract to Lord Shiva and Ambika to shower blessings unto attaining Himself. Ambika is the de facto goddess of Rukmini and she prayed to her for getting Krishna as the husband. Ambika helped Rukmini and she knows Krishna is her master too and everything happened by the will of Krishna. All the devotees of Krishna like Rukmini, Ambika, Shiva are the eternal associates of the Lord and they're ready to follow His commands. Lord Krishna enjoys the right delegation in the right time to his right sets of devotees. We pray to Ambika to obtain the service of Rukmini Dwarakadhish in the material world.

Rudra in Sri Chaitanya-caritamrta and Chaitanya Bhagavat

Lord Shiva is mentioned in Caitanya Caritamrta as he was deeply involved with Lord Gauranga's pastimes. Lord Shiva and Lord Gauranga are eternally connected with the divine mood of the rasa of servitude, friendship, brother-in-law and also Gopis. Lord Gauranga did not miss to visit the Shiva Kshetra whenever he travelled the region. He visited Lingaraj temple as well as numbers of other Shiva temples. In one instance, as per the Sri Chaitanya Caritamrta SCC Madhya 9.68 *Shiva-kāñcī āsiyā kaila Shiva daraśana,* All the places of Shivalinga and Shiva's temple are very much dear to Lord Chaitanya. We should not disrespect any of the Shiva Linga and we should always beg to Shiva Linga that please award us pure devotional service to Lord Gauranga. Lord Gauranga instructed Sanatana Gosvami in Banaras and Kanchipuram is the southern Banaras and he taught Gopala Bhatta in these areas and made pure devotees. Whenever Lord Chaitanya visited the holy places of Shiva linga, He used to offer full obeisances unto the deity and Lord Shiva and Gauri were eager to come and serve Gauranga in humble mood. This is the true reciprocation of the transcendental relationship, when one knows the true identity, there is no competition, in the material world, we don't know our identity and we fight for the position and generally bring Lord Shiva to our position and think that one is superior than others by doing some menial activities. One could argue here that Lord Gauranga performed the worship to Lord Shiva like "*Vandana karila ". As per SC*C 9.76, that means he offered obeisances and worship to Lord Shiva. There is nothing wrong in doing so, it is the highest etiquette and Lord Chaitanya was playing a role of a Vaisnava and not as Vishnu. Lord Krishna worshiped His parents also in Vrindavan. We should know these things in a proper context so that we don't get an incorrect conclusion of the true identity of the two Lords. Lord Chaitanya also visited a temple of Lord brahma and Shiva Ganga near Kumbakonam, named after the brother of Ravana.

When Lord Caitanya was living with his mother in Navadvipa and many sweet pastimes occurred in the house and with many devotees. One day a great devotee of Lord Shiva visited the house of Lord Gauranga as mentioned in CC Ādi 17.99, *prabhura aṅgane nāce, ḍamaru bājāya*, Lord Gauranga transformed himself into Lord Shiva and started playing the damaru and other manifestations. No one could imitate the extraordinary symptom of Lord Gauranga. One will be amazed to see the rasa with Lord Shiva and with the same mood, one should humbly respect Lord Shiva.

We want to understand the meaning of incarnation and the combination of both the Lord into one. Technically there is no difference between Sada-Shiva and Shiva and Rudra. They are one and the same. Similarly, Sada-Shiva is an incarnation of Maha Vishnu. It is mentioned in the Chaitanya caritamrta that Advaitaacharya is an incarnation of Sada-Shiva as well as Mahavishnu. Srila Prabhupada said in various places that both answers are right, and Advaita Acharya is an incarnation of Sada-Shiva.

Not only in Chaitanya caritamrta, but also in Chaitanya Bhagavata, there are several descriptions of Lord Shiva, In Chaitanya Bhagavata, CB Ch 9 Text 107

Gaya giya kasi gela Shiva rajadhani

Yanhi dhara vahe ganga Uttara vahini

He went to Gaya and then to Lord Shiva's abode, Kasi, where the Ganges flows towards the north.

Text 118

Shiva-kanci visnu kanci gela nityananda

Dekhi hase dui gane maha maha dvanda

Lord Nityananda then visited Shiva-kanci and the adjoining Visnu-kanci. He laughed when he saw the two groups of followers quarreling there.

Text 130

Kartika dekhiya nityananda mahamati

Sri parvata gela yatha mahesa paravati

After seeing Kartikeya at Madurai, the most intelligent Nityananda went to Sri-saila, the abode of Shiva and Parvati.

Text 131

Brahmane brahmani-rupe mahesa Parvati

Sei sri-parvate donhe karena vasati

Shiva and Parvati reside on this mountain in the forms of a brahmana couple.

Text 133

Prama santosa donhe atithi dekhiya

Paka karilena devi harasita haiya

They were most satisfied to receive such a guest, and Parvati happily cooked for the Lord.

Sri Krishna Chaitanya Carita Maha Kavya by Murari Gupta

tatraiva rudrena muni-pravira , kartu hi sahajyam avatariyan tatheti ta praha harih surari / so 'pi pranamyiisu jagama htah 23

"In this avatar of Yours, the heroes among the sages together with Rudradeva shall also descend to give Your assistance." "So be it," Sri Hari replied to the sage amongst the gods. Then swiftly, the sage jubilantly bowed before the Lord and departed. Thus, ends the Third Sarga entitled "Narada Muni Pleads for the Lord's Descent," in the first section of the great poem Sri Caitanya Carita.

Vriddha Shiva (Shiva Doba)

Nityananda disclosed various confidential places to Srila Jiva Goswami about the mystical meaning of those places. They advanced to the bank of the holy Ganges in a joyful mood, at the border of Mayapur, Jiva rolled to the ground in ecstasy after seeing the Vriddha Shiva temple. This temple is near to Mahaprabhu ghat, where Lord Caitanya completed his daily bath as Mother Ganges performed severe austerities at the Vriddha Shiva temple to obtain Gauranga's mercy for His personal association. It is widely known that a beautiful Shiva-linga was instituted in this range, which is now revered by all the devotees, and this site is stationed behind the birth site of Sri Chaitanya Mahaprabhu. Because of the ancient old linga at this place, it is also known as Vriddha Shiva, or Kshetrapala, the guardian of the Mayapur holy dhama. Lord Nityananda glorified the Shiva Linga as how Lord Shiva was eternally serving Lord Gauranga and his wife Praudha Maya's energy. By the instructions of Nityananda to Jiva Goswami, Praudha Maya and Vriddha Shiva will come here and perform their obligations of being present in the spiritual abode as per the plan of Lord's desire." There are several Ghats and hidden potent places that were constructed by Visvakarma on Krishna's command. At this ghat, one will be able to realize five Shiva holy places with five lingas. The unique four Ghats are famous in Mayapur and they are very gorgeous too. Furthermore, whoever takes a bath in any of the ghats is reassured of all touches of melancholy. A pond called Shiva-Doba will be perceived, and visible to the realized one, demonstrating the Ganges' preceding bank. In this same manner, by the Lord's divine will, the devotees will reveal to the entire world, the lost places. I am trying my best to inform you about the holy Dham Mayapur and Lord Shiva's eternal residence in such an elevated spiritual abode.

Rudra in Padma Purana (Gita-Mahatmya)

The Glories of Chapter One of the Bhagavad Gita from the Padma Purana

Parvati said, "My dear husband, you know all the transcendental truths, and by your mercy, I have heard the glories of the Supreme Personality of Godhead, Lord Krishna. Oh Lord, now, I long to hear from You the glories of the Srimad Bhagavad-Gita, which was spoken by Lord Krishna, and by hearing which, one's devotion to Lord Krishna increases."

Lord Shiva replied, "That person, Whose body is the color of a dark rain cloud, whose carrier is the king of birds, Garuda, and Who is lying on Ananta-Sesa, the thousand-headed serpent, that Lord Vishnu, Whose glories have no limit, I always worship. My dear Parvati once after Lord Vishnu had killed the demon Mura, He was resting peacefully on Ananta-Sesa, when the bestowed of all good fortune of the universe, Sri Lakshmi, respectfully inquired from Him.

The seven texts from the Padma Purana is so glorious that we can know the internal mood of Lord Shiva. He is explaining the meanings to mother Gauri on the topic of Srimad Bhagavad Gita.

gita-shastram idam punyam, yah pathet prayatah puman
vishnoh padam avapnoti, bhaya-shokadi-varjitah (1)

One who, with a regulated mind, recites with devotion this Bhagavad-gita scripture, the bestower of all virtue, will attain a holy abode such as Vaikuntha, the residence of Lord Vishnu, which is always free from the mundane qualities based on fear and lamentation.

gitadhyayana-shilasya, pranayama-parasya ca
naiva santi hi papani, purva-janma-kritani ca (2)

If one reads Bhagavad-gita very sincerely and with all seriousness, then by the grace of the Lord the reactions of his past misdeeds will not act upon him.

maline mocanam pumsam, jala-snanam dine dine
sakrid gitamrita-snanam, samsara-mala-nashanam (3)

One may cleanse himself daily by taking a bath in water, but if one takes a bath even once in the sacred Ganges water of Bhagavad-gita, for him the dirt of material life is altogether vanquished.

gita su-gita kartavya, kim anyaih shastra-vistaraih
ya svayam padmanabhasya, mukha-padmad vinihsrita (4)

Because Bhagavad-gita is spoken by the Supreme Personality of Godhead, one need not read any other Vedic literature. One need only attentively and regularly hear and read Bhagavad-gita. In the present age, people are so absorbed in mundane activities that it is not possible for them to read all the Vedic literature. But this is not necessary. This one book, Bhagavad-gita, will suffice because it is the essence of all Vedic literature and primarily because it is spoken by the Supreme Personality of Godhead.

bharatamrita-sarvasvam, vishnu-vaktrad vinihsritam
gita-gangodakam pitva, punar janma na vidyate (5)

By drinking the Ganges waters of the Gita, the divine quintessence of the Mahabharata emanating from the holy lotus mouth of Lord Vishnu, one will never take rebirth in the material world again. In other words, by devotionally reciting the Gita, the cycle of birth and death is terminated.

sarvopanishado gavo, dogdha gopala-nandanah
partho vatsah su-dhir bhokta, dugdham gitamritam mahat (6)

All the Upanishads are like a cow, and the milker of the cow is Lord Shri Krishna, the son of Nanda. Arjuna is the calf, the beautiful nectar of the Gita is the milk, and the fortunate devotees of exceptional theistic intellect are the drinkers and enjoyers of that milk.

ekam shastram devaki-putra-gitam
eko devo devaki-putra eva
eko mantras tasya namani yani
karmapy ekam tasya devasya seva (7)

There need be only one holy scripture, the divine Gita sung by Lord Shri Krishna: only one worshipable Lord-Lord Shri Krishna: only one mantra-His holy names: and only one duty-devotional service unto that Supreme Worshipable Lord, Shri Krishna.

Rudra in Sri Satvata-Tantra

Sri Satvata-Tantra was spoken by Lord Shiva. We can find some important verses in the scripture Sri Satvata-Tantra.

Text 67

Kalatra putra mitresu

Dhane geha gavadisu

Yan mamatasrvayam krsne

Krttam tan madhyamam smrtam

The conviction that I shall give to lord Krishna my wife, children, friends, wealth, cows, and other things...

Patala Six – Sri Krishna Sahasranamam – text 211

Rudro mrdha Shiva santo

Sambhu sarva-haro hara

Kapardi sankarah suli

Try-alkso bhedyo mahesvarah

He is Shiva (rudra, mrdha, Shiva, santa, and sambhu, sarva-hara, hara, kapardi, sankara, suli, try-aksa, abhedya and mahesvara)

Text 221

Sri narada uvaca

Dhanyo asmi anugrhita asmi

Tvayati karunatmana

Yatah krsnasya paramam

Sahasram nama kirtitam

Sri Narada said, I am fortunate, You, who are very merciful at heart, have been kind to me, for you have spoken to me the thousand transcendental names of Lord Krishna

Patala One – Avatara – nimitta – kathana

Text 43

Tamasa rudra-rupo' bhut

Pratisancarano vibhuh

Ete visnor gunamaya

Avatara kriyakrtah

Shiva, who is situated in the mode of ignorance, affects the dissolution of the material universe. These are Lord Visnu's incarnations that act within the three modes of nature.

Text 49

Rudrasyamsena sataso

Jata rudra-ganah prthak

Sarpas ca sataso jata

Ye ca himsra sva-bhavatah

From a part of Shiva were born hundreds of Rudras and hundreds of great serpents. These beings were all violent by nature.

Part four Bhakti-bheda

Text 7

Tada prita mana devo

Mam uvaca satam gatih

Srnusva Shiva bhadram te

Bhaktan vaksyami satvatan

Then, pleased at heart, the Lord, who is the goal of the saintly devotees, said to me, O Shiva, auspiciousness to you! Listen. I will tell this only to the saintly devotees.

Text 64

Sri Shiva uvaca

Kaya-van mansa saksat

Krsne parama puruse

Parinisthasrayam yad vai

Saranam parikirtitam

Sri Shiva said, with one's body, words, and mind to take shelter of Lord Krsna, the supreme personality of Godhead, is called surrender.

Patala five – Yuga dharma kirtanam

Text 41

Sa tata paramo devah

Sri saci devi nandanah

Devi netro dvi-bhujo gauras

Tapta-jambunada-prabhah

O child, at that time, the supreme personality of Godhead has two eyes, two arms, and a fair complexion splendid as molten gold. He is the son of Sri Saci-devi.

Part seven:- Seva-namaaparadha kathana

Text 5

Namaiva paramam danam

Namiav paramam kriya

Namiva paramo dharmo

Namaivartha prakrtitah

The holy name is the supreme gift. The holy name is the supreme pious deed. The holy name is the supreme religion. The holy name is the supreme wealth.

Text 6

Namaiva kamo bhaktanam

Mokso pi nama kevalam

Esam ca sadhanam nama

Kaminam dvija sattama

O best of Brahmanas, the holy name is the desire of the devotee. The holy name is their final liberation. The holy name is the way those who are filled with yearnings may attain their wishes.

Patala eight :- Bhakti rahasya kathana

Text 23

Ato-anya devata pujam

Tyaktva bali-vidhanatah

Sad guror upadesena

Bhajet krsna pada dvayam

Therefore, one should abandon the worship of the demigods and the presentation of offerings to them. Following the teachings of a bonafide spiritual master, one should worship Lord Krsna's lotus feet.

Rudra in Valmiki Ramayana

Bala Kanda – Visvamitra explained various incidents to Lord Rama

While entourage in the forest, Visvamitra described numerous historical events on their journey in the woods. While reaching Ganga, Rama inquired about mother Ganges, and Visvamitra explained the history of Ganga. This section is described in Mahabharat, Ramayana, Srimad Bhagavatam, and many Puranas.

The presiding deity of the Himalayas, Himavan, begot two daughters by Mena, the daughter of Mount Meru, named Ganga and Uma. Ganga was adopted by celestial God like Brahma for the universal welfare, and Uma was given in charity to Lord Shiva,

Skanda was born from Ganga and Agni with the semen of Lord Shiva.

Bhagiratha pleased Lord Shiva to bear the force of Ganga flow unto the earth.

Visvamitra performed severe austerities to obtain celestial weapons from Shiva as Arjuna did in Mahabharat; however, Visvamitra was puffed up after receiving the benediction from Shiva. Later on, he was submissive by the interaction with the sage Vasistha.

Sita picked up the Shiva bow so quickly as it was offered to Devavrata, the forefather of Nimi, and it was handed over to him by the demigods.

Yuddha Kanda

Lord Shiva then embraced Rama, saying, "My dear Lord, by slaying the incomparably mighty Ravana, you have performed a magnificent feat that they will be glorified throughout the three worlds until the time of dissolution.

Pointing to the sky, Lord Shiva said, "O Rama, see how your father is waiting there, seated upon his celestial chariot. Having been delivered by your mercy, he now resides on Indra's planet. Go quickly with Laksmana and be reunited with Maharaja Dasaratha, for he has come here just to see You.

Uttara Kanda

Lord Shiva said: "I grant that Hanuman will never be killed by me or one of my weapons."

RUDRA IN VYASA'S MAHABHARATA

Adi Parva – History of Draupadi

Lord Shiva blessed Draupadi to receive five husbands. Draupadi was a daughter of a brahmin in her past life. She was not able to find a suitable husband so prayed to Lord Shiva, and Shiva was pleased with her worship and appeared Infront of her. She requested, "O foremost of the demigods, I desire to have a good husband. Therefore, I request you to please give me a good husband. I only wish to receive a good husband and nothing else. My single-minded desire is to find a qualified husband. Therefore, please grant me my wish so that I will be united with a suitable husband. Lord Shiva said *"Tathastu"* and told her that she will receive five good husbands. Then, Draupadi asked why so? Shiva said to her. "You asked five times for a husband, and your prayers can't be futile, and my grant is always true." In this way, Draupadi received five husbands in her next life.

Vana Parva – Ganga comes to earth – Lord Shiva appeared

Sagara worshiped Shiva and received benedictions based on the astrological influences such as to receive 60,000 sons by one wife and another son from another wife and who will perpetuate the family life.

Skanda becomes the commander chief of Indra. Skanda's installation ceremony was performed, and at that time, Lord Shiva offered him a golden necklace that had been made by Vishvakarma. Because of this great honor, as well as for other reasons, Skanda thereafter became known as the son of Lord Shiva. The red rooster given by Agni became Skanda's official emblem, and it was placed upon his flagstaff.

Arjuna's quest for a celestial weapon is mentioned in the Vana Parva and the encounter with Shiva is described here. Arjuna started his venture to obtain a divine weapon, and he performed severe austerities in the forest, and Indra advised him to please Lord Shiva. Dressed in deerskin, rags, and grass, Arjuna ate only fallen leaves and fruit every third day during the first month of his vow. And subsequently, he gave up eating at all, standing on the tips and toes, and with his arms upraised, he lived only in breathing air.

The sages of the forest petitioned Lord Shiva that Arjuna's penance is becoming overheated in this arena. And thus, we are feeling some difficulty and please go to Arjuna and cease him in his vow. Lord Shiva replied, "O Great sages, rest assured that I know all about Arjuna's intention, do not be anxious, for this very day I shall go and award him with the fulfillment of his desires.

Lord Shiva assumed the form of a sizable Kirata hunter. Taking up his bows and arrows, he went to where Arjuna was performing austerities, accompanied by Uma, disguised as a kirata woman. Boars were approaching to Arjuna, and Kirata saw the boar concealed Rakshasa wanted to kill Arjuna, Lord Shiva warned Arjuna that it is prey and Arjuna also pierced his arrows and board killed and now fighting ensures as who is the killer of the boar, kirata or Arjuna.

RUDRA IN SKANDA PURANA – EPISODES OF SIMANTA DVIPA

One of the sections I am referring to where Lord Shiva is talking to Candika, his wife, about the descent of Gaurahari in Navadvipa Mandala Dham.

Gangaya dakhine bhage navadvipe manohare kali- papa-vinasaya saci -garbhe sanatana janisyati priye misra purandaragrhe svayam phalgune paurnamasyam ca nisayam gaura-vigraha (Skanda Purana)

Lord Shiva said to goddess Candika: 'O beloved one, on the southern side of the river Ganga, is the pleasant Navadvipa dhama, Supreme Lord Krisna will appear to destroy the sins of Kali-yuga.

Rudradvip is one of the islands of Navadvip Mandala Dham; The islands are (1) Antardvīpa, (2) Sīmantadvīpa, (3) Godrumadvīpa, (4) Madhyadvīpa, (5) Koladvīpa, (6) Ṛtudvīpa, (7) Jahnudvīpa, (8) Modadruma-dvīpa and (9) Rudradvīpa. Each island has a different meaning of the nine processes of devotional service, and Rudradvip is considered as a sakhya rasa mood to the Lord. In Rudra Dvipa, all the eleven Rudras personally live there for the service of Gauranga Mahaprabhu. Lord Shiva also blessed Visnusvami on this island and inaugurated the Rurda sampradaya. All the Rudras assemble here and sing the glories of Gauranga and chief Rudra (Shiva) dances in full jubilation in the pleasure of the Sankirtana movement. Those who aspire to serve Gauranga remember the service of Lord Shiva and always submit to Rudra and Gaura.

SIMANTA DVIPA IS REPRESENTED AS SRAVANAM, HEARING

Lord Shiva said to goddess Parvati, "You are the Maya potency of Lord Sri Hari who is expert in making impossible things possible. In the form of the external Maya potency of the Lord, you hide the sun-like Lord of Antardvipa from the vision of materialistic people. Therefore Yoga-pitha is known as Mayapur (the city of Maya) on this earth planet. Mayapur is covered by Maya so that non-devotees or materialist people cannot see the brilliant Lord. Dear goddess, you are, therefore, famous as Praudha Maya everywhere."

Simanta Dvipa is one of the major islands of the Navadvip Mandala Dham in West Bengal, India. This glorification has been described in scripture with utmost care. Once upon a time during Satya-yuga, Lord Shiva happened to dance in ecstasy with the chanting of the holy name of Lord Gaurasundara. Goddess Parvati asked Lord Rudra, "What is this name, Gauranga, that you are chanting, and which is causing you to dance? My mood is tender and joyful to see your delightful dance and hear your chanting of Gauranga's name. Until now, all the hymns and prayers I have listened to stretch predicaments and difficulties to the living entities merely. Please be generous enough to tell me about Gauranga. I will adjust my life."

simanta-dvipam asadya

tvam hi devi sanatani

dadrastha sundararam rupam

gaurangasya mahatmana

The Lord replied, "All your desires will be fulfilled. None of My activities are performed without you." Lord Gauranga was about to disappear when Parvati Devi fell at His lotus feet and offered obeisances unto Him. She then put the dust of the lotus feet of the Lord upon her *"simanta"*.

RUDRA IN SRI NABADWIP DHAM MAHATMYA

mayapura sima-sesa vrddha-Shivalaya
jahnavira tate dekhe jiva mahasaya [68]

Along the Mayapur's outer boundary on the Ganga bank, Jiva saw the Temple of Vrddha Shiva.

prabhu bale, mayapure ini ksetra-pala

praudha-maya sakti adhisthana nitya-kala [69]

Nityananda Prabhu said, "In Mayapur, Vrddha Shiva is the protector of the Dham. His consort, Praudha Maya, resides with him eternally."

praudha-maya vrddha-Shiva asi' punaraya
nija karya sadhibeka prabhura ichchhaya [75]

"By the will of the Lord, Praudha Maya and Vrddha Shiva will return and perform their duties (of revealing and protecting the Dham)."

vrddha-Shiva ghata haite tridhanu uttara
gaurangera nija-ghata dekha vijna-vara [97]

"O best of the wise, see Sri Gauranga's ghat ten metres north of Vrddha Shiva's ghat."

ei ghate dekha jiva pancha Shivalaya
pancha-tirtha linga pancha sada jyotirmaya [105]

"O Jiva, see the five Shiva Temples at this ghat. Five effulgent lingams always reside here in these five holy places."

Shiva-doba bali khata dekhite paibe
*sei khata ganga-tira baliya janibe [*120]

"A pond known as Shiva Doba will be visible. Devotees will recognize that pond as the previous bank of the Ganga."

SHIVASHTAKAM BY SRI CHAITHANYA MAHAPRABHU

This ashtakam is found in the book chapter 12 of Sri Krishna Chaitanya Carita Mahakavya by Murari Gupta, a great devotee of Lord Chaitanya Mahaprabhu and Chaitanya Mahaprabhu composed and sang this song very nicely.

Sri Shivashtakam is composed by Sri Caitanya Mahaprabhu. A person who lovingly hears with rapt attention this beautiful eightfold prayer to Sri Shiva can quickly gain Sri Hari-Prema as well as transcendental knowledge, the realization of that knowledge, and unprecedented devotional potency.

The author of this magnificent prayer is undoubtedly one of the greatest exponents of Bhakti Marga. Love of Godhead or being intoxicated in Krishna consciousness is his method for attainment to the ultimate destination. His chosen path is devoted to Lord Krishna. It is indeed an excellent task by Murari Gupta to capture such a beautiful prayer on Lord Shiva by Sri Chaitanya Mahaprabhu.

Namo namasthe tridaseshwaraya,
Bhoothadhinathaya mridaya nithyam,
Ganga tharangothida bala Chandra,
Choodaya Gauri nayanothsavaya 1

Salutations and salutations to him, Who is the Lord of the thirty gods,
Who is the Lord of all beings,
Who is perpetually gracious,
From whose head the waves of Ganga are born, Who wears the crescent of the moon
And who is the feast to the eyes of Gauri,

Sutaptha chamikara Chandra neela,
Padma pravalambudha kanti vasthrai,
Sa nrutya rangetha vara pradhaya,
Kaivalya nadhaya, vrusha dwajaya. 2

Salutations and salutations to Him,
Who is like the moon resembling the molten gold, Who wears a dress of the color of blue lotus and rich cloud,
Who gives boons while he is dancing,
Who is the Lord of salvation, And who has a bull in his flag?

Sudhamsu suryagni vilochanaya,
Tamo bhidhe they jagatha Shivaya,
Sahasra shubramsu sahasra rasmi,
Sahasra sanjjtwara thejasesthu 3

Salutations and salutations to Him, who has moon, sun, and fire as his eyes,
Who is the universal Shiva who dispels darkness
And who by his thousand beamed power,
Defeats thousands of moons and suns.

Nagesa rathnojjwala vigrahaya,
Shardula charmasuka divya thejase,
Sahasra pathropari samasthithaya,
Varangadha muktha bhuja dwayaya. 4

Salutations and salutations to Him,
Whose form shines like the gem,
In the head of the king of snakes, Who wears the skin of a tiger,
Who has an effulgent form,
Who stands amidst a lotus
With one thousand petals,
And who wears lustrous
Amulets in his two hands,

Sunoopura ranjitha pada padma,
Ksharath sudha bhrutya sukha pradaya,
Vichithra ratnogha vibhushithasya,
Premanam eva adya harau videhi. 5

Salutations and salutations to Him,
Who has anklets with bells tied to his lotus feet,
Who gives flowing nectar from his hands,
To his servant like devotees and make them happy,
And who dresses himself in rare gems, With a request, Please grant me your love, Lord Hari.

Sri Rama Govinda Mukunda Shaure,
Sri Krishna Narayana Vasudeva,
Ithyadi namamritha pana mathra,
Bringadhipay akhila dukha hantre, 6

Salutations and salutations to Him, who is the Lord of his bee-

like devotees,
Who chant of the names like Rama,
Govinda, Mukunda, Shauri, Krishna,
Narayana, Vasudeva and others like them, Which would completely destroy all sorrows.

Sri Naradadhya satata sugopya,
Jignanasitaya asu vara pradaya,
Thebhyo harer bhakthi sukha pradaya,
Shivaya sarvaya Gurave Nama. 7

Salutations and salutations to Him,
Who raises confidential curiosity,
In the minds of Sage Narada and others,
Who grants boons fast,
Who blesses his devotees with devotion to Hari,
And who is the teacher of everyone.

Sri Gauri nethothsava mangalaya,
Thath prana nadhaya rasa pradhaya,
Sada samuthkantha Govinda Leela,
Gana pravinya namosthu thubhyam. 8

My salutations to you who is an expert in singing,
Who is the feast to the eyes of his consort Gauri, Who is the Lord of the soul and is attractive, And who is always interested in the playful acts of Govinda,

Ethath Shivasyashtakam adbhtham mahat,
Shrunvan hari prema labhathe sheegram,
Jnanam cha vijnanam, apoorva vaibhavam,
Yo bhava purna paramam samadharam. 9

He who filled with loving feelings hears, this exceedingly pleasant octet on Shiva,
Would soon get the grace and love of Hari, get knowledge, and divine realization.

LORD RUDRA IN BRAHMA-SAMHITA

The meaning of Samhita means joining like the yoga, joining your heart to the Supersoul utilizing the prayer, hymns, mantra, etc. After the bewilderment from Sri Krishna in Vrindavan, Brahma composed various prayers, and the best of them is Brahma-Samhita. He is also mentioning about Lord Shiva in these beautiful prayers. Brahma has given the relationship of Maya Sakti, illusion with the Lord. By this illusion, He got bewildered of Lord Krishna's position, and the same Maya is going to act upon all living beings unless he is fully surrendered to the Lord. As per Śrī Brahma-saṁhitā 5.8, *tal-liṅgaṁ bhagavān śambhur jyotī-rūpaḥ sanātanaḥ*

Lord Brahma is personally praying and glorifying Lord Krishna in these hymns, and specifically, he is mentioning the word linga and Bhagavan. Brahma is a self-realized soul, and he is also an incarnation of God. Lord Brahma is stating that the masculine symbol, the original form of Lord Sambhu, in the shape of a linga or the genital form and Maya the shadow potency of the Lord is intermingled with the linga in the function of the expansion of the material world. In any tangible creation, to produce something like in a garden, we need the seed as *bija* and the land, water, sunlight, and pleasant ambiance. These are all secondary manifestations of the garden, so that the results of the effort to produce the real fruit. Brahma is stating the words *"yoni"* and *"linga"*; both combine to assist in procreating all the living beings. Even though Lord Brahma is the real creator of the material world, He is still mentioning the position of Sambhu and in front of Krishna, and Krishna is nodding the statement. Both the Lord is in one sense non-different, Lord Shiva and Lord Vishnu. The radiance of Lord Vishnu is always eternal, and reflections of spiritual light are still eternal. Sambhu takes care of the further expansion with the help of his consort Gauri.

In another sense, Maha Vishnu is the supreme enjoyer, Purusha, and the *pradhana* and *Prakriti* are the secondary creation of the world. Lord Shiva and Sakti acted as the principal-agent for further expansion. In-text nine, *liṅga-yony-ātmikā jātā imā māheśvarī-prajāḥ,* Lord Shiva and Shakti are the unified representation of the male and female as we might have seen in the temple of Shiva linga with the yoni. This unique feature replicates the sex energy, and the same perverted power drives the birth and growth of the total population. The varieties of living beings are generated from the same principles from the Shakti and Shiva, by the sexual union.

In text 10, liṅga-rūpī maheśvaraḥ tasminn āvirabhūl liṅge, Sambhu is the primary god of the material universe, and he is the Lord of Pradhana. Only by the touch of the efficient cause Maya Devi, the creation made a show, and the manifestation starts here. Lord Brahma is making it clear that Lord Shiva is not the original Purusha; however, Krishna is the original Purusha. Lord Shiva is receiving the energy and intelligence from Lord Sankarsana. Sambhu expands the ego as Rudra type in all the living beings, and by dint of such association, people fell prey to Maya with the ahamkara ideology. Lord Shiva and Shakti always perform the task in cooperation with the will of the Lord Vishnu, and there is no separate identity and there will be no other than one intention of the Lord.

Lord Brahma clearly defined the places of abode of all the Lords, and he did not want to mention his own abode; however, he pointed from where he was speaking the greatness of each dham. Generally, the current world with fourteen planetary systems is called Devi dham, and above them is Mahesh dham. And above the all dham *is Vaikuntha Loka, and ultimately top is Goloka Dhama. In text 43, "goloka-nāmni nija-dhāmni tale ca tasya devi maheśa-hari-dhāmasu teṣu teṣu.."*

One section of the Mahesh Dham is Mahakala Dham, and it's filled with darkness, and on the other hand, the Sada-Shiva Loka is full of light and the marginal abode of Lord Shiva is in between the spiritual world and material world. Lord Brahma mentioned about the distinction between Shiva and Krishna, there is no such difference, and he quoted these prayers *kṣīraṁ yathā dadhi vikāra-viśeṣa-yogāt,* Lord Krishna or Vishnu is like milk and Lord Shiva is yogurt, and there are transformations of milk by the acidic process. Lord Shiva is always subservient to Lord Vishnu, and there are no two gods. God is always one, and Krishna is the fountainhead of all incarnations, and Lord Brahma clarified the point, and Shiva is not a living entity either. Sada-Shiva is entirely spiritual, and Rudra is the manifestation in the mundane world to assist in destroying the world as per the cosmic cycle. Lord Brahma or any living being could attain the fifty qualities of God, Lord Shiva could attain fifty-five, five more than any living person or especially Brahma. Lord Vishnu has sixty qualities of opulence, and Lord Krishna has sixty-four qualities in full.

RUDRA AS MENTIONED IN THE VARAHA PURANA

bhairavena svarupena devakarye yada pura |

nartitam tu maya so.ayam sambandhah krurakarmanAm ||

kshayam ninishata daityanattahaso maya kaitah |

yah pura tatra ye mahyam patita ashrubindavah |

asamkhyatastu te raudra bhavitaro mahltale || 71.(56-57)||

Meaning: In ancient times, I danced by (assuming) my terrible form for the sake of the devas, and this (form of) mine became associated with or suited for difficult deeds. For the destruction of the Daityas, who wished to rule, I laughed. Then, by my fallen teardrops were raised innumerable fierce beings from the earth.

Rudra earlier said that while the people of rajasic/tamasic paths resorted to him, he did not endorse that path. That being the case, he now explains how he became associated with these people.

Brahmana aham pura srrishtah proktashcha srrija vai prajah |

avijnanasamartho.aham nimagnah salile dvija || 73.2||

Meaning: In ancient times, I was created by Brahma, who told me to beget offspring. Not possessing the knowledge (to do so), I immersed myself in water (for tapas), O Dvija!

This story is found in the Bhagavatam where Rudra is born, and Brahma sends him off to do tapas for begetting offspring. The Varaha Purana elaborates on what type of tapas Rudra did.

tatra yavat kahanam chaikam tishthami parameshvaram |

angushthamatram purusham dhyayan prayatamanasah || 73.3||

Meaning: There, as long as (in that state), with a pure mind abiding in param isvara (Narayana) at every moment, I meditated on the purusha, having the size of a thumb.

This is the "angushtamatra vidya" of the Upanishads.

tavajjaiat samuttasthuh pralayagnisamaprabhah |

purusha dasha chaikashcha tapayantomshubhirjalam || 73.4||

Meaning: Then, I saw 10 purushas and one (the chief), rising out of the water, with a radiance resembling the pralaya Agni, also making the waters glow with heat.

maya prrishtah ke bhavanto jaiaduttlrya tejasa |

tapayanto jaiam chedam kva va yasyatha samshata || 73.5||

Meaning: I asked them who they were, who rose out of the water so resplendently, and how did they make the waters foam so brilliantly with heat.

evamukta maya te tu nochuh kimchana sattamah |

evameva gatastushnim te nara dvijapumgava ||

tatasteshamanu mahapurusho.ativashobhanah |

sa tasmin meghasamkashah pundarlkanibhekshanah ||

tamaham prrishtavan kastvam ke cheme purusha gatah |

kim va prayojanamiha kathyatam purusharshabha || 73.(6-8)||

Meaning: Thus spoken by me, those beings, full of heat, did not say anything whatsoever and left, O best of sattvikas. Then, of those beings (stayed), a mahapurusa was extremely beautiful, with the appearance of a cloud, with lotus-eyes. I asked him – "Who are you and who are these beings who left? What is the purpose (of your visit) here, please explain, O bull amongst purushas!

purusha uvacha |

ya ete vai gatah purvam purusha dlptatejasah |

adityaste tvaram yanti dhyata vai brahmana bhava || 73.9||

Meaning: Those resplendent purushas who left earlier, they are the "Adityas" who quickly attain the ones (plural) that are mediated by Brahma, Oh Bhava!

The purushas were the indriyas that shine on account of illumining external objects and are hot due to attachments. They are called "Adityas" since they are sun-like, as they make objects shine.

Brahma, during shrishti, meditates on account of desire. The indriyas attain the objects constituting the desire which are meditated upon by Brahma for the purpose of creation.

Shiva is referred to as Bhava because brings forth knowledge of Vishnu.

srrishtim srrijati vai brahma tadartham yantyaml narah |

pratipalanaya tasyastu srrishterdeva na samshayah || 73.10||

Meaning: Brahma indeed orchestrates the creation, and for that purpose, these (ami) "naras" (indriyas) attain. It is for the protection of that creation, without a doubt. The meaning of "naras" – that which is imperishable is "nara". According to Sri Pillai Lokacharya, anything that does not lose its nature or characteristic is called "imperishable" or "nara". The indriyas, when controlled from sense objects, nonetheless indulge in other things like the experience of Brahman or the bliss of the individual self. So, they are always engaged in shining out external objects – be it sense objects, Paramatma, or our own bliss. Since they never lose this character, they are called "naras".

Now Bhagavan has explained who these purushas were. The second question is, who is that Paramatma, who is the cause of creation? For it is known by Rudra that Brahma is not Paramatma, so the next line of questioning is about Paramatma, as seen below.

shambhuruvacha |

bhagavan katham janIshe mahapurushasattama |

bhaveti namna tatsarvam kathayasva paro hyaham || 73.11||

Meaning: Shambhu (one who is immersed in the bliss of Narayana) asked: O excellent mahapurusha, how can that bhagavan (who created Brahma) be known? Please tell me, who has the name of Bhava, that (state) of being superior to all (in knowledge).

"Bhava" means that which brings forth. Rudra recognizes how the mahapurusha called him "bhava" and stakes his claim that he is superior to all in knowledge, which makes him worthy of knowing about bhagavan.

Of course, Rudra already knows who this Paramatma is – the question should be taken as – "what qualities and nature of Paramatma are to be meditated upon?"

(There is no incongruence that Rudra is referred to in the third person here as "Shambhu uvacha". One must note that the original narrator of the Rudra Gita is Varaha Bhagavan, and the listener is Bhudevi. So, Varaha narrates the dialogue between Bhadrasva and other rishis, which in turn relate the conversation about Rudra and Agastya, and in this dialogue, Rudra recounts a dialog between himself and Bhagavan. Due to the multifaceted nature of this narration, it is to be presumed that it is Varaha, the original narrator, who uses the third person for Rudra here, switching to it to highlight his qualities by names like "shambhu" etc. In most cases, Bhagavan refers to himself in the third person, so there are no problems there).

evamuktastu rudrena sa puman pratyabhashata |

aham narayano devo jalashayI sanatanah || 73.12||

Meaning: When asked by Rudra; thus, the person replied – "I am the luminous god Narayana, who is ancient, who reclines on the waters (of the milky ocean).

RUDRA SUKTAM

Suktam (set of mantras contained in the Vedas) and Rudra Sukta are found in Rg and Yajur Veda. We might know about the beautiful purusha sukta prayer; similarly, the Rudra suktam is also a beautiful rendition for the pleasure of the Lord.

It occurs in the Taittirīya Saṁhitā of the Kṛṣṇa Yajurveda in the 4th kāṇda (chapter), 5th praśna (topic) and it is considered as one of 108 Upaniṣads.

Śrī Rudram is divided into 11 anuvākas (passages) and consists of 37 ṛks (verses) in various Vedic chandas (meters) in anuvāka 1, 10 and 11. Anuvākas 2 to 9 and the last line of anuvāka 11 consists of 130 yajus (sacrificial formulas).

Some examples are noted here.

śreṣṭho jātasya rudra śhariyāsi tavastamastavasāṃ vajrabāho |

parṣi ṇaḥ pāramaṃhasaḥ svasti viśvā abhītī rapaso yuyodhi ||

Meaning: Rudra (Destroyer of the Disease of Samsara)! You, the most praiseworthy of all the Gods who are born, such as Brahma, etc., who are more durable than the strongest, have appeared in the form of a ferocious lion with arms resembling thunderbolts. You will remove the disease (i.e., obstacles to knowledge of Brahman) for the well-being (i.e., provide knowledge) of all beings in the universe and carry us over samsara to the other side, i.e., Sri Vaikuntha.

The name *"shaktimatam sreshta"* in the *sahasra-nama* shows that he is the most praiseworthy of the gods. Brahma, Rudra,

Indra, etc. are samsaris and have births, hence denoted as "jatasya". The Narayanopanishad says, "*Naranayat brahma jayate, narayanat rudro jayate, Narayanat indro jayate*".

So, "*Jatasya*" denotes the gods, including Vishnu, who, unlike the others, is born of his own will, and hence, He is the greatest. This is the interpretation as coined by sages for the name "*shaktimatam sreshta*".

If you would explore Narsimha and Rudra more in this below *suktam*, the meaning will be much more precise now. These aspects are mentioned in Rudra Sukta of Rg Veda, rks as follows:

ṛdūdaraḥ suhavo mā no asyai babhruḥ suśipro rīradhan manāyai ~ Narasimha has a pleasing nature, who is the supporter of the worlds (and hence the protector from tapatrayam), with beautiful jaws and possessing teeth to chew the asuras as Narasimha, not give us unto the ego or attachments arising from the wayward mind, i.e., may you destroy such ego and attachments.

śukrebhiḥ pipiśehiraṇyaiḥ ~ He has a shining form with golden ornaments and makes others shine as well.

niṣkaṃ yajataṃ viśvarūpam ~ He has a necklace, i.e., the vaijayanti garland studded with five gems representing the tanmatras and has the universe as his body.

GARUDA PURANA – RUDRA PRAYER TO NARASIMHA

Garuda Purana is vast in its description of the Lord and its pastimes. I have selected a section where Shiva's prayers to Narasimha and the rendition is always beautiful as both the Lords are amazing and Lord Narasimhadev is the protector of the devotees.

The Garuda Purana contains a stuti composed by Shiva in praise of Narasimha, invoking the latter to stop the sapta-matrikas from devouring the universe. The following things are manifested at a glance, upon reading this stuti:

This is an apparent reference to the fact that Shiva worships Narasimha, i.e., Sankarshana.

The meanings of the stuti echo the Rudra Suktam of Rg Veda, Satarudriyam of Yajur Veda, and Nilarudra Suktam of Atharva Veda, thus establishing that Narasimha is indeed the devata for the Rudram and Shiva is the Rishi.

We thus have the proof from the words of Shiva himself that the devata to which all praise by the names of "Rudra", "Shiva", "Shambhu", "Soma" and "Ishana" in the Veda refer to Narasimha only since this stuti matches these sections perfectly.

Let's focus on the deeper side of the meaning of the stotra.

Shiva invokes Narasimha to stop the matrganas created by the former for the destruction of Andhakasura, from devouring the universe.

The inner meaning: Shiva is an upasaka, i.e., a bhakti yogi who is attempting to conquer several vices like avidya, ruchi, vasanas, etc. by virtue of yoga. These vices are represented by the matrganas. But no matter how high the strength of a yogi is, the pull of samsaric attachments is so strong that it not only overwhelms him but after succumbing to the old vices, he starts to inflict harm on himself and on others.

Thus, Yogi's effort to perform yoga is similar to how Shiva endeavored to destroy Andhaka (Note that Andhaka means ignorance or samsara). Owing to the pitfalls and delicate as well as arduous nature of upasana, certain vices (i.e., the mothers) are produced in the process such as attachment, lust, etc. which were supposed to be eradicated by the upasana. Then, the grace of Hari, Parabrahman, is sought by the upasaka for the successful completion of yoga, which will defeat these vices.

The Rudram explains the same in the 4th anuvakam, 1st, and 2nd mantras as follows:

Nama avyadhinibhyo vividhyanti bhyascha vo namo |

Meaning: Salutations to One who is of the form of the objects of desire and Salutations to the one who is of the type of diseases (anubhoktavyam) that arise from them.

Nama uganabhya strumhati bhyascha vo namo |

Meaning: Salutations to the form of superior qualities like medha, anasuya, vidya, etc, and salutations to (these qualities) which crush the ruchi and anubhoktavyam.

This stuti is the essence of these two mantras.

In Srimad Bhagavatam 8.7.29, it is mentioned as follows,

mukhāni pañcopaniṣadas taveśa

yais triṁśad-aṣṭottara-mantra-vargaḥ

yat tac chivākhyaṁ paramātma-tattvaṁ

deva svayaṁ-jyotir avasthitis te

"O Lord, the five important Vedic mantras are represented by your five faces, from which the thirty-eight most important Vedic mantras have been generated. Your Lordship, being celebrated as Lord Shiva, is self-illuminated. You are directly situated as the supreme truth, known as Paramātmā."

The five mantras mentioned in this connection are as follows: (1) Puruṣa, (2) Aghora, (3) Sadyojāta, (4) Vāmadeva, and (5) Īśāna. These five mantras are within the category of thirty-eight special Vedic mantras chanted by Lord Shiva, who is therefore celebrated as Shiva or Mahādeva. In general, people follow the principle of aghora, and they are prominently found in Rishikesh, Haridwar area. Lord Shiva is very much affectionate towards all the devotees who live near the bank of the Ganges and worship in the method mentioned in the Srimad Bhagavatam. Shiva is non-different from Lord Vishnu and the unique qualitative incarnation of Lord Vishnu like milk and yogurt transformation principles. This fact is corroborated by a Vedic mantra: patiṁ viśvasyātmeśvaraṁ śāśvatam. Shivam acyutam. The Supersoul is called by many names, of which Maheśvara, Shiva, and Acyuta are especially mentioned.

"The mantras referred below are called mukhāni pañcopaniṣadas taveśa. Māyāvādīs take all these mantras seriously in worshiping Lord Shiva. These mantras are as follows: (1) tat puruṣāya vidmahe śāntyai, (2) mahā-devāya dhīmahi vidyāyai, (3) tan no rudraḥ pratiṣṭhāyai, (4) pracodayāt dhṛtyai, (5) aghorebhyas tamā ... , (6) atha ghorebhyo mohā ... , (7) aghorebhyo rakṣā ... , (8) aghoratarebhyo nidrā ... , (9) sarvebhyaḥ sarva-vyādhyai, (10) sarva-sarvebhyo mṛtyave, (11) namas te 'stu kṣudhā ... , (12) rudra-rūpebhyas tṛṣṇā ... , (13) vāmadevāya rajā ... , (14) jyeṣṭhāya svāhā ... , (15) śreṣṭhāya ratyai, (16) rudrāya kalyāṇyai, (17) kālāya kāmā ... , (18) kala-vikaraṇāya sandhinyai, (19) bala-vikaraṇāya kriyā ... , (20) balāya vṛddhyai, (21) balacchāyā ... , (22) pramathanāya dhātryai, (23) sarva-bhūta-damanāya bhrāmaṇyai, (24) manaḥ-śoṣiṇyai, (25) unmanāya jvarā ... , (26) sadyojātaṁ prapadyāmi siddhyai, (27) sadyojātāya vai namaḥ ṛddhyai, (28) bhave dityai, (29) abhave lakṣmyai, (30) nātibhave medhā ... , (31) bhajasva māṁ kāntyai, (32) bhava svadhā ... , (33) udbhavāya prabhā ... , (34) īśānaḥ sarva-vidyānāṁ śaśinyai, (35) īśvaraḥ sarva-bhūtānām abhaya-dā ...

, (36) brahmādhipatir brahmaṇodhipatir brahman brahmeṣṭa-dā … , (37) śivo me astu marīcyai, (38) sadāShivaḥ jvālinyai."

LORD SHIVA – SATYAM SHIVAM SUNDARAM

Master

Lord Shiva is considered the spiritual master of the entire world and a Mahajan (one of the twelve great personalities). The meaning of master is one who commands and gives the real directions for people in general, in another way having or showing very great skill or proficiency in spiritual understanding. No one can surpass the importance of Lord Shiva as the master of all the population; he can lead the mode of ignorance of people and tries to elevate them in spiritual life by his influence. As we find the beautiful verse describing Lord Shiva as the great personality out of the twelve important spiritual masters of the world. SB 6.3.20

svayambhūr nāradaḥ śambhuḥ

kumāraḥ kapilo manuḥ

prahlādo janako bhīṣmo

balir vaiyāsakir vayam

Lord Brahmā, Bhagavān Nārada, Lord Shiva, the four Kumāras, Lord Kapila [the son of Devahūti], Svāyambhuva Manu, Prahlāda Mahārāja, Janaka Mahārāja, Grandfather Bhīṣma, Bali Mahārāja, Śukadeva Gosvāmī and I myself know the real religious principle.

Husband

Lord Shiva is the eternal husband of Sati, Uma or Parvati. Either in the earlier millennium as Sati and later re-incarnate as the daughter of the mountain. Lord Shiva is an ideal husband who gives guidance, support, protection, care, and love. In chapter three, we can find a pleasant conversation between Sati and Shiva in Srimad Bhagavatam Canto four, and how all of us take lessons from such discussions. I am going to share a few instructions based guidance so that it is useful for both the husband and wife.

When Shiva appeared in the material world via the medium of Lord Brahma, then he was destined to marry Sati, the youngest daughter of Daksha. Lord Shiva instructed on the moral code of guidance in terms of relationship management between in-laws. One can gauge the mood of reciprocations of affection and respect by their bodily gestures and mental situation. Daksha had already insulted Lord Shiva for not offering him respect; the envy and grudges in the heart of Daksha were still carrying forward without any sign of cooling down. Lord Shiva is the omniscient Lord who knew well that he tried to advise Sati in social etiquette. One should not go to the places one is not respected either by her husband or the relatives in a proper receptive manner. It is better to avoid the situation; otherwise, such an incident could ring a strained relationship between the families.

Generally, people with material motivation are puffed with the six god-given qualities like education, money, beauty, popularity, family heritage, and youthfulness. Daksha possessed all of the classes in full, and he was thoroughly proud of his social position, and he forgot to behave in general standard towards Lord Shiva. Sati is the half-body of Lord Shiva; as per Vedic customs, a wife is considered the Vama Bhaga or the left part of the husband's body, and both carry forward the mission of life, i.e., attaining love of Godhead. Nothing is still pending for Lord Shiva and Sati; both are in real sense the Lord of the universe as well as the surrendered souls to Lord Krishna. After explaining the social custom, Lord Shiva said to Sati about the spiritual etiquette; we offer a seat, water, greeting with kind words to any guests coming to our house. Better than all of this is offering obeisances to the superiors and of course to the saintly personalities. Without any reservations, one should offer whatever in his possessions to serve the towering figures. If any relatives or friends happen to come to one's house, one should greet them with folded hands and always remember the Supersoul within the body and offer all respects to them.

Lord Shiva explained that even though the body of Sati was given by her father, Daksha, you are still entirely spiritual, and there are no questions of bodily relationships; we should transcend beyond the thought process of physical contact and offer all respects considering the Supersoul within. However, Lord Shiva advised that Sati should not go to the house of her parents as Daksha is still envious and possibly would not respect as per the etiquette, and this would hurt the heart of Sati. Sati being affectionate towards her parental home and other paraphernalia, neglected the real import of Lord Shiva's instructions. With this, we could take a lesson that the wife should seek guidance from an ideal husband only who is surrendered to the Supreme Personality of Godhead like Lord Shiva. Other than Lord Krishna, no one could surpass Lord Shiva in the position of an ideal husband.

Father

Lord Shiva is a true spiritual master who always thinks of the welfare of every living being; he is a true husband and the ideal father. Lord Shiva has two sons named Kartikeya and Ganesha. Parvati loves Ganesha as he is the younger one, even though some purana stated differently. Lord Shiva tackled both his sons very nicely and always gave guidance based on their temperament. As usual, there is always a fight between Ganesha and Kartikeya, who is the favorite of their parents and who is better; naturally, we see the same scene in our household affairs also. We should take guidance from Lord Shiva as how he managed his two sons nicely.

One day, there is a gift of fruit that one will be completely wise and intelligent by eating this. Whenever something comes to your home, if you have more than one kid, then there is a fight to claim for the fruit or cake. Lord Shiva tried to examine both the brothers' talent and say that whoever circles the world faster is eligible to receive the fruit. Without a moment of loss, Kartikeya started with his peacock and set for the journey to complete a cycle of the world. However, Ganesha knew well that he had a mouse as his carrier, and he was fat too, so he could not win the race. He found an intelligent way to resolve it and circled three times centering Lord Shiva and Gauri. He came back, sat in front of his father, and told him that he had finished his world tour already. Lord Shiva was surprised by the move of Ganesha and did not say any words. Mother Parvati smiled and kept silent, and all of them were waiting for Kartikeya to return.

After a few days, upon the arrival of Kartikeya, he fell at the lotus feet of his father and summoned that he had finished the world tour, and he needed the reward of the fruit of knowledge. Lord Shiva and Parvati examined both parties' claims and world tour experience. Ganesha said that whoever circles three times to their parents, or the Lord of this universe is undoubtedly completing the world tour without a doubt. As per the scripture, Ganesha was right, and he won the race and was rewarded with the supreme fruit. By eating that fruit, Ganesha became the most knowledgeable in the three worlds, intelligent and talented also. Lord Shiva blessed him to be the remover of all obstacles of all humanities. Kartikeya was not afraid and left home and subsequently became the commander-in-chief of the demigods. Lord Shiva blessed Kartikeya to be more skilled in the military arts also. Lord Shiva is equal to everyone and what to speak of his own sons, so in this example, we know that how Lord Shiva managed to employ both his sons for the welfare of the humanities and demigods for the protection of the heavenly world.

Devotee friendly

There are numerous descriptions of Lord Shiva as he is the most affectionate and easily pleasing personality. As we know, how he blessed a hunter in the jungle when he offered a bael leaf without his knowledge on the Shivaratri day. In Srimad Bhagavatam, it is described that Lord Shiva offered benedictions to a demon Bhasmasura (Vrtasura) as whoever he touches his hand, he will be killed, and how the same demon wanted to try with Lord Shiva, the boon and Lord Vishnu saved the situation. This is the mercy of Lord Shiva. We all know that Ravana got strength from Lord Shiva even though he tried to deflect the Kailash mountain. Lord Shiva forgave the Prajapati Daksha even though he insulted severely. In all the situations, we understand that Lord Shiva is always favoring the devotees. Lord Shiva is the protector of the Dham of Lord Vishnu and protects Krishna Bhaktas in all circumstances. As per SB 1.12.23, when Parikshit Maharaj was compared with Lord Shiva at the time of his birth as most munificent "*prasāde giriśopamaḥ*", He will be munificent like the Lord of the Kailāsa Hill, Shiva.

RUDRA GITA

SB 4.24.27

śrī-rudra uvāca

yūyaṁ vediṣadaḥ putrā
viditaṁ vaś cikīrṣitam
anugrahāya bhadraṁ va
evaṁ me darśanaṁ kṛtam

Lord Shiva said: You are all the sons of King Prācīnabarhi, and I wish all good fortune to you. I also know what you are going to do, and therefore I am visible to you just to show my mercy upon you.

SB 4.24.28

yaḥ paraṁ raṁhasaḥ sākṣāt
tri-guṇāj jīva-saṁjñitāt
bhagavantaṁ vāsudevaṁ
prapannaḥ sa priyo hi me

Lord Shiva continued: Any person who is surrendered to the Supreme Personality of Godhead, Kṛṣṇa, the controller of everything — material nature as well as the living entity — is actually very dear to me.

SB 4.24.29

sva-dharma-niṣṭhaḥ śata-janmabhiḥ pumān
viriñcatām eti tataḥ paraṁ hi mām
avyākṛtaṁ bhāgavato 'tha vaiṣṇavaṁ
padaṁ yathāhaṁ vibudhāḥ kalātyaye

A person who executes his occupational duty properly for one hundred births becomes qualified to occupy the post of Brahmā, and if he becomes more qualified, he can approach Lord Shiva. A person who is directly surrendered to Lord Kṛṣṇa, or Viṣhṇu, in unalloyed devotional service is immediately promoted to the spiritual planets. Lord Shiva and other demigods attain these planets after the destruction of this material world.

SB 4.24.30

atha bhāgavatā yūyaṁ
priyāḥ stha bhagavān yathā
na mad bhāgavatānāṁ ca
preyān anyo 'sti karhicit

You are all devotees of the Lord, and as such I appreciate that you are as respectable as the Supreme Personality of Godhead Himself. I know in this way that the devotees also respect me and that I am dear to them. Thus no one can be as dear to the devotees as I am.

SB 4.24.31

idaṁ viviktaṁ japtavyaṁ
pavitraṁ maṅgalaṁ param
niḥśreyasa-karaṁ cāpi
śrūyatāṁ tad vadāmi vaḥ

Now I shall chant one mantra which is not only transcendental, pure and auspicious, but is the best prayer for anyone who is aspiring to attain the ultimate goal of life. When I chant this mantra, please hear it carefully and attentively.

SB 4.24.32

maitreya uvāca

ity anukrośa-hṛdayo
bhagavān āha tāñ chivaḥ
baddhāñjalīn rāja-putrān
nārāyaṇa-paro vacaḥ

The great sage Maitreya continued: Out of his causeless mercy, the exalted personality Lord Shiva, a great devotee of Lord Nārāyaṇa, continued to speak to the king's sons, who were standing with folded hands.

SB 4.24.33

śrī-rudra uvāca

jitaṁ ta ātma-vid-varya-
svastaye svastir astu me
bhavatārādhasā rāddhaṁ
sarvasmā ātmane namaḥ

Lord Shiva addressed the Supreme Personality of Godhead with the following prayer: O Supreme Personality of Godhead, all glories unto You. You are the most exalted of all self-realized souls. Since You are always auspicious for the self-realized, I wish that You be propitious for me. You are worshipable by virtue of the all-perfect instructions You give. You are the Supersoul; therefore I offer my obeisances unto You as the supreme living being.

SB 4.24.34

namaḥ paṅkaja-nābhāya
bhūta-sūkṣmendriyātmane
vāsudevāya śāntāya
kūṭa-sthāya sva-rociṣe

My Lord, You are the origin of the creation by virtue of the lotus flower which sprouts from Your navel. You are the supreme controller of the senses and the sense objects, and You are also the all-pervading Vāsudeva. You are most peaceful, and because of Your self-illuminated existence, You are not disturbed by the six kinds of transformations.

SB 4.24.35

saṅkarṣaṇāya sūkṣmāya
durantāyāntakāya ca
namo viśva-prabodhāya
pradyumnāyāntar-ātmane

My dear Lord, You are the origin of the subtle material ingredients, the master of all integration as well as the master of all disintegration, the predominating deity named Saṅkarṣaṇa, and the master of all intelligence, known as the predominating deity Pradyumna. Therefore, I offer my respectful obeisances unto You.

SB 4.24.36

namo namo 'niruddhāya
hṛṣīkeśendriyātmane
namaḥ paramahaṁsāya
pūrṇāya nibhṛtātmane

My Lord, as the supreme directing deity known as Aniruddha, You are the master of the senses and the mind. I therefore offer my obeisances unto You again and again. You are known as Ananta as well as Saṅkarṣaṇa because of Your ability to destroy the whole creation by the blazing fire from Your mouth.

SB 4.24.37

svargāpavarga-dvārāya
nityaṁ śuci-ṣade namaḥ
namo hiraṇya-vīryāya
cātur-hotrāya tantave

My Lord, O Aniruddha, You are the authority by which the doors of the higher planetary systems and liberation are opened. You are always within the pure heart of the living entity. Therefore I offer my obeisances unto You. You are the possessor of semen which is like gold, and thus, in the form of fire, You help the Vedic sacrifices, beginning with cātur-hotra. Therefore I offer my obeisances unto You.

SB 4.24.38

nama ūrja iṣe trayyāḥ
pataye yajña-retase
tṛpti-dāya ca jīvānāṁ
namaḥ sarva-rasātmane

My Lord, You are the provider of the Pitṛlokas as well as all the demigods. You are the predominating deity of the moon and the master of all three Vedas. I offer my respectful obeisances unto You because You are the original source of satisfaction for all living entities.

SB 4.24.39

sarva-sattvātma-dehāya
viśeṣāya sthavīyase
namas trailokya-pālāya
saha ojo-balāya ca

My dear Lord, You are the gigantic universal form which contains all the living entities' individual bodies. You are the maintainer of the three worlds, and as such You maintain the mind, senses, body, and air of life within them. I therefore offer my respectful obeisances unto You.

SB 4.24.40

artha-liṅgāya nabhase
namo 'ntar-bahir-ātmane
namaḥ puṇyāya lokāya
amuṣmai bhūri-varcase

My dear Lord, by expanding Your transcendental vibrations, You reveal the actual meaning of everything. You are the all-pervading sky within and without, and You are the ultimate goal of pious activities executed both within this material world and beyond it. I therefore offer my respectful obeisances again and again unto You.

SB 4.24.41

pravṛttāya nivṛttāya
pitṛ-devāya karmaṇe
namo 'dharma-vipākāya
mṛtyave duḥkha-dāya ca

My dear Lord, You are the viewer of the results of pious activities. You are inclination, disinclination and their resultant activities. You are the cause of the miserable conditions of life caused by irreligion, and therefore You are death. I offer You my respectful obeisances.

SB 4.24.42

namas ta āśiṣām īśa
manave kāraṇātmane
namo dharmāya bṛhate
kṛṣṇāyākuṇṭha-medhase
puruṣāya purāṇāya
sāṅkhya-yogeśvarāya ca

My dear Lord, You are the topmost of all bestowers of all benediction, the oldest and supreme enjoyer amongst all enjoyers. You are the master of all the worlds' metaphysical philosophy, for You are the supreme cause of all causes, Lord Kṛṣṇa. You are the greatest of all religious principles, the supreme mind, and You have a brain which is never checked by any condition. Therefore I repeatedly offer my obeisances unto You.

SB 4.24.43

śakti-traya-sametāya
mīḍhuṣe' haṅkṛtātmane
ceta-ākūti-rūpāya
namo vāco vibhūtaye

My dear Lord, You are the supreme controller of the worker, sense activities and results of sense activities [karma]. Therefore You are the controller of the body, mind and senses. You are also the supreme controller of egotism, known as Rudra. You are the source of knowledge and the activities of the Vedic injunctions.

SB 4.24.44

darśanaṁ no didṛkṣūṇāṁ
dehi bhāgavatārcitam
rūpaṁ priyatamaṁ svānāṁ
sarvendriya-guṇāñjanam

My dear Lord, I wish to see You exactly in the form that Your very dear devotees worship. You have many other forms, but I wish to see Your form that is especially liked by the devotees. Please be merciful upon me and show me that form, for only that form worshiped by the devotees can perfectly satisfy all the demands of the senses.

SB 4.24.45-46

snigdha-prāvṛḍ-ghana-śyāmaṁ
sarva-saundarya-saṅgraham
cārv-āyata-catur-bāhu
sujāta-rucirānanam

padma-kośa-palāśākṣaṁ
sundara-bhru sunāsikam
sudvijaṁ sukapolāsyaṁ
sama-karṇa-vibhūṣaṇam

The Lord's beauty resembles a dark cloud during the rainy season. As the rainfall glistens, His bodily features also glisten. Indeed, He is the sum total of all beauty. The Lord has four arms and an exquisitely beautiful face with eyes like lotus petals, a beautiful highly raised nose, a mind-attracting smile, a beautiful forehead and equally beautiful and fully decorated ears.

SB 4.24.47-48

prīti-prahasitāpāṅgam
alakai rūpa-śobhitam
lasat-paṅkaja-kiñjalka-
dukūlaṁ mṛṣṭa-kuṇḍalam

sphurat-kirīṭa-valaya-
hāra-nūpura-mekhalam
śaṅkha-cakra-gadā-padma-
mālā-maṇy-uttamarddhimat

The Lord is superexcellently beautiful on account of His open and merciful smile and His sidelong glance upon His devotees. His black hair is curly, and His garments, waving in the wind, appear like flying saffron pollen from lotus flowers. His glittering earrings, shining helmet, bangles, garland, ankle bells, waist belt and various other bodily ornaments combine with conchshell, disc, club and lotus flower to increase the natural beauty of the Kaustubha pearl on His chest.

SB 4.24.49

siṁha-skandha-tviṣo bibhrat
saubhaga-grīva-kaustubham
śriyānapāyinyā kṣipta-
nikaṣāśmorasollasat

The Lord has shoulders just like a lion's. Upon these shoulders are garlands, necklaces and epaulets, and all of these are always glittering. Besides these, there is the beauty of the Kaustubha-maṇi pearl, and on the dark chest of the Lord there are streaks named Śrīvatsa, which are signs of the goddess of fortune. The glittering of these streaks excels the beauty of the golden streaks on a gold-testing stone. Indeed, such beauty defeats a gold-testing stone.

SB 4.24.50

pūra-recaka-saṁvigna-
vali-valgu-dalodaram
pratisaṅkrāmayad viśvaṁ
nābhyāvarta-gabhīrayā

The Lord's abdomen is beautiful due to three ripples in the flesh. Being so round, His abdomen resembles the leaf of a banyan tree, and when He exhales and inhales, the movement of the ripples appears very, very beautiful. The coils within the navel of the Lord are so deep that it appears that the entire universe sprouted out of it and yet again wishes to go back.

SB 4.24.51

śyāma-śroṇy-adhi-rociṣṇu-
dukūla-svarṇa-mekhalam
sama-cārv-aṅghri-jaṅghoru-
nimna-jānu-sudarśanam

The lower part of the Lord's waist is dark and covered with yellow garments and a belt bedecked with golden embroidery work. His symmetrical lotus feet and the calves, thighs and joints of His legs are extraordinarily beautiful. Indeed, the Lord's entire body appears to be well built.

SB 4.24.52

padā śarat-padma-palāśa-rociṣā
nakha-dyubhir no 'ntar-aghaṁ vidhunvatā
pradarśaya svīyam apāsta-sādhvasaṁ
padaṁ guro mārga-gurus tamo-juṣām

My dear Lord, Your two lotus feet are so beautiful that they appear like two blossoming petals of the lotus flower which grows during the autumn season. Indeed, the nails of Your lotus feet emanate such a great effulgence that they immediately dissipate all the darkness in the heart of a conditioned soul. My dear Lord, kindly show me that form of Yours which always dissipates all kinds of darkness in the heart of a devotee. My dear Lord, You are the supreme spiritual master of everyone; therefore all conditioned souls covered with the darkness of ignorance can be enlightened by You as the spiritual master.

SB 4.24.53

etad rūpam anudhyeyam
ātma-śuddhim abhīpsatāmyad-bhakti-yogo› bhayadaḥ
sva-dharmam anutiṣṭhatām

My dear Lord, those who desire to purify their existence must always engage in meditation upon Your lotus feet, as described above. Those who are serious about executing their occupational duties and who want freedom from fear must take to this process of bhakti-yoga.

SB 4.24.54

bhavān bhaktimatā labhyo
durlabhaḥ sarva-dehinām
svārājyasyāpy abhimata
ekāntenātma-vid-gatiḥ

My dear Lord, the king in charge of the heavenly kingdom is also desirous of obtaining the ultimate goal of life — devotional service. Similarly, You are the ultimate destination of those who identify themselves with You [ahaṁ brahmāsmi]. However, it is very difficult for them to attain You, whereas a devotee can very easily attain Your Lordship.

SB 4.24.55

taṁ durārādhyam ārādhya
satām api durāpayā
ekānta-bhaktyā ko vāñchet
pāda-mūlaṁ vinā bahiḥ

My dear Lord, pure devotional service is even difficult for liberated persons to discharge, but devotional service alone can satisfy You. Who will take to other processes of self-realization if he is actually serious about the perfection of life?

SB 4.24.56

yatra nirviṣṭam araṇaṁ
kṛtānto nābhimanyate
viśvaṁ vidhvaṁsayan vīrya-
śaurya-visphūrjita-bhruvā

Simply by expansion of His eyebrows, invincible time personified can immediately vanquish the entire universe. However, formidable time does not approach the devotee who has taken complete shelter at Your lotus feet.

SB 4.24.57

kṣaṇārdhenāpi tulaye
na svargaṁ nāpunar-bhavam
bhagavat-saṅgi-saṅgasya
martyānāṁ kim utāśiṣaḥ

If one by chance associates with a devotee, even for a fraction of a moment, he no longer is subject to attraction by the results of karma or jñāna. What interest then can he have in the benedictions of the demigods, who are subject to the laws of birth and death?

SB 4.24.58

athānaghāṅghres tava kīrti-tīrthayor
antar-bahiḥ-snāna-vidhūta-pāpmanām
bhūteṣv anukrośa-susattva-śīlināṁ
syāt saṅgamo 'nugraha eṣa nas tava

My dear Lord, Your lotus feet are the cause of all auspicious things and the destroyer of all the contamination of sin. I therefore beg Your Lordship to bless me by the association of Your devotees, who are completely purified by worshiping Your lotus feet and who are so merciful upon the conditioned souls. I think that Your real benediction will be to allow me to associate with such devotees.

SB 4.24.59

na yasya cittaṁ bahir-artha-vibhramaṁ
tamo-guhāyāṁ ca viśuddham āviśat
yad-bhakti-yogānugṛhītam añjasā
munir vicaṣṭe nanu tatra te gatim

The devotee whose heart has been completely cleansed by the process of devotional service and who is favored by Bhaktidevī does not become bewildered by the external energy, which is just like a dark well. Being completely cleansed of all material contamination in this way, a devotee is able to understand very happily Your name, fame, form, activities, etc.

SB 4.24.60

yatredaṁ vyajyate viśvaṁ
viśvasminn avabhāti yat
tat tvaṁ brahma paraṁ jyotir
ākāśam iva vistṛtam

My dear Lord, the impersonal Brahman spreads everywhere, like the sunshine or the sky. And that impersonal Brahman, which spreads throughout the universe and in which the entire universe is manifested, is You.

SB 4.24.61

yo māyayedaṁ puru-rūpayāsṛjad
bibharti bhūyaḥ kṣapayaty avikriyaḥ
yad-bheda-buddhiḥ sad ivātma-duḥsthayā
tvam ātma-tantraṁ bhagavan pratīmahi

My dear Lord, You have manifold energies, and these energies are manifested in manifold forms. With such energies You have also created this cosmic manifestation, and although You maintain it as if it were permanent, You ultimately annihilate it. Although You are never disturbed by such changes and alterations, the living entities are disturbed by them, and therefore they find the cosmic manifestation to be different or separated from You. My Lord, You are always independent, and I can clearly see this fact.

SB 4.24.62

kriyā-kalāpair idam eva yoginaḥ
śraddhānvitāḥ sādhu yajanti siddhaye
bhūtendriyāntaḥ-karaṇopalakṣitaṁ
vede ca tantre ca ta eva kovidāḥ

My dear Lord, Your universal form consists of all five elements, the senses, mind, intelligence, false ego (which is material) and the Paramātmā, Your partial expansion, who is the director of everything. Yogīs other than the devotees — namely the karma-yogī and jñāna-yogī — worship You by their respective actions in their respective positions. It is stated both in the Vedas and in the śāstras that are corollaries of the Vedas, and indeed everywhere, that it is only You who are to be worshiped. That is the expert version of all the Vedas.

SB 4.24.63

tvam eka ādyaḥ puruṣaḥ supta-śaktis
tayā rajaḥ-sattva-tamo vibhidyate
mahān ahaṁ khaṁ marud agni-vār-dharāḥ
surarṣayo bhūta-gaṇā idaṁ yataḥ

My dear Lord, You are the only Supreme Person, the cause of all causes. Before the creation of this material world, Your material energy remains in a dormant condition. When Your material energy is agitated, the three qualities — namely goodness, passion and ignorance — act, and as a result the total material energy — egotism, ether, air, fire, water, earth and all the various demigods and saintly persons — becomes manifest. Thus the material world is created.

SB 4.24.64

sṛṣṭaṁ sva-śaktyedam anupraviṣṭaś
catur-vidhaṁ puram ātmāṁśakena
atho vidus taṁ puruṣaṁ santam antar
bhuṅkte hṛṣīkair madhu sāra-ghaṁ yaḥ

My dear Lord, after creating by Your own potencies, You enter within the creation in four kinds of forms. Being within the hearts of the living entities, You know them and know how they are enjoying their senses. The so-called happiness of this material creation is exactly like the bees' enjoyment of honey after it has been collected in the honeycomb.

SB 4.24.65

sa eṣa lokān aticaṇḍa-vego
vikarṣasi tvaṁ khalu kāla-yānaḥ
bhūtāni bhūtair anumeya-tattvo
ghanāvalīr vāyur ivāviṣahyaḥ

My dear Lord, Your absolute authority cannot be directly experienced, but one can guess by seeing the activities of the world that everything is being destroyed in due course of time. The force of time is very strong, and everything is being destroyed by something else — just as one animal is being eaten by another animal. Time scatters everything, exactly as the wind scatters clouds in the sky.

SB 4.24.66

pramattam uccair iti kṛtya-cintayā
pravṛddha-lobhaṁ viṣayeṣu lālasam
tvam apramattaḥ sahasābhipadyase
kṣul-lelihāno' hir ivākhum antakaḥ

My dear Lord, all living entities within this material world are mad after planning for things, and they are always busy with a desire to do this or that. This is due to uncontrollable greed. The greed for material enjoyment is always existing in the living entity, but Your Lordship is always alert, and in due course of time You strike him, just as a snake seizes a mouse and very easily swallows him.

SB 4.24.67

kas tvat-padābjaṁ vijahāti paṇḍito
yas te 'vamāna-vyayamāna-ketanaḥ
viśaṅkayāsmad-gurur arcati sma yad
vinopapattiṁ manavaś caturdaśa

My dear Lord, any learned person knows that unless he worships You, his entire life is spoiled. Knowing this, how could he give up worshiping Your lotus feet? Even our father and spiritual master, Lord Brahmā, unhesitatingly worshiped You, and the fourteen Manus followed in his footsteps.

SB 4.24.68

atha tvam asi no brahman
paramātman vipaścitām
viśvaṁ rudra-bhaya-dhvastam
akutaścid-bhayā gatiḥ

My dear Lord, all actually learned persons know You as the Supreme Brahman and the Supersoul. Although the entire universe is afraid of Lord Rudra, who ultimately annihilates everything, for the learned devotees You are the fearless destination of all.

SB 4.24.69

idaṁ japata bhadraṁ vo
viśuddhā nṛpa-nandanāḥ
sva-dharmam anutiṣṭhanto
bhagavaty arpitāśayāḥ

My dear sons of the king, just execute your occupational duty as kings with a pure heart. Just chant this prayer fixing your mind on the lotus feet of the Lord. That will bring you all good fortune, for the Lord will be very much pleased with you.

SB 4.24.70

tam evātmānam ātma-sthaṁ
sarva-bhūteṣv avasthitam
pūjayadhvaṁ gṛṇantaś ca
dhyāyantaś cāsakṛd dharim

Therefore, O sons of the king, the Supreme Personality of Godhead, Hari, is situated in everyone's heart. He is also within your hearts. Therefore chant the glories of the Lord and always meditate upon Him continuously.

SB 4.24.71

yogādeśam upāsādya
dhārayanto muni-vratāḥ
samāhita-dhiyaḥ sarva
etad abhyasatādṛtāḥ

My dear princes, in the form of a prayer I have delineated the yoga system of chanting the holy name. All of you should take this important stotra within your minds and promise to keep it in order to become great sages. By acting silently like a great sage and by giving attention and reverence, you should practice this method.

SB 4.24.72

idam āha purāsmākaṁ
bhagavān viśvasṛk-patiḥ
bhṛgv-ādīnām ātmajānāṁ
sisṛkṣuḥ saṁsisṛkṣatām

This prayer was first spoken to us by Lord Brahmā, the master of all creators. The creators, headed by Bhṛgu, were instructed in these prayers because they wanted to create.

SB 4.24.73

te vayaṁ noditāḥ sarve
prajā-sarge prajeśvarāḥ
anena dhvasta-tamasaḥ
sisṛkṣmo vividhāḥ prajāḥ

When all the Prajāpatis were ordered to create by Lord Brahmā, we chanted these prayers in praise of the Supreme Personality of Godhead and became completely free from all ignorance. Thus we were able to create different types of living entities.

SB 4.24.74

athedaṁ nityadā yukto
japann avahitaḥ pumān
acirāc chreya āpnoti
vāsudeva-parāyaṇaḥ

A devotee of Lord Kṛṣṇa whose mind is always absorbed in Him, who with great attention and reverence chants this stotra [prayer], will achieve the greatest perfection of life without delay.

SB 4.24.75

śreyasām iha sarveṣāṁ
jñānaṁ niḥśreyasaṁ param
sukhaṁ tarati duṣpāraṁ
jñāna-naur vyasanārṇavam

In this material world there are different types of achievement, but of all of them the achievement of knowledge is considered to be the highest because one can cross the ocean of nescience only on the boat of knowledge. Otherwise the ocean is impassable.

SB 4.24.76

ya imaṁ śraddhayā yukto
mad-gītaṁ bhagavat-stavam
adhīyāno durārādhyaṁ
harim ārādhayaty asau

Although rendering devotional service to the Supreme Personality of Godhead and worshiping Him are very difficult, if one vibrates or simply reads this stotra [prayer] composed and sung by me, he will very easily be able to invoke the mercy of the Supreme Personality of Godhead.

SB 4.24.77

vindate puruṣo 'muṣmād
yad yad icchaty asatvaram
mad-gīta-gītāt suprītāc
chreyasām eka-vallabhāt

The Supreme Personality of Godhead is the dearmost objective of all auspicious benedictions. A human being who sings this song sung by me can please the Supreme Personality of Godhead. Such a devotee, being fixed in the Lord's devotional service, can acquire whatever he wants from the Supreme Lord.

SB 4.24.78

idaṁ yaḥ kalya utthāya
prāñjaliḥ śraddhayānvitaḥ
śṛṇuyāc chrāvayen martyo
mucyate karma-bandhanaiḥ

A devotee who rises early in the morning and with folded hands chants these prayers sung by Lord Shiva, and gives facility to others to hear them, certainly becomes free from all bondage to fruitive activities.

SB 4.24.79

gītaṁ mayedaṁ naradeva-nandanāḥ
parasya puṁsaḥ paramātmanaḥ stavam
japanta ekāgra-dhiyas tapo mahat
caradhvam ante tata āpsyathepsitam

My dear sons of the king, the prayers I have recited to you are meant for pleasing the Supreme Personality of Godhead, the Supersoul. I advise you to recite these prayers, which are as effective as great austerities. In this way, when you are mature, your life will be successful, and you will certainly achieve all your desired objectives without fail.

RUDRA AND HANUMAN

As per the Hanuman Chalisa by Tulsidas Maharaj, a beautiful hymn suggests the relationship between Hanuman and Lord Shiva.

Sankar Suvan Kesari Nandan, Tej Prataap Maha Jag Bandan;

You are the incarnation of Lord Shiva (Shankar), and you are very dear to Shri Kesari (father of Hanuman).

Chapter 20 of Sata-Rudriya Samhita of Shiva Purana mentions that Lord Shiva was attracted to the Mohini murti avatar of Lord Vishnu and discharged semen, which was inserted into the womb of mother Anjana. As a result, Hanuman was born. However, the effect of Lord Shiva's expansion is not mentioned in Srimad Bhagavatam, although the attraction of Lord Shiva to Mohini is mentioned.

Hanuman's mother, Anjana, was a great devotee of Lord Shiva, she performed severe austerity for the pleasure of Lord Shiva. Later on, Lord Shiva pleased with her devotion and, of course, granted her a boon that her son will be a partial representation of Shiva himself. He will be accessible in the three worlds and will become a great devotee of Lord Vishnu.

So, Hanuman is Shiva's ansha, or expansion, inheriting the attribute and quality of Lord Shiva in the relationship to service of the Supreme Personality Lord Ram.

According to Ramayana (Yuddha Kandam), After Lord Rama killed Ravana in the battle, He was to return to Ayodhya to be crowned king. Ravana was a great devotee of Shiva and a half-demon and half Brahmin, so Rama was advised to pay obeisance to Shiva (for getting relieved from Brahma Hatya dosha) at Rameshwaram, South India, Tamilnadu by installing a Shiva linga within two days of the victory.

One intriguing incident was found in the Ramayana whn Hanuman was journeying to Lanka from the city of Rameswaram, the clear picture of a transcendental relationship is mentioned between Hanuman and Lord Shiva as per the Puranic shreds of evidence. Rama's devotee Hanuman was assigned the task of finding a Linga suitable for the rituals. Hanuman, with the help of the assistant from Sugriva's army, searched everywhere for the Linga, and it's believed that they could not find a linga in this place and decided to go to the site of linga, Kashi, there Hanuman was able to see our a beautiful Linga. He was not able to get that Linga, as it was guarded by Kal-Bhairava, after a battle with Bhairava, at last Hanuman could get the Linga. Meanwhile, Rama requested Sita to prepare a Lingam with Sea sand at Rameswaram as the time was running out. And Sita did so, and the rituals started with the Sand Linga. As the ceremonies were about to finish, Hanuman came with the Shiva linga and was disappointed that in his absence, the rituals were done. Hanuman requested Rama to use the Linga, which he had secured, then Rama to please Hanuman says, "you try to remove the Lingam which has been installed Hanuman, then I will use the lingam obtained by you." Hearing this, Hanuman tried his level best to uproot the Lingam, but it did not move. In the last attempt, Hanuman wrapped His tail around the Lingam and applied full force. The Lingam got uprooted and landed a few miles away, in a place called Hanuman Pallam (the pot created by Lord Hanuman).

But in this process, Hanuman loses his tail. Hanuman then realized his mistake and asked Rama and Sita to forgive him. Lord Rama told Hanuman to ask for forgiveness from Shiva and to visit Tirukurungaval, worship Lord Shiva and request Mahadev to grant his tail back to him. Tirukurungaval means the place where Shiva was worshiped by a monkey-faced God, thus Hanuman got his tail back. I used to hear this story from my south Indian friends as many of them visited this place too. When Hanuman and Bhima syndicate another spiritual identity in Kali-yuga, the new personality becomes Madvacarya, founder of the Brahma Madhvacharya Vaishnava Sampradaya.

RUDRA AND MOON

When you think of the moon and Shiva, everyone imagines the crescent moon on the top of the head of Lord Shiva. In Srimad Bhagavatam, Sukadeva Goswami describes the crescent moon position at Lord Shiva and how it is well decorated. We can find from Srimad Bhagavatam, SB 4.6.36, *candra-lekhāṁ ca bibhratam*, on his head, Chandra as the half moon is present to glorify Lord Shiva.

Sometimes ago, the god of Moon, Chandra or Soma married the twenty-seven daughters of Prajapati Daksha. Chandra was more inclined to one of his wives named Rohini, and this caused an uncomfortable situation for the sisters. Later on, they complained to their father Daksha about the affectionate behaviors of Chandra towards Rohini only. Daksha was very much disturbed by seeing the partiality attitude of Chandra. Without further consideration, he cursed that he will lose his beauty of full bloom by such negligence towards his wives. Chandra lost his glories with the curse of his father-in-law Daksha and with no hope of gaining the lost beauty went to the creator of this world, Lord Brahma, however, Lord Brahma asked him to worship Lord Shiva for a remedy. Chandra went to the Prabhas Kshetra in Gujarat, India and prayed to Lord Shiva with severe austerities. Pleased with his prayers and devotion, Lord Shiva appeared before Chandra and asked for a boon, and Chandra explained the entire situation to Lord Shiva. Lord Shiva being omniscient of all causes thought for a moment and replied to Chandra, as Daksha is a great Prajapati and his curse cannot be invalid however I can adjust you to wane and wax in a cyclic period so that you become glow like a full moon, Purnima and wane and wax for the 27 days. Lord Shiva out of affection, carried the crescent moon on his head for coolness and rewarded the demigod who was in disappointment. Chandra was extremely pleased with the boon and blessings of Lord Shiva. Lord Shiva is also known as Chandrasekhar, Chandracuda, and Chandrakaladharan, etc. As Chandra or Soma worshiped with a linga of Shiva in this place of Prabhas Kshetra, this is also popularly known as Somanatha, and Somanatha Linga is one of the twelve Jyotirlingas.

Once, the moon was afflicted with consumption because of the curse of Dakṣa, but just by taking a bath at Prabhāsa-kṣetra, the moon was immediately freed from his sinful reaction and again resumed the waxing of his phases.

Moon-god is a famous demigod in the historical evidence as Lord Krishna appeared in the soma dynasty. All the vegetation is also possible in the moonshine's earthly planets. Material scientists have tried to reach the moon's planet; however, it was not sure where they landed because the moon is full of variety, and possibly the result can't be deserted by the astronauts' observation. By approaching the heavenly procedures of formalities and blessings from Lord Shiva or the Moon-god, one is eligible to reach out to the planet.

RUDRA AND NARADA

As both Rudra and Narada are born from Lord Brahma, and both are also Mahajana, they are celebrated as the true preachers of the Sanatana Dharma. Various scriptures mention how Narada glorifies Lord Shiva. As per Srimad Bhagavatam, Lord Shiva is speaking the glories of Lord Krishna to the assembled sages, including Narada muni also. This is mentioned in SB 4.6.37 *upaviṣṭaṁ darbhamayyāṁ* as Lord Shiva is seated in the straw mattress, Lord Shiva is speaking about the absolute truth eternally even though during the time of his wife's death and he is not lamenting for any such loss of life as he is genuinely the Yogi. In this verse *nāradāya pravocantaṁ*, Lord Shiva is speaking primarily to Narada muni; both are in complete ecstasy in hearing about the *"Om Tat Sat"*. Whenever there is a discourse of Srimad Bhagavatam occurring in this universe, there is always a speaker and an audience, Lord Krishna spoke to Arjuna, Maitreya spoke to Vidura, and Sukadeva spoke to Parikshit Maharaj. In this connection, Narada is the recipient of the knowledge from the spiritual master Lord Shiva. Narada acts as the message carrier for all great personalities for any critical news either good, bad or intriguing news, Narada arrived Kailasa hill and informed about the loss of Sati in the arena of the sacrifice of Daksha, Shiva being the *trikalanja*, knows past, present, and future of any events was very sorry to hear the news from Narada Muni. He was furious about the disrespectful behavior of Daksha and his followers. Even though Sati, the personification of the material energy, is competent enough to kill Daksha, out of humility and social etiquette, she did not retaliate against him; however, she quit her body.

Narada muni has many interactions with Lord Shiva. In one of the episodes from Shiva Purana, it is mentioned that Narada asked Lord Brahma about the ways of pleasing Lord Shiva so that one can ultimately attain the highest goal gradually. There are various tirtha yatra or pilgrimage places mystery is revealed by Narada like the glories of Kasi. Narada has offered beautiful prayers to his spiritual master Mahadeva like this "*guror gurur me shambhus ca.*" Narada muni is the son of Brahma, and his worshipable Lord is Vishnu, and his spiritual master is Mahadeva. Before composing the Narada Pancharatra, Mahadeva's prayer is also mentioned: "*vidhi-putro narado' ham, pahca-ratram samarabhya*". If Narada muni, the spiritual master of the three worlds, consider Lord Shiva to his spiritual master, we should pray at the footsteps Narada Muni and advance in religious life.

RUDRA AND BRAHMA

Lord Brahma is the father of Lord Shiva in this material world. Both of them are also technically the Mahajan and even considered the *gunavatara* incarnation of the supreme being. As per Srimad Bhagavatam, a conversation between Lord Shiva and Lord Brahma is noted in the Srimad Bhagavatam SB 4.6.41; it is mentioned that the interactive dialogue between Lord Brahma and Lord Shiva. It is customary for a son to offer obeisances as Lord Krishna offers obeisances to his father, Vasudeva. Lord Shiva offered his respectful obeisances to Lord Brahma. Lord Brahma knows very well that the position of Lord Shiva, *namaskṛtaḥ prāha śaśāṅka-śekharaṁ kṛta-praṇāmaṁ prahasann ivātmabhūḥ*. There is always Vaishnava etiquette in such dealings and the exalted personalities like Lord Shiva and Lord Brahma exemplified by such actions.

Lord Brahma is highly advanced in such dealings of psychology. This was a description when Lord Shiva lost his wife and how Brahma smiling addressed Lord Shiva with the starting of his glorification. "The material world is the spider's network, and as I am creating it so meticulously, you Lord Shiva destroy it without any effort. Your glories are fathomless, and I can't even try to understand your unlimited glories. Also, you took charge of the mode of ignorance, and you are the knower of religion, yoga, and sacrifice." Lord Brahma is soliciting the favor of Lord Shiva so that he could bestow his blessings to the aggrieved demigods, brahmins in the Daksha Yajna. Lord Brahma knew very well that no one could advance either materially or spiritually by offending Lord Shiva. He knows it very well, and he knows that Lord Shiva is also Ashutosh, who can be pleased very easily. There are no questions of grudges and envy in the heart of Lord Shiva. It's like a crystal clear and so transparent and deep the heart of Lord Shiva that one can deep dive into it, remain entirely motionless and merge in the brahman satisfaction. Brahma had a different role to play here and expressed his prayer to Lord Shiva for achievement and how the *varnasrama* system was inaugurated by Lord Shiva and how the meaning of sacrifice is inaugurated by Lord Shiva. Without the presence of Lord Shiva, the result of the sacrifice is fruitless. Lord Brahma addressed him repeatedly that, "You are the controller and protector of the entire world; your benign presence is needed in the sacrifice of any gods." So, pleased with Brahma's sweet words, Lord Shiva desired to cause a favorable environment in the devastated Daksha sacrifice, and the sacrifice could progress further. Lord Brahma gave an example of milk and yogurt in his earlier prayer already, and he is pointing out that you are non-different from the Lord. If the three Lords, Brahma, Mahesvara, Vishnu wanted to do good for the people, who else can stop and the trinity of divinity prevails in the entire world.

In Srimad Bhagavatam SB 1.7.18, *yāvad-gamaṁ rudra-bhayād yathā kaḥ,* just to save his life, as Brahma fled in fear from Shiva. Sukadeva Goswami described the reason for the fear of Brahma from Lord Shiva. Shiva is *dharma-vatsala* and He protects the religious principles and when he found out that Lord Brahma being sexually inclined towards his daughter, he wanted to punish Brahma. Lord Brahma is very much afraid of Shiva as he knew well that Shiva is very angry, and he could pierce his trident in his neck. As per Vamana Purana, Surya is also envious and irritated with a demon named Vidyunmali who was gifted by Lord Shiva with a bright and illuminated golden plane. Upon receiving the golden throne, there is no question of night in one part of the world, this incident is like that of Priyavrata Maharaj, who obtained a golden chariot and reduced the power of Surya or sun. Being angry with the demon, Surya tried to melt the airplane so that the existence of the plane vanished and then his reputation of sun, the powerful planet remains. Shiva, being very much angry with Surya, He tried to kill Surya with his trident, No one could surpass the power of Rudra, Surya found no hope other than taking shelter at the lotus feet of Lord Shiva. Surya dev went to the Banaras temple and surrendered at the pilgrimage place, Kasi. Lokarka temple in Kashi is famous and this story reveals the power of Rudra.

RUDRA AND THE SNAKES

Whenever we see the deity of Lord Shiva, we find a snake associated with Shiva's neck or in the Shiva temple or on the top of the Shiva Linga or the top of the Shiva temple architecture. What does the snake represent? If we pay proper attention, we will find out that the snake is coiled around three times in the neck of Lord Shiva, symbolizing past, present, and future. This resembles the same feature of three depressions of Lord Vishnu's abdomen, where the entire universes lie. Lord Shiva is known as *Trikalanja*, meaning, knower of past, present, future. He holds the neck in his neck showing the world that Shiva is the controller of the time.

Matsya Purana suggests the Shiva wearing the snakes as a necklace and sign of compassion to the most fallen. In the current age, Kali Yuga, mostly Lord Shiva, found that a single snake around his neck, however, many more snakes in his body are described in the Puranas. The five-headed snake starting a canopy over Shiva-linga is the ideal audience for the visitors. We find various tales associating snakes and Lord Shiva in the scriptures such as Skanda Purana, Padma Purana, etc.

Snakes are two types, Nagas, and Sarpas, "*Sarpanam asmi Vasukih, anantas casmi naganam*". Lord Vishnu lies in the causal ocean on the bed of Ananta Sesa. Here the expansion of Vasuki is also serving Lord Shiva, and many of us have been worshiping such a form of combination in the traditional temples. Lord Shiva also drank the poison *kalakuta* from the churning of the ocean with the help of Vasuki. Lord Shiva turns out to have blue-throated and is also called as Nilakantha. He is known as Pasupatinath, which means "lord of all creatures," and that he controls all the animals, beasts, birds, and reptiles. Since the snake is feared by most of us, Lord Shiva wanted to show to the world as the fear is controlled by me, so there is no need to worry about the fear when you surrender to the Supreme Lord. There is a magnificent temple Pasupatinath in Nepal, and the Lord is worshiped opulently.

As the "Nagas" clan is cultured to adapt poison (venom) and turned into a diamond (*mani*), sometimes, the scientific explanation was given that the heat from poison in Shiva's throat is again channeled into the body of Vasuki. Likewise, there are other snakes that form anklets and bracelets of Shiva out of respect.

Anyone has an evil past, unbelievable karmic reactions, no good behavior, and still surrenders to Shiva, all the poisonous effects like snakes are removed from him. As Lord Shiva gave protection to the snakes when they were in danger and seek for protection from Shiva, he awarded the place in Kailash. When the Kailash is still very cold, they need to get the warmth of the body temperature and Lord Shiva, without any hesitation awarded the place in His own body, shelter to all the snakes. Even during the gift ceremony to Parvati after her marriage, Lord Shiva presented jewels, anklets, and various ornaments in the forms of snakes. Snakes also enlighten the Kailash with their hood even though Lord Shiva himself is completely effulgent as good as Brahma Jyoti. Thus, snakes expanded in numerous types of ornaments. This event is mentioned in the Skanda Purana. Shiva making ornaments from serpents are also mentioned in the Padma Purana and the Matsya Purana. As per Srimad Bhagavatam, the head of the *śiśumāra* form is in reverse directions. Its composition form appears like that of a coiled snake resembling the neck of Lord Shiva for the symbolic representation of the art of meditation of the Kundalini Yoga.

In Srimad Bhagavatam, fourteen planetary systems are described like Patala, Atala, Vitala, Satyaloka, Tapaloka, etc. One of the planetary systems below our planet earth is called Vitala in between Patala and earth. Lord Shiva and Parvati eternally live on this planet Vitala, the storehouse of all goldmines. If you are interested in finding gold in this material world, then please explore to know about the Vitala planet. Many demons, snakes, and other lower forms of the creature live on this planet, and they decorate the body with the gold. By the sexual union of Parvati and Shiva, secretion of the reproductive outcome produces the massive amount of gold as we know the sperm generated from Lord Shiva during the time of seeing the Mohini murti and gold, silver, copper and other mines are produced.

RUDRA AND THE CREMATORIUM

When we imagine heaven or the kingdom of God, then we paint beautiful gardens, flowers, lakes, palaces, music, poetry, and opulent services around the ecosystem. Now we speak of crematorium and God, and they live in such filthy places, we may doubt how such contrast remains in God and lower state of life. People generally shun those who roam around the *smasana* or crematorium. Is His position of Shiva affected with such living conditions or glorified? When we see the picture of Lord Krishna assuming the role of a driver of Arjuna's chariot, his position never got affected. Of course, it did not, because He is Achyuta and infallible. Similarly, Shiva is the master of the material world, and He could do whatever is not even attainable by the highest demigods, He lives in the Kailasa Hill where Parvati takes a bath in the holy Ganges, He is showing us the compassionate father being kind to His children by associating with them. Shiva is the controller of the mode of ignorance. He is always helpful to the people who are degraded and fallen in the ordinary sense and whose practices and behaviors are abominable. There is a tantric system followed by such living beings contaminated with envy and cruelty. Shiva never left them in such a situation, and He gives hope to those people bereft of higher spiritual values. Generally, religious values are more recognized and perceived in the mode of goodness, and this mode is controlled by Lord Vishnu. Lord Shiva uses a platform to uplift them to higher values by continually trying his best to raise their consciousness level. In the crematorium, ghosts, demons, rakshasa, and many haunted beings live as they are entirely under the control of *tamo guna* or mode of ignorance. When Daksha, out of anger expressing his viewpoint about Lord Shiva, concocts the meaning of Shiva as "inauspicious" even though Shiva is the most auspicious and by chanting the name of Shiva, one becomes auspicious. Daksha is projecting Shiva's views being garlanded with bones, skulls, ashes on his whole body. It looks so fearful as he is crying, laughing, dancing, acting so awkward in the midst of the fallen souls. What else one can be concluded from the position of Lord Shiva by experiencing such behavior. No one can understand the inner meaning of a great personality like Lord Shiva, what to speak of even a great Prajapati like Daksha.

Drunkards, Marijuana smokers, drug dealers, and many intoxicant addicted people act crazily in this world. Lord Shiva is the hope for them, and Lord Shiva is always eager to give his association brings to a higher system of life by dint of his expertise. However, the followers of the mode of ignorance are so doomed that they don't come to the sense unless mother Kali chops them with her *khadga*. All the demigods work under the directions of Lord Vishnu, so as Yamaraja and Shiva. We should glorify the position of Yamaraja and Shiva as they are managing such a risky department. Unless one is highly elevated and compassionate, it is not possible to give one's association to the fallen souls. It is the mercy of Shiva that he is living in the crematorium and offering all kinds of solace to the people for upgrading to a higher mode of life. Shiva is always auspicious and transcendental even though He lives in either crematorium or Kailasa hills. On his lips, Shiva is always chanting the name of Rama, Rama, Rama.

Shiva is *Bhasmanga's* embodiment personality, which means Shiva smears ash of the cremation grounds on his body. Shiva is Digambar, who is clothed as the sky. Shiva is *Smashaanavaasi*, which means that Shiva resides in *Smashan* (burial ground). Shiva is *Smashananatha*, which means Shiva is God for the burial ground. Shiva is beyond the worldly things, and he stays in Rudra Kshetra, the burial ground. Shiva is free from this cycle of life and death, so he is untouched. Shiva is telling us that the beautiful physical body we always boast of, will turn into a pile of ash one day. So, stop giving importance to mundane things, and evolve above your physical body. Every living being born one day has to reach the burial ground one beautiful day; this is inevitable. Shiva smears ash on his body since the ultimate truth of life is ash. Shiva is the only God who stays with you when you are alive and even after you pass away. He smears our dead ash on His body, and thus dissolves us into Him. Legends say that when any person dies, it's true that only the physical body passes away, but the soul will be forever. The souls in the burial grounds cry and miss their loved ones, so Shiva stays with them and provides the much-needed relief to the departed souls.

Lord Shiva isn't bound by time. He is here and everywhere when we are born; he will be there when we are dead. He will be there during the whole process. Burial grounds are not as detrimental as opposed to general acceptance. It is the place where the soul gets freedom from the body and otherworldly things. It is the place where the soul realizes how it has wasted all that time on earth. It is the place where it determines to behave well in the next life. It's a new beginning. It is the point where something ends, and something starts at the same time. So, Shiva is there to guide souls in the process, through the sadness and realization and then the preparation for the next life.

It is to be understood that the first Shiv Sutra and its import is as follows corroborated with the teachings of the second chapter of Bhagavad Gita. Shiva is liberated awareness. This body, such as a *shareer*, is that which withers away. *Shmashan* (funeral ground) is the cusp that separates the perishable material body and the imperishable soul. Only in *shmashan* can liberated awareness be experienced. *Jeevit Mariye Bhavjal Tariye.* Die while being alive and cross the ocean of suffering. The imagery of Shiva roaming crematorium grounds represents the need to realize the perishable nature of the body and forsake all attachment to it, in order to inhere in the lasting bliss of liberated awareness.

SANKARACHARYA AND LORD SHIVA

Lord Chaitanya admitted that Shankaracharya was an incarnation of Lord Shiva, and it is known that Lord Shiva is one of the greatest devotees, a Mahajan of the Bhagavat school. There are twelve mahājanas, high authorities on devotional service, and Lord Shiva is one of them. Why, then, did he adopt the process of Māyāvāda philosophy? The answer is given in the Shiva Purāṇa, where Lord Shiva told his wife Parvati about the appearance of a brahmin boy. From the Padma Purāṇa, it is learned that Shankaracharya is Lord Shiva, and who can be a more excellent devotee than Lord Shiva? Lord Shiva is considered to be the foremost Vaishnava.

CC Madhya 6.180

ācāryera doṣa nāhi, īśvara-ājñā haila

ataeva kalpanā kari' nāstika-śāstra kaila

"Actually, there is no fault on the part of Shankaracharya. He simply carried out the order of the Supreme Personality of Godhead. He had to imagine some kind of interpretation, and therefore he presented a type of Vedic literature that is full of atheism.

CC Madhya 6.181

svāgamaiḥ kalpitais tvaṁ ca

janān mad-vimukhān kuru

māṁ ca gopaya yena syāt

sṛṣṭir eṣottarottarā

"[Addressing Lord Shiva, the Supreme Personality of Godhead said:] 'Please make the general populace averse to Me by imagining your own interpretation of the Vedas. Also, cover Me in such a way that people will take more interest in advancing material civilization just to propagate a population bereft of spiritual knowledge.'

This is a quotation from the Padma Purāṇa, Uttara-khaṇḍa (62.31).

CC Madhya 6.182

māyāvādam asac-chāstraṁ

pracchannaṁ bauddham ucyate

mayaiva vihitaṁ devi

kalau brāhmaṇa-mūrtinā

"[Lord Shiva informed goddess Durgā, the superintendent of the material world:] 'In the Age of Kali I shall take the form of a brāhmaṇa and explain the Vedas through false scriptures in an atheistic way, similar to Buddhist philosophy.'"

Sankaracarya is the original propounder of the *Mayavada Bhasya* philosophy. It formulates the oneness of the living being and the supreme being, and there is no difference between the two entities. Secondly, he preaches that the transformation of this material world is simply an illusion and false. All the arguments will lead to confusion. People will be deprived of the actual treasure, such as cloudy commentary to suit the needs of the Karma Kanda and mental speculators and pseudo devotees of God.

This verse is a quotation from the Padma Purāṇa, Uttara-khaṇḍa (25.7).

Śaṅkarācārya preached the Mayavada Bhasya in southern India and the philosophy spread across the continents, and it was the will of the Lord as well as Lord Shiva to come and challenge the Buddhist ideology, his messages are filled with impersonalism or monism or merging into the absolute whole. No matter how much we try to imitate or concoct the original ideas or message of the Lord in the form of Vedas and Vedanta sutra, it's not possible to conclude, and sincere seekers of the God will eventually come to the path of bhakti, there is no doubt about it. This is the internal mood of Lord Shiva and Sankaracarya. Sankaracarya mentioned several quotations that Narayana is not from this mundane world. There is no need to speculate on His sweet form and excellent qualities, they are beyond debate, but when we search through our own limited mind and senses, all possibilities to be confused and misdirected, One should pray to Sankaracarya to give the best of the gem, the substance of all the Vedas and not the falsity.

Śaṅkarācārya repeatedly stressed the mantra *"tat tvam asi"* and pointing out that you are same as the supreme and there is no difference between you and God, people would like to be mesmerized with the idea of superiority and oneness. They forget their limitations and deficiency being as a spirit soul. In the corporate world, we often see the height of self-proclamation and self-promotional qualities are manifested so that people cherish their desires with the process. In spirituality, if we apply the same principle, one will be doomed. Instead, one has to seek the spiritual substance from the real Lord. Before the creation of the material world, who was there, this question will agitate the mind of the neophyte, however, Sankaracarya knew very well that Narayan was beyond the conception of the current cosmos and the entire mundane universe, he is the Lord of the spiritual world. No one has produced or created Him. In Bhagavad Gita, eighth chapter Lord Krishna says, one should aspire to attain him, and Sankaracarya is indirectly proving the point, only the smart and intelligent catch the real import of Sankaracarya.

One may still question the validity of Sankaracarya's position in defeating Buddhism. If Buddha is the incarnation of Lord Vishnu, then why did Lord Shiva challenge one incarnation of the Lord. The mystical appearance of the Lord is tough to understand. The *saktyavesha* incarnation appears in the mortal world to serve one purpose; Buddha appeared to eradicate the slaughterhouse concept. Many people in the name of religion sacrificed animals and ultimately satisfying their tongue only. Buddha is very merciful, and being the savior of the animals, he preached the gospel of not following the Vedas and no God in existence. Most likely, many people were converted as *sunyavadi* by following the doctrine of Lord Buddha however by the sweet will of Lord Chaitanya as predicted to appear in this age of Kali, they all became pure devotees of Lord Krishna. The presence of clouds is certainly prominent whenever the rain comes, as well as the sight of lightning. By order of Lord Krishna, Lord Shiva appeared as Śaṅkarācārya and defeated the gospel of Buddha and re-established the belief in the Vedas again. People are so deviant in their understanding that there is no scope of accepting the form of the Lord, even though it is approved, people will consider as low style, To maintain a higher status quo in the society, formless, oneness, thinking oneself as good as God was the ideal people followed in those days. It was easier for Śaṅkarācārya to convert all Buddhist and atheists to be a follower of his teachings.

These descriptions can be found in the discussion between Lord Shiva and Parvati in Padma Purana. Lord Shiva is saying in ancient ages that he forecasted his appearance in the mortal world as a brahmin boy and defeated the Buddhist philosophy. All the appearances of Lord Vishnu are mentioned in Vedas and Puranas and Jayadeva Goswami's poem of *dashavatara* song. Śaṅkarācārya also picked a few points from the Buddhist philosophy and made some adjustments in his teachings. Only Shiva knows what he is doing based on the needs of the people. Many demons receive various benedictions as per their wishes, Lord Shiva is fulfilling different beings' desire in the form of convictions, vada, and argumentations. Lord Chaitanya even reemphasized the value of devotion, and there is no necessity of following neither to Buddha nor to Śaṅkarācārya. One has to focus on Om and Hare Krishna *maha-mantra* to come to the highest stage of spiritual standards. Śaṅkarācārya did not forget the mood of His master Lord Krishna he preached inherently, *gupta-tattva* of worshiping to Govind. He understood very well that the science of debate, argumentations, comparative studies, and many more philosophical speculations is not going to save one from death's most significant danger and repeated birth and death cycle. He knew very well that only one person, Lord Narayana, Lord Govind, could act as the savior. Furthermore, Sankaracarya composed the beautiful poem for these followers if someone understands the message, then he will be fortunate, and Śaṅkarācārya will be highly pleased if he worships Govind.

bhaja govindaṁ bhaja govindaṁ

govindaṁ bhaja mūḍha-mate |

samprāpte sannihite kāle

nahi nahi rakṣati ḍukṛṅkaraṇe ||

Worship Govinda, worship Govinda,

Worship Govinda, oh fool!

At the time of your death,

Rules of grammar will not save you.

PREGNANCY IMPACT BY LORD RUDRA

Many times, Vedic reference is given for regulated sex life as someone is involved for procreation must adhere to the Vedic scriptures and must not engage in the three Sandhya transient times of the day, such as morning, noon and evening twilight period. Generally, it is said that possibly bad omen will happen, or someone demoniac is going to be born in such an inauspicious time. We can take a referential point from Diti's request for procreation during an odd time of the day. As per Srimad Bhagavatam ŚB 3.14.34, Diti is telling her husband Kashyap that his pregnancy could be disturbed by Lord Rudra or his associates as quoted" *na me garbham imaṁ brahman,"* the meaning is "why Lord Rudra would kill her embryo?" Is it true that Rudra killed the embryo? The essential point is any irreligious activities performed in the evening, especially sexual intercourse; it is not considered auspicious because the three Sandhya is dedicated to performing Gayatri. Even the demon-like Ravan was also performing Gayatri during the evening time and the monkey king Vali used to do his Gayatri in this period. One should not engage in affairs of procreation in the evening period. Diti was, by the will of the Lord, engaged in sexual relations with her husband, Kashyap, and she was very much apprehensive that her embryo would be killed by the Rudra. It is said that "*bhūtānām ṛṣabho' vadhīt,"* Lord of all the living beings might be enraged by such regulations, and he could cast some demoniac creature into her womb or else it would be killed. If anyone desires to produce highly pious children, one must refrain from sex in such a period in the evening time during the sunset. Diti was religious and very much aware of all the ethical principles, and she could not know to commit an offense by transgressing the moral code of conduct with higher values in spiritual life. By adopting the Varnasrama system and following the path of the religious system, Rudra blessed such souls, if there is any violations of the system then there is a possibility of obtaining a demoniac child. Shiva is Rudra as well as Ashutosh also. He is easily pleased with the people having a little bit of inclination towards dharma or chanting of the holy name of Rama. Diti knew that Shiva or the agents of Rudra or Bhutanath might spoil the pregnancy she had achieved in a wrong period of the day. At the same time, she knew that Shiva is also Ashutosh, she pleaded unto her husband Kashyap Muni to tackle the situation by satisfying Lord Shiva. Kashyap Muni is an ardent devotee of Lord Shiva and He will keep his prayers without a doubt. We should take lessons from the incident that how to produce children who will oblige to the religious path, the system of *garbhadhana* samskara and pregnancy planning should be done based on the Vedic values. The details of the rituals or samskara are mentioned in Vedic scriptures and one could follow it.

One could obtain better progeny by engaging in Vedic rituals and praying to the supreme Lord so that the population will be filled with devotees of the Lord and expand the mission of the *Sanatana Dharma.*

MAYAVADA BHASYA AND LORD SHIVA

Mayavada Philosophy, which says Krishna has no form, but He assumes a form for facility of devotional service. Mayavada Bhasya is a commentary by Śaṅkarācārya advocating that one impersonally considers oneself the Supreme Lord. Such Māyāvāda philosophical commentaries upon the Vedānta-sūtra are merely imaginary, but these -bhāṣya, establishes the *viśiṣṭādvaita-vāda* philosophy. Interpretations of Vedanta made by the followers of Shankaracharya are neither Mayavada nor Satvatta. Lord Shiva is speaking to Parvati in the context of the preaching of the Mayavadi Bhasya. "My dear wife, hear my explanations of how I have spread ignorance through Māyāvāda philosophy. It is recommended that one give up all activities to achieve freedom from karma. In this Māyāvāda philosophy, I have described the *jīvātmā* and *Paramātmā* to be one and the same." Each philosophical thought process differs in the subtle argument or, in conclusion, *Siddhanta* of the Sastra is one and establish "*satyam param dhimahi*".

There are six schools of philosophy, Vedanta darshan is coined by Vyasa, and Sankaracraya here refuted the conclusion of Vyasadeva. In the Shiva Purāṇa, it is stated that Lord Shiva said to Pārvatī that in the Kali-yuga, in the body worshipers of Lord Shiva are Māyāvādī followers. Lord Shiva himself says, "*māyāvādam asac-chāstram.*" *Asat-śāstra.* Bhṛgu Muni cursed that persons who worshiped Lord Shiva would become followers of this Māyāvāda *asat śāstra,* among the worshipers of Lord Shiva there is a section who live a devilish life. Sankaracarya knew very well that he could not do any word jugglery interpretation on the Srimad Bhagavatam literature. He made his famous commentary known as Saririka Bhasya, just like in Vaishnava school; we have the Govinda Bhasya. Saririka Bhasya teaches about the merging in the absolute, and there is no distinction between soul and Supersoul and focuses on the oneness. Even the followers of Sankaracarya deride the glories of Srimad Bhagavatam and also argue the literature's authenticity. Srila Vyasadeva has written this excellent literature for advanced living beings, or the liberated souls. There is no question of its conclusion or the importance of establishing the goal of human beings' life. Narayan is not the creation of the mundane world nor he is a product of this mortal cosmology. Narayana is always transcendental, and Sankaracarya has mentioned it several times, Alas, many arguments put forth by the followers to dismiss the glories of Narayana and the Srimad Bhagavatam. Srimad Bhagavatam is the real hope, and it acts as our mentor, father, master, and lover in all situations of life and how we can miss the transcendental boat in this dark age of Kali. *māyāvādi-bhāṣya śunile haya Sarva nāśa* [Cc. Madhya 6.169]. Anyone who tries to understand Māyāvāda is undoubtedly doomed.

LORD SHIVA IS ASHUTOSH

The meaning of Ashutosh is one who is easily pleased, and Lord Shiva is known as Ashutosh. Lord Shiva gives benedictions to unworthy recipients and makes no distinctions between a demon, demigod, or a human. Lord Shiva offered various boons to many demons in the past. With the power obtained from Lord Shiva, demons became very aggressive and tried to manipulate the system and ultimately defeated Lord Vishnu. Because Lord Shiva is very compassionate to the fallen, He always ensures they receive what they ask; however, Lord Vishnu offers the boon what the recipients might need. Even though He is Ashutosh, Lord Shiva is also known as *dharma-vatsala*. Of course, the word *dharma-vatsala* refers to a person whose additional significance. Sometimes Lord Shiva has to deal with persons who are in the modes of passion, and they worship Lord Shiva for some material profit; they sometimes obey the religious principles. As soon as Lord Shiva sees that his devotees are following religious beliefs, he blesses them. The Pracetās, sons of Prācīnabarhi, were naturally very pious and gentle, and consequently, Lord Shiva was pleased with them. Lord Shiva is happy with any person doing or even acting in the name of doing; also, he blesses them.

Once upon a time, there was a beggar whom Parvati wanted to bestow mercy by giving some wealth. Considering Parvati's request, Lord Shiva kept some jewels in a cloth container and remained on the side of the road where the beggar was traveling. Unfortunately, the beggar, at the same time, thought how wonderful and mysterious that the blind man walked without the vision and closed his eyes. He passed through the jewel cloth box and missed the opportunity, Lord Shiva is eager to give everyone, and especially he is anxious to give Krishna Prema; however, we are becoming unfortunate and not taking His mercy. There is an argument that how Lord Shiva resides in His linga as some rats' pass urine and stool over the Shiva-linga, and Lord Shiva does not even protest, there are no questions of Shiva being in the linga. This argument was put forward by *Arya samaj.* Lord Shiva is generous, noble, and liberal towards his children, a mother or father won't protest when the child urinates or passes stool in his body. The innocent rats have no clue, and they are mere rodents, and Lord Shiva forgives any mistakes done by his children.

LORD SHIVA AND THE RUDRAKSHA MALA

As we know, *Adhokshaja* means, beyond the conception of "A" and "Ksha" as every word of this universe is generated within the syllables of *"A"* and "*Ksha*". Similarly, It is believed that the *Rudraksha* means everything embedded within the bead, the Rudra principle in the *"A"* and *"Ksha.*" This bead also encompasses the mysteries of the complete evolution of Cosmos. In Srimad Bhagavatam 4.6.38 *kṛtvorau dakṣiṇe savyaṁ pāda-padmaṁ ca jānuni bāhuṁ prakoṣṭhe' kṣa-mālām āsīnaṁ tarka-mudrayā.* Lord Shiva's left leg was placed on his right thigh, and his left hand was placed on his left thigh. [This sitting posture is called vīrāsana.] In his right hand, he held rudrākṣa beads, and his finger was in the mode of argument. Followers of Lord Shiva always wear a Rudraksha mala for spiritual advancement and peace of mind. The meditation position and thoughtfulness of Lord Shiva brings good health, wisdom, and spiritual enlightenment to the entire humanity.

Lord Shiva once was performing a deep transcendental meditation unto Lord Sankarsana for the happiness of all living beings. After the prayer of the demigods, He opened His majestic eyes with the most auspicious glances unto the surrendered souls, and subsequently, teardrops fell on the Earth. These tear droplets appropriated the form of seeds that later became Rudraksha trees. Rudraksha from now meant 'The Tear of Lord Shiva.' The dehydrated fruits from the Rudraksha tree configured as Rudraksha beads are thus used as spiritual beads and put on for massive spiritual gains. The scientific meaning of Rudraksha is called "*Elaeocarpus ganitrus roxb*" trees. It could grow almost 70 ft and is found in the Gangetic plain in the foothills of the Himalayas in India. Lord Vamanadev also was gifted with a *rudraksha* mala by Sarasvati as per Srimad Bhagavatam. 8.18.16. *kamaṇḍaluṁ veda-garbhaḥ kuśān saptarṣayo daduḥ akṣa-mālāṁ mahārāja sarasvaty avyayātmanaḥ*, O King, Lord Brahmā offered a water pot to the inexhaustible Supreme Personality of Godhead, the seven sages offered Him *kuśa* grass, and Mother Sarasvati gave Him a string of Rudrākṣa beads.

Devotees of Lord Vishnu wear Tulsi beads and chant on Tulsi beads; however, devotees of Lord Shiva wear a Rudraksha bead and chant on those beads.

LORD SHIVA'S RESIDENCE – KAILASH MOUNTAIN

Mount Kailash is also found on the planet earth, it is located in the heavenly planet next to Kuvera's planet as well as Lord Shiva resides in Vitala planets. Mount Kailash on Earth is 21,778 ft high peak in the Kailash Array, which forms part of the Trans Himalaya in Tibet. Nowadays, with the help of the Govt of India and China, there is a provision to go on a pilgrimage to the Kailash *Manasarovar yatra.*

The Kailash mountain is located near Lake Manasarovar and Lake *Rakshastal*, adjacent to the foundation of the longest Asian rivers: the Indus, Sutlej, Brahmaputra, and *Karnali* (an offshoot of the Ganges) in India. Mount Kailash is holy in four major faiths: Bon, Buddhism, Hinduism, and Jainism. In Hinduism, it is customarily known as the abode of Lord Shiva, who resided there with his consort Goddess Parvati and their children, lord Ganesh and Lord Kartikeya.

Kailash Hill is the eternal residence of Lord Shiva, and many people claim that there is no form of God, no residence, no qualities, Lord Shiva lives in the Kailash, and it has expanded unto the earthly planet also as well as below Earth in Vitala planet, Lord Shiva resides. Actual Kailash in this material world is near to the Kuvera planet, Yaksaloka, in the upper planetary systems. As per the Vedic literature, this world is divided into fourteen planetary systems, and upper ones are called Swarga Loka, and there are innumerable planets for each god, like Agni, Indra, Surya, Chandra, etc. Shiva Loka is known as Kailash Loka, and per Srimad Bhagavatam, this location is in the upper planetary systems and near to Kubera's Loka. Lord Shiva and Kuvera are very friendly so that the Kuvera appeared as the father of Advaita Acharya, an incarnation of Lord Sada-Shiva and Mahavishnu. If God's planet or residence is void or sunya, then how perfect analysis and descriptions are given in the Srimad Bhagavatam in such details.

One will wonder about the varieties found in the Kailasa hills. After the death of Sati, Lord Shiva was performing his austerity and penances in the Kailash hill under a banyan tree, measuring almost 800 yojana's height and 600 yojana's breadth. Lord Brahma and all the important demigods are planning to approach Lord Shiva for pacification and obtaining his mercy. Lord Brahma is setting an example to ask for forgiveness from the saintly personality or from the supreme Lord in case of mistakes. Daksha was also killed in the episode of the insulting behaviors towards Lord Shiva and his associates. They are flying in their respective carriers, such as swan is the carrier of Brahma, and other demigods are flying in their airplanes. Airplanes are decorated with ornaments, jewels, and musical arrangements for a better ambiance. Of course, the airplane is not like the one in earthly planets, run by fuel only, some of the airplanes run by mantra or by will, *Pushpaka vimana* of Kuvera runs by will and command only. The mystery of the upper planetary systems is unknown to modern scientists, then how can one even approach the spiritual world, which is beyond the coverings of the egg-shaped layers of earth, water, fire, ego, etc. When all of the demigods are flying in the sky, they are in complete harmony, and there is no need for GPS and traffic management as the sky and ether are controlled by the rulers only. They know the system and the means, and there is nothing hidden for the demigods. However, the demigods are amazed to see the beauty of the Kailasa Hill as it was so marvelous in its opulence, gardens, rivers, fruits, animals, lakes, and many other elements of opulence existed in the hills. When the demigods entered the arena of Kailasa Hills, they found all kinds of lotuses, blue, red, pinkish, and many more varieties indivara, kusuma, etc. One could notice that flowers around the lake and top of the mountain peak like kadamba, malli, ketaki, champa, mandara, kumuda, and many more flowers, making it as Holi in the top of the hills. Lakes are filled with clear water, lotus, and surrounded by innumerable birds. Swans, geese, cuckoo, and birds are roaming around various lakes and waterfalls in the Kailasa Hills. The whole atmosphere is enlivening to the mind. Not only the fruits and birds but lots of animals like reindeer, kasturi(nusk) deer, elephants, lions, and tigers are enjoying the beautiful and serene environment. All kinds of auspicious plants and trees are decorating the Kailasa hills, mango, banana, banyan, bilva, jackfruit, berries, amla, and many more. Even though demigods live in the heavenly planets as Indra has a beautiful garden, *nandan-kanan*, he was envious upon seeing the beauty of the Kailasa hills. All around the hills, minerals, jewels, and herbs are fully manifested in the hills and glorifying the presence of Lord Shiva and its associates. When the bees are running around different fruits to collect the honey, the cuckoo is singing the glories of Lord

Shiva, and as if performing the morning rituals, it captivated the mind of the demigods. Some of them used to visit the Alakananda lake for enjoyment. Lord Shiva is generous and merciful, and he has allowed the demigods to come and compete with their wives in the lake, Alakananda. There were special sections of the Alaknanda, where the Saugandhika flowers sprouted and made the whole environment fragrant. Generally, that's the place of Mother Gauri's bathing places, as some demigods are describing among themselves and filled with joy and sorrow because mother Sati is no more, and she left her body in the Daksha yajna. Sati used to take bathe in this lake, and it is the Ganges only because Gange's origin is from the hair of Lord Shiva and she has the first drop at this spot and the beautiful lake formed from the Ganges water is known as Alakananda in the heavenly kingdom, and Sati used to bless the Ganges by her presence and bathing with her husband. Lord Krishna has various sporting activities in the lake Radha Kund in Vrindavan Dham. All the demigods remember the uncommon glories of Lord Shiva and Sati feeling morose that how they could manage to meet Lord Shiva and ask for forgiveness on behalf of the Prajapati Daksha. They are feeling confident because Lord Brahma is leading the journey with them, and Kailasa hill has such a magnanimous effect that one's anxiety and doubts are dispelled by the divine mercy of the Lord. Alakananda is the emanations from the lotus feet of Vamanadeva, Lord Krishna, and it has sanctified the whole of Kailasa hills. In earthly planet, we go to the Ganges for purifications, and saintly people take a bath to give mercy to us, *tīrthī-kurvanti tīrthāni* (Bhāg. 1.13.10), the *theerthapada* is Lord Krishna's lotus feet, and the sanctified place is very auspicious for the fallen souls. Even demigods take pleasure in drinking the water of the Alakananda, the sanctified place in the material world. Kailasa Hills is as close to Goloka Dham as Lord Shiva is as close to Lord Krishna, and there are *Kalpa-vriksha* and Desiree trees that are available by the sweet will of Lord Krishna. These trees are not even found in Brahma Loka or Svarga Loka; however, these trees are available in Kailash Hills. Kinnaras, Gandharvas, Yakshas are always singing the glories of Lord Shiva, and they are getting the benefit of the musical ambiance and the mercy of Lord Shiva. One will aspire to visit such holy places of Kailasa hills; however, on the earthly planet, we can visit the place on the border of Nepal, Tibet, and India.

LORD SHIVA AND THE BAEL (WOOD APPLE)

Bilva or Bael tree is the most worshipable offering to Shiva Linga and even to Goddess Parvati or both Shakti and Shiva. Bael or Bilva is known as a wood apple tree in an English dictionary and a tropical fruit *Aegle marmelos*. Bael is the only affiliate category of the monotypic genus Aegle nomenclature. I am fortunate to see a beautiful Bael tree in my home, native place in Odisha, India, and we used to get a lot of fruits from these trees. Bael is a deciduous plant or sometimes grows a mid-sized tree with drooping branches around it.

Bael Patra or Bilva leaf is considered the most sacred leaf for offering *archana* to Lord Shiva. Their joint of three leaves signify the symbol of three Supreme Lord, Brahma, Vishnu and Maheshwar. So, if it is offered to Lord Shiva, with the proper recitation of Mantra, Lord Shiva is pleased shortly. It is also known as three modes of nature are under the control of the Supreme Lord, and three eyes of Lord Shiva depicted in the triangular shape of the Bael leave as it is protracted as His Trishul, the trident.

Once Jaya, Vijaya, Jayanti, and Mangalaruna, the companions of Parvati, were frequently requesting her to take them on an excursion to Mandarachal, the most outstanding of mountains. Parvati agreed to their proposals as she is eager to serve their moods. She immediately summoned the great lion and mounted upon it along with her friends. On reaching the Mandara mountain, Parvati and others stepped down on the mountain and surveyed the elegant vicinity of the mountain. Due to the voyage and long journey from Kailash, sweat droplets pebbled on the forehead of Parvati. As she streaked them off, the sweat beads fell on the rocky territory of Mandara and suddenly transformed into a tree, having three leaves in a single spring, as if smack of a trident, or the three eyes of Bholenath.

Upon seeing the beautiful tree, Gauri was in perfect amusement and surprise; she told her companions that this tree is so beautiful, and it is captivating her mind upon looking into it. Her companions could understand their mistress's extreme happiness with the newly developed tree in the rocky mountain. Of course, it is born from the energy of the personification of this universe's material energy. She wanted to name the tree as the tree pierced from the rock and sprouted just next to her, so she uttered Bilva or Bael. Even the leaves and all parts of the tree will be extremely dear to me, and whatever is dear to Parvati, it is most precious to Lord Shiva. So we offer the leaves in the worship of Bhava and Bhavani. Whoever lives near the tree or touches the leaves on one's forehead, Yamaraja, the God of death, can't reach that person. Meditating on the situation, she expanded and implanted energy of all her expansions onto the tree.

"Oh, great tree! Goddess Girija is residing in your roots. Dakshayani is present in the main stem. Maheshwari is present in the branches, Parvati in the leaves, Katyayani in the fruit, Gauri in the outer bark, Aparna in the inner bark, Durga in flower, and Uma in the twigs. The other nine core Shaktis, at the behest of Bhavani, have occupied the place on its thorns for the protection of devotees. This tree is the most beloved to Shiva since his Shakti resides in all of its parts! Obeisances to this Bilva tree, the abode of Devi Jagadambika!"

This Bael tree is beneficial for medicinal purposes. As per the Ayurveda school methods, the bark of Bilva assuages Vāta; leaves are valuable in cardiac disorders, gastrointestinal, lymphatic, and other disorders. The immature fruits are astringent, bitter, improve digestive fire and check diarrhea. There are countless other divisions about the significant rise of

Bilva leaves. Adi Shankar would unfold the exceptional hymns in the glory of Bilva popularly known as "*Bilvashtakam.*" Bael or Bilva to Shiva is what Tulasi is to Vishnu. Their arrangement echoes the three-eyed appearance of Shiva, or the three indentations of the trident, or the three types of physiques, to the three kinds of such abodes as Bhur, Bhuva, and Svarga.

It is customary to say that those who seek material opulence, comfort, gold, diamond, better living standards are advised to worship Lord Shiva as he is easily pleased and award such benedictions. We could find the contrast of the situation where Lord Shiva lives under a Bael tree, and his devotees live in a luxurious environment. Lord Shiva is transcendental to happiness and distress, and he is ever satisfied under the Bael tree. Even in the tenth canto of Srimad Bhagavatam, The Bael tree glorifications are mentioned while the Gopis are in search of Krishna after the disappearance of Krishna from the rasa Lila. Gopis cried in search of Krishna, and they are asking even the deer and kadamba tree as well as Bael tree because they thought the tree could witness the whereabouts of Govinda. Bael trees are also found on the bank of the Yamuna based on the conversation of the Gopis and the Bael tree during the Rasa Lila pastimes. We can see that the Bael tree is located in Vraj Mandal with Krishna's pastimes, as Sukadeva Goswami is answering to Parikshit Maharaj.

LORD SHIVA AND THE DAMARU

Shiva's *Tandava* is the cosmic dance, and his Damaru, a cone shaped drum with the circular design at the two ends, represents the cosmic sound. Sound is transmitted via the ether and the ignition from the false ego. Damaru is a symbol of infinity, endless and the eternal time. It represents that the universe is expanding and collapsing. from where it is expanding, it is collapsing there only. It's a continuous process. It is said in Shiva Mahapurana that the sounds from the Damaru beat the rhythm of the cosmic vibrations, and the energy is activated by the divine Mother or Shakti.

The whole universe is resting on the Pranav mantra or the first word of the universe "Omkar". There are various brahman like Daru Brahma in Jagannath, *Shabda Brahma* as Pranav and the sound of the Damaru, Anna Brahma as the *mahaprasad* of Lord Jagannath and offered to the shakti, Vimala. Sa Re Ga Ma is the basis of the sound vibration and all musical composition, the sound of Damaru is non-different from the Sa Re Ga Ma and the Pranav Mantra. Shiva is the emblem of the dance and music and Bharatanatyam originated from the Damaru of Lord Shiva and composed by the sages. Shiva *Tandava* is very popular, and the rhythm of such uncommon creation comes from the sound of the Damaru and this is the gift to the world. Lord Rudra used the Damaru when he was extremely angry at the death of His dear wife, mother Sati. Lord Shiva used the Damaru when he used it in the procreation of the first son Kartikeya. Damaru sound is the composition of the world, emotions of the entire humanity, the Pranavas, Om and all kinds of music available in the world. Everyone loves music and we should thank the sound of the Damaru as the origin of the mundane world musical creations and the sustenance of cosmology. The movement of the sun and moon occurs due to the sound of the Damaru also.

Jatatavee gala jwalapravaha pavitha sthale

Galae..valambya lambitaam bhujanga tunga malikaam

Damad damad damad damanninaadavaddamavaryam

Chakara chandatandavam tanotu naha Shivaha Shivam.

Damaru is a symbol of infinity (the endless time). It represents that the universe is expanding and collapsing, from where it is expanding, it is collapsing there only. It is a continuous process.

Damaru creates cosmic rhythm and influences the movement of energy in the universe. Such a beautiful verse which is found in Shiva Purana.

In Srimad Bhagavatam, when Markandeya Rsi saw Lord Shiva, he described the Damaru also. You can refer to the Srimad Bhagavatam ŚB 12.10.11-13

ātmany api Shivaṁ prāptaṁ taḍit-piṅga-jaṭā-dharam

try-akṣaṁ daśa-bhujaṁ prāṁśum udyantam iva bhāskaram

vyāghra-carmāmbaraṁ śūla-dhanur-iṣv-asi-carmabhiḥ

akṣa-mālā-ḍamaruka-kapālaṁ paraśuṁ saha

bibhrāṇaṁ sahasā bhātaṁ vicakṣya hṛdi vismitaḥ

kim idaṁ kuta eveti samādher virato muniḥ

"Śrī Mārkaṇḍeya saw Lord Shiva suddenly appear within his heart. Lord Shiva's golden hair resembled lightning, and he had three eyes, ten arms, and a tall body that shone like the rising sun. He wore a tiger skin and carried a trident, a bow, arrows, a sword, and a shield, along with prayer beads, a Damaru drum, a skull, and an ax. Astonished, the sage came out of his trance and thought, "Who is this, and where has he come from?"

It is fascinating to note how Krishnadas Kaviraj Goswami explained the mood of Lord Chaitanya when he saw a devotee of Lord Shiva come near to his home. As per Sri Chaitanya Caritamrta, CC Ādi 17.99

āra dina Shiva-bhakta Shiva-guṇa gāya

prabhura aṅgane nāce, ḍamaru bājāya

On another day, a great devotee of Lord Shiva, chanting of Lord Shiva's qualities, came to Lord Caitanya's house, where he began dancing in the courtyard and playing his ḍamaru [a musical instrument].

CC Ādi 17.100

maheśa-āveśa hailā śacīra nandana

tāra skandhe caḍi nṛtya kaila bahu-kṣaṇa

Then Lord Chaitanya, adopting the mood of Lord Shiva, got on the man's shoulders, and thus they danced together for a long time.

Lord Chaitanya exhibited the mood of Lord Shiva in Navadvip Dham, as mentioned by the author Krishnadas Kaviraj Goswami. Lord Chaitanya, out of His causeless mercy, exhibited many incarnations such as Varaha, Narasimha, Vishnu, etc., and now he is acting like Lord Shiva. This is not difficult for Lord Chaitanya as He declared in Gita that He is Sankara. From our understanding, we should not conclude that we should act like Lord Shiva or Lord Shiva worship is the same as Chaitanya worship. Milk and yogurt are two substances with the root of milk, and One cannot get the same result by drinking yogurt in place of milk. Lord Shiva himself says that *Vishnu Mukti Pradayata*, Vishnu is the savior and Mukunda, the giver of liberations, and (Lord Shiva) I can recommend any sincere seekers to Him as a guru or spiritual preceptors. There is no denial from Lord Chaitanya in this context. Any devotee should not compromise on the chanting of the name of Shiva or Kali and Krishna to be the same. One should always aspire to chant the holy name of Lord Hari so that Hara will be pleased with your actions, and ultimately you will attain the Prema of Hari.

UNIFIED VISION FOR THE TRIMURTI - LORD SHIVA, BRAHMA, AND VISHNU

We find various scriptures and understand that the position of Lord Vishnu as the eternal master and Lord Shiva and Lord Brahma are the servitor gods. They are as close as a god but not the supreme personality of Godhead.

Padma Purana states *"Shivasya sri-visnor ya iha guna-namadi-sakalam*

dhiya bhinnam pasyet sa khalu hari-namahita-karah"

One should be careful to discriminate against the three principal deities as well as must guard against the protocol of not considering them equal and on the one level. As per *Vaishnava Siddhanta*, it is an offense to consider the gods Brahma or Shiva to be the same as Vishnu and think oneself that chanting of name Shiva or Rudra or Brahma is same as Vishnu or Rama.

Similarly, we find the verse in Sri Chaitanya caritamrta as follows,

yas tu nārāyaṇaṁ devaṁ

brahma-rudrādi-daivataiḥ

samatvenaiva vīkṣeta

sa pāṣaṇḍī bhaved dhruvam

[Cc. Madhya 18.116]

"'A person who considers demigods like Brahmā and Shiva to be on an equal level with Nārāyaṇa is to be considered an offender, or pāṣaṇḍī.'"

In this age of Kali, every aspect of the philosophical conclusion is cloudy or distorted, and people only give a statement or judgment based on convenience and social customs. If someone visits a town or village in India, then based on the social custom, some deities, *Gramyadeva*, or the local saints become prominent; They set the standards and tone for the common man to follow. However, an intelligent person should always aspire to learn the conclusion of the Vedas and the learned scholars. We can have many opinions based on the inclinations towards a particular faith, and one cannot ascertain the singular truth from such ambiguity. The best formula is to render services to a learned scholar, and they will eventually impart the knowledge. Srimad Bhagavad Gita, Krishna demands from Arjuna to surrender to Him only, and there is no superior truth. Is Brahma the creator only? Is Shiva the destroyer only? Is Vishnu the maintainer only? How could the disturbed mind of the ages come to a steady answer who is the Lord of all beings? There are many instances in the historical evidence that Lord Vishnu is the supreme Lord in all circumstances. Lord Shiva is the master of the mode of ignorance, Lord Brahma is the master of the mode of passion, and Lord Vishnu is the master of the mode of Goodness. The government has many departments to function its activities; similarly, Lord Vishnu has many departments to function the material world in an efficient manner, and all the crucial demigods are delegated for a special function. One should not bewilder in understanding the ideas of power and interactions of the demigods to the God and being fixed in the vision that Shiva is the greatest Vaishnava and Brahma is also a Vaishnava and Lord Vishnu is the ultimate resort and shelter of the universe. This is the true vision of a seeker of the absolute truth. In this age of Kali, there is only one mantra, the savior of the whole world and all the demigods recommend the same and are pleased by chanting of the holy name of Krishna and Rama in the form of *"Hare Krishna Hare Krishna Krishna Krishna Hare Hare - Hare Rama Hare Rama Rama Rama Hare Hare."* This is the original formula to set the vision in one's life. Our vision should be like that of Uddhava and entirely focus on the chanting of the holy name of the Lord.

LORD SHIVA AS A TAMASI OR TAMO GUNA ADHIKARI

There are three types of *gunas* in the material world, such as modes of goodness, passion, and ignorance. As Vishnu is for the controller of goodness, Brahma is the controller of passion, and Shiva is the controller of ignorance. Shiva is offering his association to the most fallen persons of the world, like the ghosts, rakshasas, pisacas, etc. Generally, we find a picture of Lord Shiva engaged in deep meditation. This image depicts that Lord Shiva is always meditating upon Lord Sankarsana in a trance for the welfare of humanity. Lord Shiva oversees the destruction of the material world whenever it is needed.

Brahma is the creator of the world; Shiva is the destroyer and Maintenance; the most challenging task was governed by Lord Vishnu. Sometimes Rudra and his worshipable Lord, Ananta, or Sankarsana are known as *tamasi.* Lord Shiva is the maintainer and the master of the modes of ignorance; that's the reason for his name as *tamasi.* Truly Shiva is auspicious and beyond the modes of material nature. We know about the three states of qualities such as ignorance, passion, and goodness. Beyond the state of goodness is called *visuddha-sattva. sattvaṁ viśuddhaṁ vasudeva-śabditam,* one must come to the stage of understanding Vasudeva as all in all, and He is transcendental to all the modes then the same being is situated in the *vishuddha sattva* state. Lord Shiva is eternally in the state of the *vishuddha sattva* state. One the contrary, one will be bewildered to see Lord Shiva with the shakti *ghoraya*, i.e all kinds of dangerous energies, Lord Shiva is associating with all kinds of dangerous energies. The inner mood of Lord Shiva is complete trance, and the external behavior is a manifestation of anger, ignorant modes, and many more. Lord Shiva is also in charge of the *tamo-guṇa,* or the mode of ignorance in this material world as found in this verse; *yā devī sarva-bhūteṣu nidra-rūpaṁ saṁsthitā.* Lord Shiva is in associations of all kinds of dangerous energies and dangerous beings, but Lord Shiva is not affected by such association, and he is beyond such jurisdictions of thought process. There is no doubt about Shiva's position as the spiritual master of the entire world, and one should aspire to get the instructions from Lord Shiva. He is truly the best of all yogis.

In Srimad Bhagavatam SB 2.7.39, *ante tv adharma-hara-manyu-vaśāsurādyā māyā-vibhūtaya imāḥ puru-śakti-bhājaḥ,* but at the end there is irreligion, and then Lord Shiva and the atheists full of anger, etc. All of them are different representative manifestations of the energy of the supreme power, the Lord.

DOES LORD SHIVA DRINK MARIJUANA (GANJA)?

Many of us wonder whether Lord Shiva consumes the Bhang or Ganja or Cannabis or Marijuana. If Lord Shiva consumed halahala poison, then he can consume any poisonous leaves as the snakes, dhutura, and ark plants receive the poison from the bit slippery from his hand during the time of churning. Although there was such a significant quantity of poison that it spread all over the universe, Lord Shiva took all of them in his palm, and drank it without any difficulty or suffocation. He did not lose his consciousness also and remained as cool as before. One should not try to imitate Lord Shiva. Lord Shiva can do whatever he likes, but those who try to imitate Lord Shiva by smoking ganja and other poisonous things will certainly be killed because of such activities.

Kṛṣṇa can eat any amount of poison. Even Kṛṣṇa's greatest devotee, Lord Shiva, he can also drink any amount of venom. But the people who follow the path with their sense gratification attitude think that "Lord Shiva smokes gāñjā and he can drink the ocean of poison." So, let us also try to follow the footsteps of Lord Shiva by smoking gāñjā." This is not the highest level of understanding; however, Lord Shiva still wants to bring them to the right path as long as they come to the intellectual consideration of the absolute truth.

Śrīla Śukadeva Gosvāmī continued about the position of Shiva as the savior of the whole world: After informing Bhavānī in this way, Lord Shiva began to drink the poison, and Bhavānī, who knew perfectly well the capabilities of Lord Shiva, gave him her permission to do so. Lord Shiva has no entertainment in consuming the ganja or some material products because He is always beyond the sense of duality of this world.

The reason for bringing this point forward is based on the cult of *aghoris* worship of Lord Shiva, and they firmly believe that Lord Shiva is the one who created *ganja* as a remedy for some incurable diseases and to cure fluctuating human minds. So, it is a ritual for them to smoke *ganja*. Nearly a few people believe this myth to some extent.

Legends refer to the great festival of Lord Shiva, every year in February, Maha-Shivaratri, Hindus from India, and Nepal assemble in Kathmandu for consuming ganja or marijuana. Millions of Hindus gather near the temple of Lord Shiva, known as Pasupatinath, echoing the name of Lord Shiva by chanting *Bam Bholenath, Bam Bholenath, Bam Bam Bholenath, Har Har Mahadev!*

THE REAL MEANING OF SHIVA RATRI

Shivaratri means the night dedicated to worshiping Lord Shiva or also called as the night of Lord Shiva. Shivaratri is celebrated on the thirteenth night of the Krishna paksha or the waning lunar cycle of the month of Phalguna (Feb/Mar). Technically, there will be twelve Shivaratri in a year, and the most important is the Shivaratri, which falls in the month of Phalguna, mostly in Feb/Mar. Numerous puranic incidents describe the Shivaratri as the wedding ceremony day of Shiva and Parvati; some Puranas describe it's a day of annihilation where Lord Shiva perform the *Shiva-tandava* dance for cosmic annihilation, few other Puranas describe it as the drinking of the Halahala poison from the churning of the milky ocean. He was named as Nilakantha on this auspicious day. No matter whatever the reason, every devotee should celebrate the Shiva Ratri, and it would ultimately award the highest spiritual benediction. On Maha Shivaratri, followers of Shiva, as well as other religionists, wake up before sunrise and take a ceremonial bath, preferably in the sanctified waters of Mother Ganga. By observing fasting, offering the Bela-leaf or Jala-Abhishek to the linga and *Panchamrta* Abhishek to Shiva Linga, these various offerings are very pleasing to the Lord, One can chant the mantra *"Om Namah Shivaya"* or the most pleasing mantra to Lord Shiva in this age of Kali is chanting of the maha-mantra "*Hare Krishna Hare Krishna Krishna Krishna Hare Hare Hare Rama Hare Rama Rama Rama Hare Hare.*"

They also offer abir, gulal, white flower, lotus flower. Devil's trumpets (dhutura) and Bael Leaf (belpatra) hold a lot of importance; it is recommended to offer 108 Bael leaves unto the Shiva linga with holy Ganga water. This is most pleasing to Lord Shiva, and He can award anything desirable. Limited Bael leaves are kept on the uppermost portion of the Shivalinga to calm the linga in the higher divine energy which is on high state of energetic heat in its substance. It is believed that devotees who offer a trifoliate Bael Patra to the Shivalinga are certainly the recipient of blessings from Lord Shiva. Enthusiast persons also offer incense sticks, ghee lamps, offer white cloth, a variety of sweets, any five fruits and *panchamrita.*

Once upon a time, a *Nishada* king went for hunting to the jungle along with his dogs, after the day-long search, he could not find any prey for this day, tired and lost in the wilderness, he took rest in a place where it happened to be a Shivalinga, and he washed the linga and being awake the whole night with full devotion to Lord Shiva. After that, he returned home, and sometimes later the king left his body, during the passage of the soul from the body, there is a fight between Yamaraja and Shivagana, and by the will of Lord Shiva, the *Nishada* king was able to be transported to the Kailasa loka to stay forever with Lord Shiva. A similar incident could be found in several Puranas about the hunter who lost his way and climbed to a nearby tree by the fear of a lion, and he jumped onto the top of the tree. Due to fear, he could not sleep the entire night and used to drop a trifoliate leaf, and this happened to be Bael leaf, and on the ground, there was a Shiva Linga, and the night was the Shiva Ratri. With all the combination, the hunter got the *ajnata sukriti* and received the benediction of Lord Shiva by offering the Bael leaf to Shiva Linga and ultimately moved to the abode of Lord Shiva. Nanda Maharaj traveled to Ambikapur near the bank of Sarasvati in Gujarat to celebrate the Shiva ratri, He was accompanied by all the cowherd men along with Krishna and Balarama. Nanda Maharaj, father of Krishna is celebrating Shiva ratri then what to speak of us rejecting the glories of Shiva ratri. Vaishnavas are always eager to celebrate the glorious occasion or the divine night for the pleasure of Lord Shiva and its worshipable master Lord Krishna. Sukadeva Goswami mentioned very nicely in the tenth canto and pointed out as "deva ratra" for Shiva ratri. Nanda Maharaj was rescued from the snake's clutches in the Sarasvati river. We find many references about Shiva ratri as found below from *(Hari Bhakti Vilasa 14/187 from Gautamiya Tantra)*

Shiva Ratri Vrtama Krsna catur-dasyantu Phalgune
Vaisnaver api tat Karyam Sri krishna Priyate sada

On the fourteenth day of the dark fortnight of the month of Phalguna, for the pleasure of Lord Shri Krishna, a Vaishnava should always take a vow to fast.

CRITICISM AGAINST LORD SHIVA

Sometimes, people tend to offend Lord Shiva that he was agitated by seeing the beauty of Mohini, but Lord Shiva is above such rules, and this happened by the will of Yogamaya only as he is the controller of the Mahamaya. When we compare Lord Shiva and Thakura Haridasa and their different response to sex agitation, we found that Haridas Thakur controlled the sex desire at a much higher level than Lord Shiva. However, one should not think that Lord Shiva is degraded and try to criticize him.

We try to bring the position of great personality to our level and try to compare based on such level and consciousness. We will fail to estimate the greatness of such a rare situation. Lord Shiva has never fallen from his devotional platform or the true sense, his position as a spiritual master of a sampradaya, a qualitative incarnation of Lord, and so on. Lord Shiva is attracted by sex desire towards Mohini murti; such an incident should not bring our level of thinking towards Lord Shiva; he is the real *dhira* person whenever Lord Vishnu desires so, no one could check the strength of the Vishnu-Maya. Lord Shiva is the controller of Maha-Maya and the husband of Maha-Maya in the form of Durgadevi. In any way, one should not criticize any Vaishnavas, what to speak of Lord Shiva, even though there are minor irregularities in the behavior of a Vaishnava, it should be compromised and encouraged for further advancement in the spiritual path. Lord Shiva or Lord Brahma are highly advanced personalities, and we should remain humble at their lotus feet and not prone to develop hostility nor try to criticize the great actions performed by them even though they appeared contrary to the Vedic injunctions. Lord Shiva could remain in a very filthy place and still be in the *vishuddha-sattva* state; ordinarily, we cannot imitate such behavior. Sun can purify the contaminated places on the Earth and bring forth pure rain. It has the power as Lord Shiva. The only hope for us to glorify Lord Shiva with no reservations and ask for the boon of Krishna-Prema. Lord Shiva is Ashutosh, and he can grant it to us the same with little effort. So why do we miss the opportunity and involve ourselves in criticizing such an elevated Vaisnavara?

Lord Shiva acted very calmly during the period of heavy criticism by king Citraketu, and it is mentioned in Srimad Bhagavatam SB 6.17.

Citraketu appreciated the exalted position of Lord Shiva, and therefore he remarked at how wonderful it was that Lord Shiva was acting like an ordinary human being. He appreciated Lord

Shiva's position, but when he saw Lord Shiva sitting in the midst of saintly persons and acting like a shameless person, he tried to glorify indirectly with an apparent contrast of criticism. Citraketu did not offend Lord Shiva like Dakṣa. Dakṣa considered Lord Shiva an insignificant being. It is clear that Citraketu wanted to criticize the behavior of his friend Lord Shiva because Lord Shiva was sitting with his wife on his lap. Parvati cursed Citraketu in this regard as she could not tolerate such harsh remarks from Citraketu; however, Lord Shiva did not take this matter seriously. Upon hearing the instructions of Lord Shiva, Pārvatī must have been very much ashamed for therefore she cursed him, but when she understood the teachings of Lord Shiva, she was embarrassed.

Srila Prabhupāda mentioned that there is no harm in worshiping Shiva. Lord Shiva is also called Mahādeva. Amongst the demigods, he is the chief. So, if we worship Lord Shiva, it is not condemned; however, we pray to Lord Shiva for obtaining the love of Krishna. It is not good etiquette to disrespect Shiva out of ignorance and false pride. We offer our utmost respect to Lord Shiva. But that does not mean that he is the Supreme Lord.

In Srimad Bhagavatam, Lord Vishnu is talking about the position of the three deities as ŚB 4.7.50

Lord Vishnu replied: Brahmā, Lord Shiva and I are the principal cause of the material manifestation. I am the Supersoul, the self-sufficient witness. But impersonally, there is no difference between Brahmā, Lord Shiva, and Me.

In all situations, a Vaishnava should not criticize Lord Shiva by any means rather appreciate the position of Lord Shiva in relationship to Lord Krishna; that will be a real success.

LORD SHIVA AND GODDESS KALI

Goddess Kali is the energy of Lord Shiva, and she is the personification of the material energy or the shadow potency of the spiritual power. The famous picture of goddess Kali is raising her tongue out in amazement and stepping on Lord Shiva. It is fascinating to know why this happened. We can also confirm from Srimad Bhagavatam that goddess Kali saved the pure devotee Jada Bharata from the clutches of the rogues and thieves who wanted to offer him as a human sacrifice. Her form is dangerous to view, and demons are not spared of her wrath, so there is no need to worship Kali rather than chant the Hare Krishna mantra incessantly. As per Srimad Bhagavatam ŚB 5.9.18.

bhṛśam amarṣa-roṣāveśa-rabhasa-vilasita-bhru-kuṭi-viṭapa-kuṭila-daṁṣṭrāruṇekṣaṇāṭopāti-bhayānaka-vadanā hantu-kāmevedaṁ mahāṭṭa-hāsam ati-saṁrambheṇa vimuñcantī tata utpatya pāpīyasāṁ duṣṭānāṁ tenaivāsinā vivṛkṇa-śīrṣṇāṁ galāt sravantam asṛg-āsavam atyuṣṇaṁ saha gaṇena nipīyāti-pāna-mada-vihvaloccaistarāṁ sva-pārṣadaiḥ saha jagau nanarta ca vijahāra ca śiraḥ-kanduka-līlayā.

"Intolerant of the offenses committed, the infuriated goddess Kālī flashed her eyes and displayed her fierce, curved teeth. Her reddish eyes glowed, and she displayed her fearsome features. She assumed a frightening body as if she were prepared to destroy the entire creation. Leaping violently from the altar, she immediately decapitated all the rogues and thieves with the very sword with which they had intended to kill Jaḍa Bharata. She then began to drink the hot blood that flowed from the necks of the beheaded rogues and thieves, as if this blood were liquor. Indeed, she drank this intoxicant with her associates, who were witches and female demons. Becoming intoxicated with this blood, they all began to sing very loudly, and dance as though prepared to annihilate the entire universe. At the same time, they began to play with the rogues and thieves' heads, tossing them about as if they were balls."

From this verse, we can learn that even Goddess Kali wanted to save and assist the devotees of Krishna. Jada Bharat was a pure devotee, and he was kept in the hand of dacoits for offering it to Goddess Kali. Dacoits prepared everything, and on the night of Amavasya, they were ready to offer the human sacrifice to Goddess Kali. But such behavior is not acceptable by Goddess Kali even though people offered goats, animals, etc.; she did not like to accept it. Out of formality, she indirectly fulfilled their wishes so that they can come to their senses. Goddess Kali is very much aware of the protections of pure devotees of Krishna; we should be thankful to mother Kali that she is helping every devotee of Krishna to practice their devotion with sincerity. Goddess Kali punishes the *sadhaka* if there is any minor discrepancy in the rituals, why not directly worshiping Lord Krishna, who is the reservoir of all pleasures. Animal sacrifice is forbidden; Buddha stopped it because human society was taking due advantage of the Veda for the tongue's satisfaction, and the same example was given by Goddess Kali, and she appeared herself from the deity form and chopped all the dacoits.

Once upon a time in ancient ages, a demon named Rakta Beeja was mighty as he received the benediction that as soon as the blood came from his body, clones or duplicates would be born from his body. He was close to invincible in battle with demigods; lately, demigods approached Goddess Durga to protect them. The ferocious form she assumed so named as "Kali," chopper in her hand, the hair lashed madly about causing great gusts to carry off a few of the gods supposed to accompany her. She turned about and lifted her ten arms to the unlimited blue atmosphere, laughing all the time frantically. She was enraged with the bad behavior of the demon Rakta Beeja. Goddess attacked the demon with her chopper, as soon as she killed, blood came out from the body of Rakta Beeja, thousands of Rakta Beeja were born from the blood. As he received the boon, blood gushed out and touched the Earth; then new Rakta Beeja was born, she tried to kill the thousands of Rakta Beeja, with her wonder, millions of Rakta Beeja were produced by such killing. Goddess Kali is all-powerful to destroy any demons in the material world; nothing could stop her.

Finally, she exterminated him and drank all his lifeblood until he fell down unconscious. By doing such ghastly actions for a long time, Goddess Kali turns out to be furious and uncontrollable with blood yearning after this episode. She started pirouetting the dance of devastation and overlooked that She had already slain the demon. She butchered whoever came in Infront of her. Seeing this horrific incident, the demigods were perturbed and approached Mahadeva for intervention in this matter. Shiva is even the controller of Shakti in this material world, and he is the one who could control goddess Kali. Upon examining the situation, Shiva could understand that Kali is beyond any direct or straightforward approach. So, Lord Shiva went and put down among the carcasses where the Goddess was twirling. Accidentally, Kali stepped on Shiva and when she comprehended her blunder. It is then her tongue instantly came out of awkwardness, and she was comforted by Shiva's divine intervention. She was very sorry that Her blood longing had prohibited Her from identifying her own master.

In Srimad Bhagavatam, SB 1.15.9, *tenāhṛtāḥ pramatha-nātha-makhāya bhūpā*, the Maha Bhairava worship is mentioned as it was performed by king Jarasandha. Since Jarāsandha possessed demonic qualities from birth, naturally, he became a great devotee of Lord Shiva, the Lord of all ghostly and demoniac men. Rāvaṇa was a great devotee of Shiva, and so also Jarāsandha. He used to sacrifice all arrested kings before Lord Mahābhairava (Shiva), and by his military power, he defeated many small kings and captured them to butcher before Mahābhairava. There are many devotees of Lord Mahābhairava, or Kālabhairava, in the province of Bihar, formerly called Magadha.

LORD SHIVA AND KAMADEVA

Kamadeva is known in the English language as cupid or *madana*, Krishna is called madana-mohana. Kamadeva is also called kandarpa, and in Brahma Samhita, Krishna is known as kandarpa koti kamaniya, which means Krishna cannot be equal to millions of cupids in beauty and He is much more than this. No matter what the comparison, Kamadeva is the God of love in this material world. Kamadeva's glories are mentioned in Matsya Purana, Vishnu Purana, Srimad Bhagavatam, Rg Veda, and Atharva Veda. In Srimad Bhagavatam, Kamadeva is known as Smara and appeared as Pradyumna in Dvaraka Lila. In order to avoid confusion of the quadruple expansion of Pradyumna and Kamadeva, Jiva Gosvami mentioned in Krsna-sandarbha that Kamadeva merged in the body of Pradyumna. Lord Krishna also mentioned in Bhagavad-gītā (10.28), prajanaś cāsmi kandarpaḥ: Krishna says that I am Kandarpa or Smara or Cupid. Kamadeva's birth is mysterious as he appeared as the son of Dharma, the son of Lord Brahma and mostly known as the one of the opulence of Lord Krishna. In Rg Veda (RV 9.113/11), Kamadeva is a portion of Lord Vishnu as corroborated with Gita.

Kamadeva has a beautiful body, he is the most handsome personality of the material world, and he enchants anyone in the mortal world. Kamadeva holds bows and arrows, and his arrows have five dimensions with the flowers of love, such as flowers of mango, jasmine, white and blue lotus, and Ashoka tree. All the flowers combined together are the symbolic fragrance of love generated in the heart of any conditioned beings and carry forward with the conception of love in this world. Kamadeva is surrounded by Gandharvas, Kinnaras, and his favorite pets are cuckoo and parrot. Spring god, Vasanta, is the order supplier of

Kamadeva and makes the world dance as they desire. No one can surpass the arrows of Kamadeva unless one is surrendered to the supreme personality of Godhead.

After the death of Sati, Lord Shiva is practicing severe austerities in the Himalayan mountain range, and Parvati is serving his linga without cessation. As Tarakasura is disturbing hugely and demigods are impatient to take corrective actions against this, the only remedy is that the son needs to be born from Lord Shiva and Parvati. Who else can break the meditation of Shiva? Finally, they begged Kamadeva to induce Lord Shiva with the arrows of love; however, Kamadeva was hesitant to go near Lord Shiva as he knew very well the power of Shiva and his anger. Nevertheless, he never declined any offer of Indra in any circumstances as he obeyed the same principle during the time of Nara-Narayana rsi austerity. Kamadeva was prepared with his armies, his wife Rati, the spring, Gandharvas, and many more followers to create a suitable ambiance for Lord Shiva to break his meditation. By the will of providence, Lord Shiva broke his meditation and looked straight to Kamadeva with anger in his mind as Kamadeva was disturbing in his deep meditation. By the wrath of Lord Shiva, Kamadeva was burnt into ashes in a moment. One can arguably say that why Lord Shiva, the most generous one, became so angry and killed Kamadeva, and even though he conquered lust, kama, however, was still unable to control his anger. One will certainly be bewildered by the activities of great personalities because lust cannot penetrate the heart of Shiva, then possibly the anger is known as Rudra by his anger only. By the divine will of the Supreme, many occurrences of incidents happen for the purpose of lessons to the society and expansion of further pastimes of the Lord. After the incineration of the wrath of Shiva, Kamadeva is also known as Atanu and Ananga because he is disembodied and has no form of a body. The soul is never neither born nor annihilated, but the body is. Rati, the wife of Kamadeva, was in complete sorrow for losing her husband; however, she remained calm and waited for Shiva to shower His mercy. Rati took birth as Mayavati in the house of a fisherman and worshiped Lord Shiva continuously, once she happened to go to the Himalayas to take the direct blessings from Lord Shiva and at the same time, the king of Nisada, Sambara went to Lord Shiva also. Even though Rati came to Shiva first, it was her due to receive the mercy first.

Similarly, Duryodhana appeared in the scene of Krishna, and Lord Krishna first noticed Arjuna. Still, he allowed Duryodhana to ask for his request. Similarly, Lord Shiva is omniscient of the situation and asked Samabara for his wish. Sambara completely forgot the reason for coming and completely attracted to Rati and begged for her hand. Lord Shiva awarded the boon to Rati, in the name of Mayavati; she went along with Sambara, but by her mystic yoga-siddhi, she was untouched by Sambara as she was eternally the consort of Kamadeva.

At the same time, by the mercy of Lord Shiva and the divine will of Lord Krishna, Pradyumna was born from the womb of Krishna, and Kamadeva also entered into Pradyumna when he was stolen by a demon and obtained by Sambara. When Mayavati saw the infant boy, the boy felt affectionately like a mother; however, Mayavati was attracted to the conjugal love. The little boy was astonished, and at the same time, Kamadeva entered the body of Pradyumna, and he was attracted to Mayawati. Mayavati explained the details about their previous birth and new birth. It is mysterious to know the details about how an infant became an adult in a day and got married. Everything in the realms of Krishna happened by the divine will of the Lord without the influence of time and space. Kamadeva is an expansion from the *citta*, or the mind of the Lord, and the arrangement made to attain a body with the same expansion of Pradyumna. All such mysterious incidents happened by the will of Lord Krishna and a mixture of the causeless mercy of Lord Shiva unto Kamadeva. Ultimately one's attainment is supreme when one deals with either Lord Shiva or Lord Vishnu. One must understand the absolute reality and its logical truth in Vedic Sastra's viewpoints. Pradyumna is the quadruple expansion of Lord Vishnu, and there is no doubt about it, and Kamadeva is the partial representation of Lord Vishnu also. Both these personalities can be one by the divine will of the Lord. Whoever hears this episode of Lord Shiva with faith and devotion will certainly conquer both lust and anger.

LORD SHIVA GLORIFIES MARKANDEYA RSI

Markandeya is the son of great sage Markanda, and he was very much sincere, devoted, austere, and knowledgeable since his childhood. There is a Purana named Markandeya Purana in his name, and Markandeya even countered his fate of death and remained immortal for many *kalpas* of Brahma. In Jagannath Puri, the place of Markandeya linga and Sarovar is very much famous. Markandeya is glorified by Sukadeva Goswami in Srimad Bhagavatam Canto twelfth chapter ten. Sukadeva Goswami even declared that anyone who hears the pastimes of Markandeya would certainly be liberated from the material pangs of life. Markandeya was blessed by Lord Krishna to give darshan of his lotus feet in a banyan leaf floating in the cosmic devastation water.

Once upon a time, a sage named Markandeya was in complete meditation with high powered austerity and mysticism. Fortunately, enough, Lord Shiva and his dear wife Gauri were traveling in the sky, and by the request of Gauri, they wanted to come and meet Markandeya rsi. Such fortune comes very rarely to a person, it happened to Pracetas, and now the mercy is manifested to Markandeya. If Lord Shiva has offered the love of Godhead to two sets of sages in Srimad Bhagavatam, then where is the question of offending him and deriding him? Such a person cannot be considered as Vaishnava. Lord Shiva and Gauri, out of their sweet will, appeared near the hermitage of Markandeya. At that time, the radiance, the fragrance and the divinity maddened the thoughts and intellects of Markandeya muni. When Markandeya saw both Lord Shiva and Parvati with all the opulence of Rudraksha bead, Damaru in his hand, snakes in his neck, he was filled with joy and happiness. He was in the union of love with the enchanting face and gorgeous presence of both Lord Shiva and Mother Gauri. By seeing them, Markandeya offered prostrated obeisances and glorified them with hymns and prayers for their pleasure.

Lord Shiva and Gauri were extremely pleased with his devotion, austerity, and humility. And certainly, the divine Lord will bestow mercy and blessings if the sage is extremely meek and humble. We should learn the art of being meek and humble so that spiritual success will be easier. As usual, Ashutosh asked him for any benedictions he liked to receive and without further asking from Markandeya rsi, Lord Shiva offered him six boons such as Markandeya will never become old, will not be inflicted with any disease, will be famous in the three worlds, will have knowledge of past, present and future, the science of self-realization, will become a spiritual teacher and preacher in Puranas. Upon receiving the benedictions, Markandeya was deeply grateful and offered repeated prayers to Lord Shiva. Lord Shiva is very pleased with Markandeya because he attained the state of equality of all spirit souls as one, and he has full knowledge of all the three principal deities Brahma, Vishnu, and Mahesvara. There is no sense of duality ideology in Markandeya, and he has full clarity and understanding of Shiva and Vishnu. He has developed a sense of true understanding of the material and spiritual world. As he is favored by Lord Shiva, Lord Krishna gave him the audience of his baby form darshan in a banyan leaf during the universal dissolution. Markandeya is a renowned sage in the Vedic history, and whoever listens or hears the glorious meeting of Markandeya with Lord Shiva will certainly be free from material nature and ultimately attain love of Godhead.

As per Skanda Purana, "*Markendeyovata Krushno darubrahma Mahodadhi – Indradyumna sarashaivam panchatirtha Vidhi smrutah*||

Markandeya, Kalpavriksha, Darubrahma, Mahodadhi, Indradyumna Sarovar are the five principal tirthas in Puri as mentioned above. In another scripture, Mukti Cintamani, it is mentioned that "*Markendayobatokrishney, Rohiniyam ca Mahodadhi, Indradyumna sare snatam punarjanma na labhyate.*" If one takes bath in Markandeya pond, Sweta Ganga, Rohini Kunda, Mahodadhi, and Indradyumna Sarovar, then one doesn't take birth in this material world. We should aspire to go to the abode of Lord Jagannath and always remain there forever.

LORD SHIVA AND BRHASPATI

Brhaspati is the spiritual master of the demigods in heavenly planets. He sets an example not only to the heavenly world but also to the earthly planets also, and his teachings are worth imbibing for our own growth. He gives guidance to the demigods as needed and performs various sacrifices for the welfare of the demigods. Demigods attain peace, prosperity, and strength by the mercy of Brihaspati. When the selection for the spiritual master was to be determined for the heavenly world, both Sukracarya and Brihaspati were in the competition, and Brihaspati was selected for the post, this angered Sukracarya and he took the position of the spiritual masters of the demons. Sukracarya is also mentioned as a Kavi in Bhagavad Gita by Lord Krishna. In Srimad Bhagavatam, ŚB 9.14.6, *haro guru-sutaṁ snehāt*, the meaning of *haro* is Lord Shiva and his affectionate behavior towards Brihaspati because he is the son of Angira and Angira is the spiritual master of Shiva. It is natural to follow one's spiritual master. On the other hand, Sukracarya and Brihaspati are natural enemies and Sukracarya needed to take the side of Chandra as he found a golden opportunity. Sukadeva Goswami pointed out that Shiva is accompanied by numbers of ghosts, demons who were eager to take part in the fierce battle.

On many occasions, we have found out that there is fighting between demons, demigods, but occasionally there is infighting between demigods also. Due to the relationship issue between soma dev (moon god) and Brihaspati about the claimant of the son and the affairs between the wife of Brihaspati and moon God. A big quarrel and dispute occurred in lieu of such a relationship, love, and emotional state of mind. Both moon god and Brihaspati accused each other of the fault, and moon god did not even return Tara, wife of his spiritual master. This happened due to the excessive pride and arrogance of the moon god who dared to kidnap his spiritual master's wife.

Upon not able to resolve, there is about to be a huge fight happening and many demigods sided each of their favorites, Sukracarya looking for the opportunity, took the side of Moon-god so that he could attack Brihaspati, his eternal enemy. King Indra, of course, inclined towards his spiritual master, took the side of Brihaspati. Lord Shiva, who also joined the hands of the war and supported Brihaspati for multiple reasons. The primary reason for supporting Brihaspati is due to him as his godbrother because Lord Shiva accepted Angira as the spiritual master. Lord Chaitanya accepted Isvara Puri as the spiritual master, similarly Lord Shiva has an eternal spiritual master in this material world named Angira; *aṅgirasaḥ sakāśāt prāpta-vidyo hara iti prasiddhaḥ*: Brihaspati is the son of Angira, and this is the main reason Lord Shiva took the side. The second reason is that Brihaspati was a brahmin, and the spiritual master of the heavenly planets and Shiva has the abode in the heavenly kingdom as Kailash Hills. Thirdly, it is injustice from moon god to kidnap the wife of his spiritual master. It is unknown at this point whether Shiva has already decorated the crescent moon or not, otherwise, how could he abandon moon god in such a situation. This episode is the most intriguing portion of Srimad

Bhagavatam, and one should be careful in knowing the subject matters by surrendering to all the spiritual masters of the world.

There is a famous Guruvayur temple in South India, which was initiated by God of Winds (Vayu) and Brhaspati (Jupiter), and the temple was installed with the help of Lord Shiva.

LORD SHIVA AS A MAHAJANA

Out of twelve great authorities in the line of teachings of the essence of the religion in the world, Lord Shiva is one of them. As per the discussion between the yamadutas and Yamaraja, He is speaking the authority of the religion, as per Srimad Bhagavatam SB 6.3.20,

svayambhūr nāradaḥ śambhuḥ

kumāraḥ kapilo manuḥ

prahlādo janako bhīṣmo

balir vaiyāsakir vayam

"Lord Brahmā, Bhagavān Nārada, Lord Shiva, the four Kumāras, Lord Kapila [the son of Devahūti], Svāyambhuva Manu, Prahlāda Mahārāja, Janaka Mahārāja, Grandfather Bhīṣma, Bali Mahārāja, Śukadeva Gosvāmī and I myself (Yamaraj) know the real religious principle."

Lord Shiva is one of the Mahajanas who is fully conversant with the transcendental knowledge and capable of delivering the entire world. Mahajana means the great personality who is aware of the great spiritual science for the great cause of human welfare. The spiritual science, the knowledge about God, is the most confidential knowledge, and one, by fortune, only meets or comes in contact with a Mahajana. One Mahajana does not contradict with another Mahajana, and they follow the footsteps of a great Mahajana or God. Their knowledge and mechanism of delivery are so sublime to suit according to the place, time, and circumstances. Mahajana should be a recognized person, and here Yamaraj himself declares to his servants about the twelve Mahajanas and Lord Shiva is one of the prominent Mahajanas who sets such high standards of code of religion that general people naturally get attracted to such principles and get benefitted.

Sometimes, people argue that if the Vedic scriptures are so complex, then what's the significance of their use? The Mahajan's role is to simplify and present the knowledge to the common mass of people without adulteration. Lord Krishna has spoken about the Bhagavat Dharma in Gita, and many followers of Gita present the same principles by following the aphorism *"mahajana yena gata sa pantha."* Great authorities in the Vedic knowledge should be strictly followed to know the real goal of life. Lord Shiva is also a Mahajan, and we should all respect the twelve Mahajanas as the propounder of the *Sanatana dharma*. Narada Muni has preached to many kings, brahmins, kshatriyas, shudras and even to animals like a snake. That's the potency of a Mahajana. Lord Rudra is million times superior to Prahlad because he knows and preaches on *asta-kaliya-lila*, the *rasa tattva* of Lord Krishna. Even though Prahlad Maharaj and Shiva are in the category of Mahajan. On the other hand, Lord Shiva always glorifies Prahlad and consider him a superior devotee of Lord Vishnu, that's the nature of a true Vaishnava and Mahajan.

LORD SHIVA WITH MOHINI

Each of us is interested to learn about new things, new innovations, new manifestation, and a new adventure. Lord Shiva, after drinking the halahala poison coming out of the churning of the milk ocean. Lord Shiva was absent during the process of obtaining the *amrita* or nectar. It is clearly to be understood that Lord Shiva is not a demigod, and neither he needs amrita to be immortal. He is beyond the laws of the material nature. He is interested in learning the absolute majestic opulence of Lord Vishnu. He was contemplating the Mohini murti of Lord Vishnu, and he was filled with joy and wonder that Lord Vishnu could do anything impossible. His curiosity and inquisitiveness were not checked further, and out of transcendental emotion, Lord Shiva told his wife Gauri that he would like to see Lord Vishnu and inquire about the Mohini murti. Mother Parvati is always obliged to her husband and nodded with the proposal.

All the Shiva *Ganas* planned for a picnic-like excursion as they all followed Lord Shiva to go to *Svetadvipa* and meet Lord Vishnu. Lord Vishnu is not accessible to even demigods; they usually come to the milk ocean shore and offer *Purusha- sukta* prayers, and then they are able to see Lord Vishnu. In this case, Lord Shiva and his associates like ghosts and goblins are even qualified to enter and see the Lord face to face. This is the mercy of Lord Shiva unto his followers. All the *bhutagana*, ghosts, Nandi, Gauri, and Lord Shiva, started for the journey to meet Lord Vishnu. Upon seeing Lord Vishnu, Lord Shiva offered various prayers: "You are the Supersoul of everyone, you are impartial, and nothing is impossible in your domain." Lord Vishnu was duly satisfied with Lord Shiva and offered seating arrangements for Shiva, Gauri and other associates of Lord Shiva. This is social etiquette, as followed by Lord Vishnu, and we can take an example on how to treat a guest and exalted guest like Lord Shiva. Lord Shiva asked his core desire in his heart to see the Mohini murti of the Lord, and how Mohini bewildered the demons. Lord Vishnu was hesitant to show this form as it's unusual, and so many of the associates are present. However, Lord Vishnu can reveal his confidence upon the request of a saintly personality like Lord Shiva. Lord Vishnu does not consider any difference between Him and Lord Shiva.

Finally, He manifested as a beautiful woman and displayed extraordinary beauty. All of the associates were struck with wonder and felt joyful within. But Vishnu Maya is so powerful that it can bewilder even Lord Shiva. Upon seeing Mohini's extraordinary beauty, her glance, the three-bend form, thin waist, the restless eyes, Lord Shiva was attracted. She was wearing a beautiful saree and was playing with a ball. As she was running after the ball, her breasts were moving to, and fro, and her two soft feet with tinkling bells were amazing to watch upon her movement. During the course of the playing, her saree got loosened, and her hair was scattered on her face. She tried to settle herself, and intermittently, she glanced upon Lord Shiva. Upon seeing the interaction of the beautiful dealings of a beautiful woman, Lord Shiva completely forgot that his wife and associates were nearby and was fully absorbed in the form of Mohini. This is also called trance but in the illusory display of Vishnu Maya. How come the ghosts nearby Lord Shiva are not affected with lust? Similarly, one can arguably ask how the demigods were not influenced by lust when Mohini distributed the nectar to them. It is the desire of Lord Shiva to be captivated by Vishnu and simultaneously the will of Lord Vishnu. Lord Vishnu made a declaration form with Shiva before showing the Mohini murti that please do not blame me if you are entrapped by the beautiful mystical woman. After a while, the cool breeze took the sari and the belt away from the opulent body of Mohini. Then she disappeared, and Lord Shiva, with full force, left the company of Bhavani and followed Mohini in the bushes. His lusty desires were so powerful that he wanted to embrace her and enjoy with her unlimitedly. Again, by seeing Mohini murti in her full-blown naked form, Shiva forcefully embraced her, and by such impulsive force, Mohini tried to escape from Shiva's arm. In this course, Shiva discharged semen, and many people say that Ayyappa was born from the semen. Gold mines and minerals in the universe were created by the discharge of the semen. After the semen's discharge, the lusty desires came to an end, Lord Shiva came to his senses, and Lord Vishnu appeared in front of him again. He was very sorry for this incident; however, Lord Vishnu mentioned that was the power of Maya. Even Parvati is the goddess of Maya in the material world; however, Lord Shiva was still captivated by Vishnu Maya. One must surrender fully to the supreme Lord in order to overcome the insurmountable fort of Maya.

LORD KRISHNA SAVED LORD SHIVA

In Srimad Bhagavatam's seventh canto chapter 10, we hear the descriptions of Tripurari which is narrated by Narada to his dear most disciple Yudhishthira Maharaj.

Yudhishthira Maharaj was curious to know about the details of Tripura and Tripurari, how Lord Shiva was named as Tripurari. And, the most interesting episode in this section is how Lord Krishna saved Lord Shiva and how he saved him, and why did he do so? Narada is fully conversant in all the historical details with a philosophical conclusion. Maya Danava built a castle in the sky and offered it to the demons. Maya is the replica of the Vishwakarma of the heavenly planet. Sukracarya is the spiritual master of demons, Brihaspati is the spiritual master of demigods. Similarly, Maya Danava is the architect or the chief engineer of demons so as Visvakarma for the demigods. He has so detailed technical knowledge in machinery, and even no great scientists could defeat him in his knowledge. During the time of forest sacrifice to the Agni by Arjuna and Krishna, Arjuna saved Maya Danava and spared his life, in reward he built the beautiful and gorgeous palace for Pandavas in Indraprastha. Maya Danava built the three invincible, invisible, inspiring residences for the demons, which constituted three layers and three divisions, thus the name was called Tripura. There is a state Tripura in India resembling the opulent as defined in the scripture. Demons are very much powerful by the strength of the residence quarter built by Maya Danava. Not only that, but Maya also built a nectarean pond inside the Tripura palace. Anyone who takes a dip into the pond will resume infinite strength and continue a new life if he is dead. This facility gives immense power for the demons as whenever they die, Maya Danava puts them into the pond, and they come alive.

Demigods were very much perturbed with the torture of the demons and petitioned to Lord Shiva for protection. If there is intellectual wisdom guidance, they approach Lord Brahma, if there is complete distress, military assistance, they approach Lord Shiva. If nothing works, they approach Lord Vishnu, the ultimate shelter of the universe. Decorated with his bow, arrows, trident, and other military assets Lord Shiva attacked the demons. All of them were vanquished in a minute. Lord Shiva thought at least he was able to control the demons in no time. At the same time, Maya Danava collected all the corpses as well as ashes and put them into the nectar pond. Suddenly the division of military armies, fully vigor and powerful, emerged from the pond and ready to attack Lord Shiva. The cycle continued for some time, and Lord Shiva got fatigued and bewildered as to how they were re-emerging again and again. Seeing the condition of Lord Shiva, Lord Vishnu appeared there and consoled Shiva that he will assist in the situation for a complete win for him. Lord Vishnu converted himself as a cow, and Lord Brahma as a calf, the cow and the calf went to the pond of Tripura and drank all the water. Even though Maya Danava was watching the incident of drinking the water from the pond, he could not prohibit the cow and calf due to the influence of Vishnu Maya. After vanquishing the water, they returned back to Lord Shiva. Lord Vishnu also awarded various weapons and ornaments such as chariot, bow, arrow, artillery, and shield, and many other forms of defense system to equip Lord Shiva. Lord Shiva was glowing and being confident, he attacked the demons and completely vanquished all the demons. Maya Danava could not do anything as the pond was dry by then. Lord Shiva easily destroyed the Tripura city, so he is popularly known as Tripurari. In such a situation, Lord Krishna saved Lord Shiva and increased his reputation as Tripurari. Yudhishthira Maharaj was very much joyful upon hearing the pastimes of the Lord from the lotus mouth of Narada.

LORD SHIVA AND DESCENT OF MOTHER GANGES

In Srimad Bhagavatam's ninth canto ninth chapter, Ganges' descent by the sincere prayer of king Bhagiratha is mentioned. Mother Ganga is also called as the Ganges for English speaking people, and both the names are the same. Out of love, people called her Ganga-Maiya also. In the sacrifice of Bali Maharaj, Lord Vamana appeared and begged for three steps however in two steps Lord Vaman covered this world and the upper world, Due to the extension of His gigantic left leg unto the tip of the universe like a balloon, from his toenail there caused a small hole. The rush of Viraja water fell into the world. It first washed the lotus feet of Lord Vamana and sanctified by the bathing of the lotus feet of the Lord. The river is known as Ganga directly which fell into the immediate planet known as Brahmaloka or Satyaloka, the planet of Lord Brahma. The *kamandalu* of Brahma was filled with the holy water of Ganges. It sanctified the whole Satya loka and heavenly planets. The appearance of Ganga was caused by Lord Vamandeva and Bali Maharaj.

Once upon a time, King Sagara performed a horse sacrifice with his sixty thousand sons. As usual, the jealous Indra stole the horse the kept it in the ashram of Kapila muni. When the sons of Sagara searched for the horse, they dig the Earth to reach the nether-lands and found the horse. They noticed that a sage is also meditating in the same place. They thought the sage to be the real thief of the horse and tried to disturb his meditations. By the offense at the lotus feet of Lord Kapiladev, all the sons were burnt to ashes by the heat produced from their own body due to the aggression. Many kings appeared in the dynasty of Sagara to help liberate the sons but in vain. Finally, king Bhagiratha worshiped Lord Brahma and pleased him to allow the Ganga to come down. Then, he worshiped Mother Ganga to come down to the Earth. There was still a problem in all aspects of how the earth is going to bear the massive flow of Ganga. Bhagiratha could not find anyone other than Lord Shiva because he knew that Shiva drank the poison from the churning of the milk ocean and could help him in this dilemma. He worshiped Lord Shiva with great austerity and devotion. Lord Shiva appeared in front of Bhagiratha and bestowed that let Ganga fall unto Earth via me and let all your wishes be fulfilled. Ganga's flow is so furious that Ganga was arrogant and fell with rapid speed on the head of Lord Shiva near the Himalayan range in India. Ganga underestimated the potency of Lord Shiva and tried to assess the power of Lord Shiva, Shiva, not only sustained the flow of Ganges rather he kept the Ganges into his matted hair and Ganga fell in love with Shiva also within the matted hair. Parvati was jealous of Ganga's activities in Shiva's hair. Lately, the mysterious Kartikeya was born via Parvati and Ganga. Ganga is also the mother of Bhisma, and there is a long story related to Ganga and Shantanu's marriage. Bhagiratha was driving with his golden chariot and made a path to Ganga to go until the point where the sons of Sagara or his forefathers were burnt to ashes. By the sprinkle of the water from the Ganges, anyone could be liberated, and so it happened, and all the sons of Sagara resumed their body and went to heaven. This is the potency of the sprinkling of Ganga water, then what to speak of its power of worship to Shiva linga or to Radha Madhav. By worshiping Radha-Madhava in Navadvipa, one would surely attain Krishnaloka or Vaikuntha without a doubt.

LORD SHIVA AND VRKASURA

In Srimad Bhagavatam's tenth canto chapter eighty-eight, it is mentioned the description of Shiva saved from the demon Vrkasura by the intervention of Krishna. We learn about the benedictions given by Lord Shiva unto Vrkasura and how it turned out to be too dangerous. To be liberal is a good thing, however, not to apply the strictness, it could be fatal. In current days, democracy sets up the government, people tend to adopt the path of liberal approach and give their opinion, but the factual outcome could be different. Lord Vishnu is very strict in awarding any boons to anyone, he considers various items and qualifications and ultimately awards the boon, and His boon is also eternal. Lord Shiva is very generous and magnanimous and always wants to please everyone who comes for a good reason or a bad reason. This is the arrangement of the divine world, whereas at least someone should be liberal enough so that demons can take due advantage of the situation. When an undue person receives more than what he deserves, they create massive disturbance in the society, ecology, environment, and traditional value system. In today's scenario, we can see how human beings are completely exploiting the plants, animals, minerals, oil, and water for their selfish enjoyment.

Once upon a time, there lived a demon named Vrka, and he desired to obtain more power, and he approached Narada muni for advice. Being omniscient, the spiritual master of the three worlds, Narada advised Vrka that it's better to worship Lord Shiva as He is Ashutosh, easily and quickly pleased, and he is powerful too, and he can award anything you need. This was music to the ear of Vrka as he was looking for such an answer, Narada muni knows well that demons won't listen to good advice; however, all fruitive results they are looking for. Vrka went to the place near the mountain Kedarnath, a beautiful place in India and one of the famous pilgrimages of Shiva in India. He found a suitable place near the bank of a creek and started worshiping Lord Shiva, and he made arrangements for the fire sacrifice as it was suggested by Narada muni. Demons also invented their new and unauthorized manner of the system in fire sacrifice to suit their needs or fulfill extravagant demand or adamant and arrogant behavior. Vrka thought it is beneficial and easier to please Lord Shiva by offering one's flesh unto the fire sacrifice. This intention and activities are generated from the mode of passion, and he started offering his own flesh in the name of Shiva. By torturing one's own body, mind, one should not offer any prayer or sacrifices to the Lord, Lord being the

Supersoul, he is not happy with such an attempt. Person born of the mode of lower thought process has no other means to adopt lowly actions and is tailored to please Lord Shiva. After offering the flesh of his own body, there is still no sign of Lord Shiva appearing on the scene. Vrka thought of offering his head or himself in the fire sacrifice so that he can please Lord Shiva; these are madness, and out of extreme greed for power, they can do anything and everything. When Vrka started to offer his own head to Lord Shiva, Shiva, out of His causeless mercy, appeared in front of Vrka, such appearance of Shiva is out of formality and compulsion and not of his affection. Lord Shiva appeared to Pracetas out of compassion, devotion, and empathy for the devotees of Lord Krishna. Lord Shiva is very sincere towards the people who are aspiring for sincere spiritual seekers. Here, in this case of Vrka, he had to appear; otherwise, his name will be defamed because Vrka is about to commit suicide.

Lord Shiva asked Vrka, "Whatever desire you have for worshiping me will be fulfilled. My words never go in vain. Please ask, dear Vrka". Shiva is merciful to the fallen souls, but sometimes the outcome is too dangerous. He knew that Krishna would tackle any situation as Lord Shiva is completely surrendered to Lord Krishna. Vṛka said, "May annihilation of the living being come to whomever I simply touch upon the head with my any hand." Lord Shiva, without any consideration, said Yes to Vrka. The immediate moment for Vrka was heavenly as he received such a great boon, and there was a great relief in his mind. Demons remain demons even though you make friendship, or you award them something substantial. The ungrateful Vrka, instead of thanking Shiva or even offering prayers to Shiva, thought about how to try this benediction upon Shiva and then enjoy Parvati later on. These foolish actions are bewildering as they try to misuse the system of divinity; however, the end result in such cases is always destructive. Losing any further moment, Vrkasura approached Lord Shiva to touch on his head. Lord Shiva was not even prepared for such demoniac action from

Vrkasura. As Lord Shiva had given many boons to the demons; however, Vrka was the worst among the demons. Lord Shiva, out of fear of such a situation, the effect of Boomerang, own good comes for the worst destruction, and runs out of the scene. Vrkasura chases Lord Shiva wherever he is fleeing in fear of Vrka. He traveled from one planet to another, Bilva Svarga, Bhu Svarga, Deva Svarga, and even *Brahmaloka* and ultimately ended up in *Svetadvipa*, the island or the planet of Lord Vishnu in this material world. It is very interesting to note that Vrka, being the demon, has the capability to come to the *Svetadvipa*. *Svetadvipa* is even not accessible to the powerful demigods of the material universe but how Vrkasura got to enter this planet. This is the power of association with a great Vaisnavara, and the same situation occurred in terms of Durvasa and Amabrish Maharaj's episode. Narada and brother of Ambarish Maharaj episode revealed the glories of even a moment of association with a pure devotee, and how one can even attain Vaikuntha by such association, *Sadhu sanga sadhu sanga sarva Sastra koi, lava matra sadhu sanga sarva siddhi hoi*. All the revealed scriptures inform us that the moment association of a pure devotee can grant access until the point of Vaikuntha, even to an unworthy demon. Then the future of the devotee is so elevated that one could not imagine the ultimate position for a pure devotee.

When Lord Vishnu saw the precarious condition of Lord Shiva and the Vrkasura chasing after him, he appeared in the scene as a beautiful Brahman boy like Vaman incarnation. Lord has innumerable form, and out of his sweet will, he took the form of a small brahman boy. Lord Shiva had the power to kill Vrka by his trident, but he did not do so because he had awarded him the boon, and it would be infamy to kill a worshiper. Lord Vishnu might have employed the Sudarsan cakra to kill Vrka, but he did not do so because he knew well how to manage the demon. Why unnecessarily employ such a powerful weapon to an unworthy fool? Lord could kill anyone by the wind, lightning, mountains, natural disease, and many other forms because all the agents of death, including the Yamaraj, are his servants and order carriers. As a small brahmin boy, he appeared on the way to Vrka, and he asked with respect, where are you going? I am glad to see you as the son of a great personality, and I know your grandfather. Anyone who speaks about your family history, that's to a stranger, the person will eventually stop and engage in a conversation. We use similar techniques in our book distribution methods by personally engaging with a human touch. Lord Vishnu shared the human touch formula to all of us. We need to be humble and personal with the demons by asking their welfare also. Vrkasura was struck with wonder upon seeing the beauty of the little brahmin, and more puzzled was how Lord Vishnu knew about his family history. The little brahmin said, ``I know everything about you, and I know you are running the marathon for a crazy person like Shiva, who has no power. He lived with the hobgoblin and lost his power after the curse of his father-in-law, Daksha." Most likely, this incident happened after the Daksha Yajna.

Vrkasura wondered why He was blaspheming Lord Shiva. Of course, not. But Vishnu was trying to calm the demon and subdue him by this transaction. Lord Vishnu in the disguise of the brahmin boy told, "I doubt the power of Lord Shiva is still valid, and you are unnecessary wasting your time by running after Him. Have you checked it yourself about the impact of the boon? Does it work? Lord Shiva is Bholenath, and he might have told you something, and it has no meaning to it." Vrkasura said, "It's impossible as Lord Shiva gave this blessing to me, and there is no doubt about it. But it seems that this boy is telling the truth. Let me try the boon on myself first." Being tricked by Vishnu, he put his hands on his own head and was shattered into the ground with a blow of ashes around the place. Lord Shiva came towards the brahmin boy and Lord Vishnu reappeared in his original form. All the demigods from the sky showered flowers upon the victory of Vrkasura and Lord Shiva thanked Vishnu for taking care of Him again. This is the power of the relationship between Lord Vishnu and Lord Shiva and how they vanquished a demoniac person like Vrkasura. We don't need to experiment on the auspicious benedictions of the Lord otherwise we fall victim of demoniac thoughts. Better to surrender to the process of devotional process directly unto the Supreme Lord.

SIVOHAM

Sivoham means I am Lord Shiva, or I will become Lord Shiva, or I will merge with Lord Shiva. The concept of oneness as there is only one concept of merging into the impersonal Brahman as a form of Lord Shiva and chant the mantra "sivoham sivoham sivoham" for the attainment of the highest stage. Srila Prabhupāda mentioned that they say *Shivaham or sivoham*, "I am Shiva." They are impersonalist. If you are Shiva, then why are you worshiping Shiva? That is an impersonalist idea. It is not the becoming process as every living being has a constitutional position in the spiritual world, and we need to awaken ourselves to know our position. Lord Shiva is in perfect knowledge of His position, and the spirit soul is not Lord Shiva. This is a false conception and will mislead the goal of spiritual life.

Lord Shiva never accepts any luxurious dress, garland, ornament, or ointment. But those who are not self-realized in the spiritual life, such persons do not understand Lord Shiva. Such people are always hankering after material comforts and enjoyment, and they seek the shelter of Lord Shiva for such boons. There are two sections of followers of Lord Shiva. One is completely in the gross materialistic concept of life desiring to obtain some material boon, and the other class desires to become one with him. They are mostly impersonalist and prefer to chant *śivo' ham*, "I am Shiva," or "After liberation, I shall become one. Devotees of Lord Shiva should worship Him and ask for the best boon from Him, i.e., devotional service to Lord Krishna. That's the real and ultimate goal of life, and this misconception of I am Shiva or will become Shiva needs to be eradicated from the consciousness.

SHIVA-JVARA AND VISHNU-JVARA

Jvara means the temperature during the time of illness; sometimes, it is said that the high temperature in any human body is sure that death is approaching. Nowadays, people fear temperature due to the COVID-19 virus issues, and Lord Shiva and Lord Vishnu also control the temperature through the agency of many demigods of the material world. One must conclude that every virus movement is also happening by the will of the demigods and the karmic reactions. At all points of time, one should surrender to the Supreme Lord for the protection and betterment of society. There are two types of Jvara, one is Shiva-Jvara, and the other one is Vishnu-Jvara. It is very interesting to note how both the Jvaras being the representative of Lord Shiva and Lord Vishnu performed a battle, and this incident is noted in Srimad Bhagavatam.

In SB 10.63.22,

vidrāvite bhūta-gaṇe

jvaras tu trī-śirās trī-pāt

abhyadhāvata dāśārhaṁ

dahann iva diśo daśa

"After Lord Shiva's followers had been driven away, the Shiva-jvara, who had three heads and three feet, pressed forward to attack Lord Kṛṣṇa. As the Shiva-jvara approached, he seemed to burn everything in the ten directions.

The various descriptions about Shiva-Jvara is also found in other scriptures and great acharya Śrīla Viśvanātha Cakravartī's commentary.

jvaras tri-padas tri-śirāḥ

ṣaḍ-bhujo nava-locanaḥ

bhasma-praharaṇo raudraḥ

kālāntaka-yamopamaḥ

"The terrible Shiva-jvara had three legs, three heads, six arms, and nine eyes. Showering ashes, he resembled Yamarāja at the time of universal annihilation."

Is it not interesting to learn how the two types of Jvara are fighting each other as if they are the most powerful weapons? God has various tools to control and rule the material nature. As the Jvara are the weapons of the two Lords, and they are in the fighting spirit as the war was ensued by Lord Shiva and Lord Krishna. We might wonder, related to the COVID-19 and Coronavirus, does Lord play any role in controlling the movement of the virus and the disease. Everything in the world is controlled by the Lord, and the growth, expansion, death of the virus is also dependent on the Lord's will and is manifested based on the sinful reactions of the society. When Shiva-Jvara was in full swing to attack Lord Vishnu, at the same time, the counter weapon was released from the lotus hand of Lord Krishna, fever weapon, Vishnu-Jvara. Both the fever weapons fought in the battle, and Vishnu-Jvara had the superior power, and it dominated the strength of the fever weapon of the Shiva-Jvara and loudly cried when caught in the grip of the rim of Vishnu-Jvara. There was no way of escaping from the fever weapon of Vishnu. Shiva-Jvara was trembling and there was no other means than to surrender the master of the Vishnu-Jvara, Lord Krishna. With folded hands, he begged at the lotus feet of Lord Krishna for protection. This could be an ideal situation as why Shiva-Jvara did not surrender to his master Lord Shiva however to Lord Vishnu.

Yamaraj instructed his servants about the Mahajanas and whoever surrenders unto Lord Krishna is not subjected to the jurisdictions of hell. Lord Shiva also gave solid instructions to all his weapons; the ultimate shelter of the universe is Lord Krishna. Remembering the instructions from Lord Shiva, Shiva-Jvara applied his mind and surrendered to Lord Krishna for protection. Secondly, he knew Vishnu-Jvara is also controlled by Lord Krishna, it is better to ask for his mercy at the crucial time in the battle. Shiva-Jvara is glorifying the Lord with all kinds of valuable prayers; whatever he heard from his master Lord Shiva, such as, "You are the most charitable personality of the three world, You are the foundation of the cosmos and You are Ananta, the unlimited etc. People in this world are suffering due to the forgetfulness of Your form and qualities. No one would achieve any success, peace or satisfaction without duly satisfying your mood, temperament. I beg down repeatedly at your lotus feet which are the refuges of all higher personalities." The Supreme Lord said: "O three-headed one, I am pleased with you. May your fear of My fever weapon be dispelled and may whoever remember our conversation here have no reason to fear you."

There are unlimited types of form in the domain of associates of Lord Shiva; Shiva-Jvara has three legs and three heads, you can't imagine such a personality; however, Sukadeva Goswami described the form in Srimad Bhagavatam. We have heard about the arrows, the bow of Shiva and his *Pasupathi Astra*, and many other weapons. Here the Shiva-Jvara is specially mentioned that at this time of death, the temperature is so high that the body collapses and the living being dies with such an attack. We might have seen the recent temperature check for the protection of the Coronavirus in the world; these are the symptoms of the Shiva-jvara. There is no other way to counterattack the Shiva-Jvara or the Vishnu-Jvara by any vaccine or medicine. The real medicine for this world is the holy name of Lord Krishna.

By chanting the holy name of Krishna and Rama, the master of Lord Shiva, who always glorifies Rama's name, we will be able to overcome these types of jvara. Lord Shiva or Lord Vishnu Jvara, or the fever weapon, is ready to employ for the people bereft of religious principles and atheistic in nature. We pray to Lord Shiva that please give protection to humanity and let all come to a superior sense so that they understand the divinity of the Vedas, positions of Lord Shiva, and the supremacy of Lord Vishnu. Shiva-Jvara has now fully realized that Lord Krishna is the only hope. He never leaves to any surrendered souls, and this will also please his master Lord Shiva eventually. Considering his plan's strategic approach, he fully begged at the lotus feet of Lord Krishna and offered innumerable prayers composed with emotions and devotions. Lord Krishna awarded the shelter to Shiva-Jvara and released him from the Vishnu-Jvara and offered all kinds of benedictions. Lord Krishna assured him freedom as he did to Arjuna "*ma suca*", do not fear any ideology, any weapon, any fever, any contamination, any virus, any temperature and just stay free and stay safe. Upon hearing the assurance from Lord Krishna, Shiva-Jvara bowed down again and returned to his master's domain.

SHIVA OR VISHNU (YOGURT OR MILK)

We have often heard Srila Prabhupada quotes the milk and yogurt in comparison to Lord Shiva and Lord Vishnu. And also, the appropriate example of one candle passing unto the other candles to show the expansions and incarnations of the Lord. Who is milk, and who is yogurt in this analogy? "Is Shiva milk or *dahī*? Lord Shiva is *"Dahi"* or yogurt, and Lord Vishnu is milk or Kṛṣṇa is milk. Yogurt is prepared from the original milk by applications of lemon or some acidic composition, milk is transformed into yogurt after some time. Similarly, Kṛṣṇa is the pure spirit, and when this pure spirit is mixed up with māyā, that is Shiva. Lord Shiva is the *māyā-adhipati*. There are many more narrations about the transformations of Lord Vishnu to Lord Shiva. This was inquired by Yudhishthira Mahārāja, "Lord Shiva, he appears to be like a beggar. He does not possess even a house. He lives underneath a tree. And the devotees of Shiva become very rich and opulent, materially, although he's a beggar, whereas Vishnu is *Lakṣmī-pati, vaikuṇṭha-pati*, and the Vaishnavas become a beggar. Wonderful and contradictory to understand that worshiping the opulent Lord Vishnu, one becomes a beggar or poor where worshiping the beggar God, Lord Shiva, becomes richer. What is this contradiction?" So, Kṛṣṇa answered, *yasyāham anugrhṇāmi hariṣye tad-dhanaṁ śanaiḥ* [SB 10.88.8]. "My first benediction to My devotee is that I take away all his riches." When the wealth is taken out, a person comes in anxiety, helpless, and perturbed, so there is no hope than the Lord. At this point. he transcends from the material conception of life and seeks to the path of real happiness. In other words, this is the mercy of Lord Vishnu to his devotees. That is Kṛṣṇa's special mercy. On the other hand, the Lord of the material universe, Lord Shiva and the husband of the material energy, Durga, bless his devotees with all kinds of sophistication, material enjoyment, comfort, power, and fame. It is the desire of the living entities and Lord Shiva to fulfill those without any impartiality and judgment of the person's qualifications. The materialistic person forgets the blessings of Lord Shiva and is wholly engrossed in the enjoyment with the matter and no scope of any kind of spiritual advancement. If you see the progress of a Vaishnava, instead of material blessing, he or she gets all the best of the benefits, i.e., spiritual benediction. We can understand the import of the blessings from the two Lords and need to be careful whatever we desire, this does not mean that Vishnu is not capable of giving material opulence as he has made the Pandavas more vibrant, Amabarish Maharaj, the richest king, Dhruva, the powerful king in this planet and may more. The same rule applies to Lord Shiva; also, He can make someone pure devotees like Pracetas and Markandeya muni, and so on.

Even Lord Brahma is explaining the concept of Shiva-tattva in Srimad Bhagavatam ŚB 4.6.42. Although Lord Brahmā had received very respectful obeisances from Lord Shiva, he knew that Lord Shiva: there is no difference between Lord Vishnu and Lord Shiva in their original positions, but still Lord Shiva is different from Lord Vishnu. The example is given that the milk and yogurt as yogurt is not different from the original milk from which it was made.

RUDRA SAMPRADAYA

Sampradaya means spiritual lineage, religious system, or the master and disciples' tradition. This is more often used in the Vedic traditional values or the ancient order of Yoga practices or transferring the secret mantra from *Guru* and *Sisya samaja*. Currently, in this age of Kali, there are four authorized Vaishnava Sampradaya. Authorized Sampradaya is capable of delivering the message of God as it is and without any interpretation and adulteration. The goal of the Vaishnava Sampradaya is one; to attain Krishna or Vishnu. However, the Sampradaya methods are different based on the mood of the Sampradaya's principal teachers. All the principal acharya believe that Krishna is the supreme personality of Godhead, and there is nothing superior to Him in both the material and spiritual worlds. The four Sampradayas are named as Kumara Sampradaya inaugurated by the four Kumara and led by Nimbarka Acharya; Sri Sampradaya was inaugurated by mother Laxmi and led by Ramanujacarya; Rudra sampradaya was initiated by Lord Rudra and led by Vishnuswami; Brahma-Madhava Sampradaya was inaugurated by Lord Brahma and led by Madhavacarya. There is a logical and philosophical relationship amongst the sampradayas, and the sweetness is revealed only to the confidential devotees.

In Bhagavad Gita, Krishna instructed to Arjuna that *evam parampara praptam*, the yoga system is valid as long as the learning is verified by the bonafide system. There are many *Apa-Smpradyas* in this age, and they are generally the offshoot, and even though they may be following to some degree, the conclusion is not established based on the four sampradayas. They should not be considered bonafide in any means. In all circumstances, we should be careful to know about the parampara and sampradaya system and learn the yogic methods from the bonafide system.

In Padma Purana, it states that *"parampara vihina e mantra nisphala"*. This verse was quoted in some of the books of the Vaisnava authors like Baladeva Vidyabhusana in the Prameya Ratnavali.

yad uktam padma-purane sampradya-vihina ye mantras te nish-phala matah atahh kalau bhavishyanti catvarah sampradayinah

shri-brahma-rudra-sanaka vaishnavah kshiti-pavanah catvaras te kalau bhavya hy utkale purushottamat (5)

That means: "Unless one is initiated by a bonafide spiritual master in the disciplic succession, the mantra he might have received is without any effect. For this reason, four Vaishnava disciplic successions, inaugurated by Lakshmi-Devi, Lord Brahma, LordShiva, and the four Kumaras, will appear in the holy place of Jagannatha Puri, and purify the entire earth during the age of Kali."

ramnujam shrih svi-cakre madhvacriyam caturmukhah shri-vish-nu-svaminam rudro nimbadityam catuhsanah (6)

Lakshmi-Devi chose Ramanujacarya to represent her disciplic succession. Lord Brahma chose Madhvacarya in the same way. Lord Shiva chose Vishnu Swami, and the four Kumaras chose Nimbarka.

The Vaishnava society authorizes the four Vishnu sampradayas; the parampara system is quite ancient and bonafide even though some sampradayas are not sufficiently distinct in community.

It's the will of the Lord to remain the parampara system for the benefit of the humanity, and it is predicted that Brahma-madhavacraya sampradaya will remain for ten thousand years in this age of Kali, we should take advantage of the situation and cross over the material ocean by connecting to the Sampradaya. Lord Krishna creates Varnasrama to function in harmony and collaboration and ultimately attain the goal of life.

Lord Shiva is known as the greatest devotee of the Supreme Personality of Godhead, Krishna. He is considered as the topmost of all types of Vaishnavas (*vaiṣṇavānāṁ yathā śambhuḥ*). Consequently, Lord Shiva has a Vaishnava sampradāya, the disciplic succession known as the Rudra-sampradāya. Just as a Brahma-sampradāya is coming directly from Lord Brahmā, the Rudra-sampradāya comes directly from Lord Shiva. Rudra sampradaya, the original teacher, is Lord Shiva, and he spoke the aspects of philosophy on pure monism, and he also spoke to Pracetas. According to Vaishnavism, Shiva, who has the Saivites school of philosophy, has dedicated his hymns and prayers to the worship of the Supreme Personality of Godhead. Being the first and foremost Vaishnava, or follower of Vishnu, he gave the instructions to many like Narada. According to the custom, Vishnuswami was fifteenth in the line of disciplic succession of the "Suddha-Advaita" or pure monism theological principles of parampara. Krishna says in Gita, *evam parampara praptam*. Without parampara, the benefit is no more applied to the recipients. The date of establishment of the Sampradaya is borderline. While some scholars date Vishnuswami to the early 15th century and others date him to the 13th century, Sampradaya's followers say that Vishnuswami was born 4500 years earlier. I am not sure about the existence of Visnuswami as per historical facts; however, he is the principal spiritual master and known as Rudra-sampradaya of Visnuswami, so as Brahma-Madhava Gaudiya sampradaya by Madhavacarya. The Sampradaya originated in Jagannath Puri, Odisha and Visnuswami received the knowledge from Lord Rudra in Rudra

Dvipa of Nadia, West Bengal. Nowadays, the existence of the Sampradaya is mostly present in Gujarat/Rajasthan through the Vallabha sampradaya. The theories of the Sampradaya was further broadcasted by Vallabha Acharya (1479–1531).

Vallabhacharya was born into a south Indian brahmin family, to a mother whose own father was a priest in the royal court of the Vijayanagara Empire. Vallabha's family fled Varanasi and settled there, and Vallabhacaya met Lord Chaitanya and got instructions and corrections in terms of Vaisnava regulations. He composed the beautiful mantra 'Krishna Saranam Mama," and this is the main mantra in the Pushtimarg society.

All the sampradayas are related to one another because the conclusion is the same: that Lord Krishna is the Supreme Personality of Godhead and the living entities are His eternal servants. Rudra-gīta also indicates that under the disciplic succession of Lord Rudra, the Pracetās achieved spiritual success. One has to be an expert in the science of spirituality and imports of the meaning; then, he is qualified to lead his disciples. On the other hand, a sincere seeker should be fortunate enough to meet a sage or a guru in the system of the bonafide parampara system. None can liberate, no matter how much they are qualified or knowledgeable, only the person who is especially favored by Krishna and the bonafide guru can enlighten the society in general.

The philosophers were known as *kevalādvaita-vādīs* generally occupy themselves with hearing the *Śārīraka-bhāṣya*, a commentary by Śaṅkarācārya advocating that one impersonally considers oneself the Supreme Lord. Such Māyāvāda philosophical commentaries upon the *Vedānta-sūtra* are merely imaginary, but there are other commentaries on the *Vedānta-sūtra*. The commentary by Śrīla Rāmānujācārya, known as Śrī-bhāṣya, establishes the *viśiṣṭādvaita-vāda* philosophy. Similarly, in the Brahma-sampradāya, Madhvācārya's Pūrṇaprajña-bhāṣya establishes *śuddha-dvaita-vāda*. In the Kumāra-sampradāya or Nimbārka-sampradāya, Śrī Nimbārka sets the philosophy of *dvaitādvaita-vāda* in the *Pārijāta-saurabha-bhāṣya*. And in the Viṣhṇu-svāmi-sampradāya, or Rudra-sampradaya which comes from Lord Shiva, Viṣhṇu Svāmī has written a commentary called *Sarvajña-bhāṣya*, which establishes *śuddhādvaita-vāda*. The knowledge of the Bhagavad-gītā must be received by the paramparā system, as it was spoken by Kṛṣṇa and as it has been received by the later ācāryas. Although there are different systems of preaching institutions. They are all in agreement that Kṛṣṇa is the Supreme Personality of Godhead. All these ācāryas are in the full spirit of distribution of revealed knowledge to one and all.

Yamarāja said that "These are the twelve Mahajans or great personalities or authorities." We have to follow the Mahajanas even though some of them did not start the guru-shishya system of preaching institution. Yamaraj has no sampradaya, however he advises the science of God to his assistants in the Patala Loka, and he recommends the four Sampradaya for initiation and accepting the bonafide system, It applies to Bhishma also. They are the knower of the Gita. Bhisma did not start an institution, however he gave the knowledge to Yudhisthira Maharaj. Technically, they act as the advisors in spiritual science and act as the Siksha Guru, and by following them, one can come to the stage of love of Godhead. In the age of Kali, we need both diksha and shiksha, so the sampradaya system is very much needed.

RUDRA'S HUMILITY IN DAKSHA YAJNA

Humility means considering oneself lower than that of grass and offering all kinds of respect to others even though, in return, nothing comes in. Humility means sharing positive gentleness to others irrespective of others' behaviors, gestures, and words. Lord Chaitanya recommends us to be humble and meek so that we overcome the difficulty in real life. By being humble, one wins the heart of others. Sometimes puffed-up and proud men's hearts melt when they meet a humbled person in their life. Lord Shiva's exemplary behavior is glorified in the transaction at the Daksha Yajna and the outrageous behavior of Prajapati Daksha. Nowadays, nationalists, political leaders, and scientists should take lessons from Lord Shiva and develop a better relationship amongst the nations, cultural background people, and so on. It is an essential quality in spiritual life so that one can advance very fast. Humility acts as an ingredient and increases the flavor of the curry in a typical analogy. Humility is the essential substance either in the civility or moral code of conduct or spiritual section of followers. When Prajapati Daksha entered the arena of the assembly, he was greeted by the demigods like Indra, Chandra, Varuna, etc., and even Brahma reciprocated greetings and favorable words towards Daksha. Daksha looked around all the corners and automatically his eyes noticed at the seat of Lord Shiva. He found out that Shiva is just sitting indifferently and there was no sign of greeting or even a formal reciprocation. By social custom, Prajapati is the father-in-law of Shiva as Shiva is married to Sati, the daughter of the Prajapati Daksha. Daksha has the expectations of receiving honor and respect from Shiva, and he had earlier relationship issues with his son-in-law on ideological viewpoints. Lord Shiva being aloof from the ritualistic Karma-Kanda activities, thought himself isolated and alone and altogether meditating on the Supreme Lord.

Devotees often ask what is to be done when someone invites to a social party; then, one should be aloof from the customs and remember the Supreme Lord for being protected by the Lord. However, Daksha took this matter very seriously, and his mind was agitated by this kind of behavior. At the same time, Lord Shiva had no intention of offending even an ant and what to speak of Daksha, and he is in his own domain of trance. So, there is no question of understanding the presence of Daksha in the assembly hall. There are two sets of expectations from two personalities, one is expecting respect based on social custom, and the other person is aloof from such a situation. When Daksha was about to address the assembly, in his welcome speech, rather he started blaspheming Lord Shiva by saying the lower standard of accusations. He said, "This personality Shiva is accustomed to staying in a crematorium, smeared with ashes, and he forgot the basic etiquette of respect and gesture. It is the most significant fault I made in my life to give the hand of my younger daughter Sati, whose complexion is white, the face is like lotus, and her eyes are like a deer cub. On the other hand, this lowly Shiva has a crazy look, bad association with ghosts and goblins, no home or opulence, his eyes look like a monkey's. Out of formality and command from my father, Lord Brahma, out of compulsion, I gave my daughter to such lowly Shiva. Overall, his heart is filled with dirty things and no sense of civility and morality."

When he spoke, there was trembling anger in the associates of Lord Shiva, such as Nandi, Bhringi, and many more. They started cursing the demigods, Daksha, and many more. The sage Bhrigu cursed the Shivagana, and curses were going back and forth. Shiva knew very well that he saw the Supersoul in everyone's heart, he did not protest anything and prayed for their welfare and left the arena in silence. Lord Shiva is equally powerful, and he could employ his trident and kill Daksha on the spot, but he did not want to do so. He brings auspiciousness for others only and nothing inauspicious is going to happen in any living beings. As Shiva considers everyone equal, and without envy, anger, grudges, he thoughtfully left the place. His bodily gesture was as grave as it was earlier, and there was no sign of resentment and frustration; instead, he exemplified the behavior of a great Vaishnav like Haridas Thakur in the quality. Such reasons attribute Lord Shiva to be the greatest Vaishnava in the world. We should take lessons from this episode and pray to Lord Shiva to grant us the humility nature so that we can respect everyone equally and advance spiritually.

ARJUN ACQUIRED THE PASHUPATI-ASTRA

Arjuna was describing to Yudhishthira after the return from the heavenly planets, and he is revealing the great details of receiving the most significant weapon known as Pasupathi Astra. The *Pashupatastra* is an enticing and most destructive subtle weapon of Lord Rudra, which can be applied by using mantra in mind, the eyes, words, or a bow like *Gandiva.* In Mahabharata, only Arjuna possessed this weapon for the war. Arjuna told Yudhisthira that how Mātali took him to the town of the *Kalakanyas*, a class of ferocious Daityas. It was called Hiraṇyapura, and even the demigods like Indra could not surmount it. Hence, the demons resided there without anxiety. The Kalakanyas were ordained to be slain by a human by Brahmā's prearrangement. Thus, Mātali admonished Arjuna to rush upon the Daityas and please Indra.

There was a deadly fight sued against those demons on the planets. Arjuna was deeply fraught by their weapons. Here and there, all around the ocean of the *Kalakanyas*, Arjuna abruptly remembered Shiva's weapon. Arjuna uttered the mantras holy to the three-eyed eternal Rudra deity. There appeared in the chorus before a massive disposition with three heads, nine eyes, six arms, and hair raging like fire. His clothes contained great serpents whose tongues whizzed back and forth. Arjuna shook off the fear and paid obeisance to that horrible form of the eternal Shiva. Then he fixed on the *Gandiva* bow the Rudra-Astra and, continuously chanting the mantras, discharged it to terminate the *Daityas.* Millions of dissimilarly shaped artilleries spread out across the combat zone as the weapon was ablaze. Many of the creatures resemble tigers, lions, and other bears and buffaloes. There were serpent-shaped weapons and others designed like elephants, cats, boars, and bulls. Concurrently, the battlefield burst up with Shiva's followers--innumerable *Guhyakas, Yakṣas, Piśācas, Bhūtas*, and other ethereal lives. The fight resembled the war of Banasura and Lord Krishna. Altogether the mantra transformed creature hurried toward the *Daityas* with terrifying rumbles. As the Rudra-Astra twisted havoc among the foe, Arjuna, the eternal friend of Lord Krishna, blazed a continuous shower of darts glaring like fire and lightning in the blue sky. It's certain that Arjuna's triumph was due only because of the presence of the Shiva's *Pasupathi* weapon. Arjuna bowed down to Lord Shiva during the warfare period and amid the combat zone. After the victory, Mātali commended Arjuna, and all of them then returned to Indra's abode. This example sets a right tone for the devotees aspiring to please Mukund the way Arjuna pleased the demigods by their service and ultimately pleasing to the Supreme Personality of Godhead. One can learn the art of pleasing to God via the medium of serving the demigods.

BANASURA, LORD SHIVA AND KRISHNA

In Srimad Bhagavatam tenth canto, chapter sixty-two recounts the meeting of Aniruddha and Ūṣā, and also Aniruddha's battle with Bāṇāsura. Of the one hundred sons of King Bali, the oldest was Bāṇāsura. He was the most powerful demon and he got the power from Lord Shiva's benediction that no one could defeat him in the battle. All the demigods including Indra used to pay respects to Banasura because of his invincible power and strength.

Banasura had a beautiful daughter named Usa, and one night she dreamed of a young man, and suddenly the dream came shattered when she awoke from the dream and found herself surrounded by maidservants. Usa's best friend, Citralekha, was a great artist, and she depicted the various person's images based on the descriptions of Usa.

Upon the capture of Aniruddha, Krishna and Balaram came to attack Banasura's kingdom. There was a fierce fight between the soldiers of Banasura accompanied by Lord Shiva, Kartikeya, many ghosts, hobgoblins, rakshasas and so on. By the will of Krishna, all the Yadav's subdued the enemies and all the thousand hands of Banasura were cut off. He was completely defeated in the battle by the strong presence of the Yadava sena, Lord Krishna and Balarama. Krishna did not want to kill a devotee of Lord Shiva and he would be the father-in-law of Aniruddha. He spared his life for the social custom and by Shiva's request. Lord Krishna loves Shiva as much He does to any of His pure devotees. Shiva also proclaimed to Banasura that the day will come where Banasura's false prestige of battling spirit will be destroyed. Lord Krishna fulfilled the same commandment of Lord Shiva also. This is the true relation between Lord Shiva and Lord Krishna as both of them are eager to satisfy each other and at the same time please all the devotees around. We should pray to Shiva and Krishna in order to advance in our spiritual life. By the mercy of Rudra, we can easily obtain the lotus feet of Lord Krishna.

ESSENTIAL TEACHINGS OF LORD SHIVA

Lord Shiva is undoubtedly the topmost Vaishnava, a Mahajan, and the *gunavatara* incarnation of the Lord. He has an authorized sampradaya where everyone can go back to Godhead by following the principles of Shiva's teachings. Śrīla Sanātana Gosvāmī has advised us to hear about Kṛṣṇa from a Vaishnava. It is very much essential for us to advance in the spiritual line by following a real Vaishnava.

avaiṣṇava-mukhodgīrṇaṁ pūtaṁ hari-kathāmṛtam

śravaṇaṁ naiva kartavyaṁ *sarpocchiṣṭaṁ yathā payaḥ*

In the material world, we find various intellectuals' persons and offering lots of information on stress management, simple living, the pursuit of happiness, a better lifestyle, a healthy fitness system, one goal, and ultimate end, etc. One should not be baffled and accept any path seemingly exciting, and then one is known to be in Maya. We should follow the path laid down by the Mahajanas, and in another instance, a new lesson we learn from Lord Shiva is that we should hear the spiritual topics from a Vaishnava only.

The second important aspect Lord Shiva is pointing out about the ultimate enjoyer of the sacrifices, as he does not enjoy the sacrifices offered in any of the Karma Kanda and he is aloof from such materialistic motivated offerings, however he is mentioning that the root is Lord Krishna. One should always aspire for liberation from this mortal world. Why Lord Rudra became angry and statement is found in Srimad Bhagavatam as follows. "If you don't try to get out of this world in your lifetime, you are making me angry." *evam aradhanam vishno sarvesam atmanas ca hi*, Vishnu or Krishna is the sum and substance of all worship. Lord Shiva is setting an example that He is chanting the name of Lord Rama always and desires the same result from everyone.

As the conversation between Lord Shiva and Parvati, we found the verse stated in the Padma Purāṇa: ārādhanānāṁ sarveṣāṁ viṣṇor ārādhanaṁ param tasmāt parataraṁ devi tadīyānāṁ samarcanam

The worship of Vishnu is the best in all respects either to any demigods, Indra, Chandra, Surya, Varuna, or Brahma, and the best result will be obtained by worshiping Lord Vishnu, this is the verdict of Lord Rudra while He is speaking to his wife, mother Gauri.

All the demigods assembled and tried to find out who is the supreme Lord and they concluded by the experiments of Bhrgu. Similarly, many people in the world question the best worship process and the person whom the worship should be offered. During the time of the Gajendra Moksha period, he was offering his prayers to God without any name; however, no one dared to accept his prayers and waited for the real Lord to come in the scene and rescue Gajendra. Another example is given in the *Rajasuya* sacrifice of Yudhishthira Maharaj. All of them are searching for the best and foremost person to worship, and ultimately, they selected Lord Krishna. Here Lord Shiva is explaining in detail to Mother Parvati the methods of worship and the best process of prayer and how the worship should be done. Out of all the demigods of the cosmos, the best is Mahadeva, and Mahadeva himself is stating that Vishnu worship is the utmost form of prayer. And he went further while explaining to Gauri that the *tadiya-seva* is even superior to Vishnu's worship. The objects related to the worship of Lord Vishnu; Lord Rudra are always transcendental. and the book written for the pleasure of Saivites, Vaishnavas. It is conforming with the *tadiya-seva* such as service to the reading of Srimad Bhagavatam, temple building, playing the musical instruments like *mrdanga, karatal*, and many more similar activities. Even worshiping them is the best form of worship, and we know that in Gurudwara, we find that Sikhs worship *Granth-sahib* and attain peace and love from the Lord and Guru and the scriptures.

Lord Shiva's position is glorified as the topmost Vaishnava, and we should seriously take his teachings. In Srimad Bhagavatam, ŚB 12.13.16

nimna-gānāṁ yathā gaṅgā
devānām acyuto yathā
vaiṣṇavānāṁ yathā śambhuḥ
purāṇānām idam tathā

Just as the Gaṅgā is the greatest of all rivers, Lord Acyuta the supreme among deities and Lord Śambhu [Shiva] the greatest of Vaishnavas, so Śrīmad-Bhāgavatam is the greatest of all Purāṇas.

No one would know the inner meaning of Lord Shiva's drinking the poison and keeping in the throat. As per the great commentary, Shiva knew very well that Lord Sankarsana resided in his heart and He did not want to disturb his master by swallowing the poison unto the heart. He wanted to keep it near his throat so that His master does not get the fumes of the poison and on the other hand he wanted to save the entire humanities including the demons and the demigods. This is the position of Lord Rudra.

Therefore, the summary of Lord Rudra's teaching and the purpose of the Rudra-Gita are meant to please the *parama-purusha* Bhagavan Krishna.

Acknowledgement

I would like to thank the following persons for their special contribution in providing the paintings of the inside sections of this book.

Aparupa-Radhika Devi Dasi (Arpita Nandi)

Sasirekha Devi Dasi (Sarita Ojha)

References

Schedule A

H. D. G. A. C. Bhaktivedanta Swami. Bhaktivedanta Book Trust. https://www.vedabase.com/

1) Srimad Bhagavatam 12.13.1
2) https://vedabase.io/en/library/sb/6/6/17-18/
3) Srimad Bhagavatam ŚB 3.12.13
4) Srimad Bhagavatam ŚB 5.25.3
5) Brahma Samhita 5.44 (partly)
6) Srimad Bhagavatam 12.13.16
7) https://vedabase.io/en/library/sb/11/3/26/
8) https://vedabase.io/en/library/sb/11/5/4/
9) CC Madhya 9.38
10) https://vedabase.io/en/library/sb/8/7/29/
11) SB 4.24.27 to 79
12) CC Madhya 6.180-182
13) Srimad Bhagavatam ŚB 12.10.11-13
14) Srimad Bhagavatam SB 2.7.39
15) Srimad Bhagavatam ŚB 5.9.18
16) Sri Chaitanya Caritamrta, CC Ādi 17.99
17) CC Ādi 17.100

18) CC Ādi 18.116

19) Srimad Bhagavatam, ŚB 12.13.16

20) Srimad Bhagavatam ŚB 5.9.18

21) Srimad Bhagavatam SB 6.3.20

22) Srimad Bhagavatam SB 10.63.22

Schedule B

https://en.wikipedia.org/wiki/Mahamrityunjaya_Mantra

https://en.wikipedia.org/wiki/Kedarnath_Temple

https://en.wikipedia.org/wiki/Guruvayurappan

https://en.wikipedia.org/wiki/Jyotirlinga

http://www.holydham.com/vriddha-Shiva-Shiva-doba/

https://en.wikipedia.org/wiki/Shiva

https://en.wikipedia.org/wiki/Sampradaya

Sri Jagannath Darshan (Odiya) by Dr. Purnachandra Mishra (Prachi Sahitya Pratisthan)

Purusottama Kshetra – by Dr. Rama Chandra Mishra

Sri Jagannath Kathamrta (Odiya) by Pujya Baba Chaitanya Caran Das Maharaj

Rg Veda (R.T.H Griffith / Parimal Publications)

Yajur Veda (R.T.H Griffith / Parimal Publications)

Sam Veda (R.T.H Griffith / Parimal Publications)

Sri Satvata Tantra (Spoken by Lord Shiva) – Kusakratha Das / Purnapranja Das RBL&S

Padma Purana

Vamana Purana

Varaha Purana

Gita Mahatmya

Shiva Purana (Hindi) – Manoj Publications (Dr. Mahendra Mittal)

Srila Vyasadeva's Mahabharat (Summarized by Purnaprajna Das)

Ramayana by Bhakti Vikas Swami

Articles and Blogs from H.H.Hanumatpreshak Maharaj

Navadvipa Mahatmya

Rudra - SRI NABADWIP DHAM MAHATMYA

(Sri Krishna Chaitanya carita Mahakavya) – Murari Gupta

Garuda Purana: Shiva's prayers to Narasimha section

www.ingramcontent.com/pod-product-compliance
Lightning Source LLC
LaVergne TN
LVHW091536060526
838200LV00036B/635
* 9 7 8 1 6 4 7 4 9 3 4 7 9 *